Genealogy

IS _MORE_
THAN CHARTS

Genealogy
IS _MORE_
THAN CHARTS

BY

LORNA DUANE SMITH

LifeTimes

COPYRIGHT © 1991 by LORNA DUANE SMITH

First Printing, 1991
Second Printing, 1992

Printed in the United States of America

Port City Press, Inc.
Baltimore, Maryland

Copies may be ordered from
LifeTimes
2806 Fox Hound Road
Ellicott City, Maryland 21042

Library of Congress Catalog Card Number 91-225528

ISBN 0-9632467-4-7

DEDICATION

Though my mother's passing set me on my journey to look for her past, it is to my husband and companion, Lee, that I dedicate this book. He has done all he can to smooth the bumps and clear the way, so I can smell the roses.

I hope we have many miles to go before we sleep.

DA

ACKNOWLEDGMENTS

This book has helped me to acknowledge first, who I am and how indebted I am for all those ancestral attributes I have been given genetically. I have found someone in my past to whom I can give credit for just about everything I know about myself.

You will never know how far I've come to believe in myself, and trust in my judgment as a person. Working with creative people, especially Grace Nelson, helped me to make things happen! So I take this opportunity to acknowledge, with thanks, everyone in my life who has encouraged me, and realized that even though I looked strong on the outside, there was a scared little girl on the inside wondering if it was going to work out.

I acknowledge all the people I've met on this journey, for I've either learned what to do, or what not to do from their example. We never stop learning, and all of us are teaching something.

Seeing the pleasure genealogy brought to Audrey and Helen Critchfield, and knowing Allie May Buxton, and Kathy Fitzpatrick survived the publishing of their books was very encouraging. Everyone should have a friend like Eleanor Jose to give technical assistance, and proofreaders like Carla and Roy Hendricks and Melinda Niles. With an "auntie in residence" like Doris Pelton, I always had a listening ear.

This book is about people, some related, some not, but all very important in my life. I'm grateful to you all for helping me grow.

INTRODUCTION

Until ten years ago, I was living a pretty normal lifestyle for a person married for 29 years, having survived three teenaged daughters. I had successfully pursued a degree in music education, returned to my hometown of Brunswick, Maryland and promoted music by teaching in the schools, directing choirs and community choruses, and giving private piano lessons.

Both my husband's and my families had lived in *town* for two generations, so it wasn't difficult to get together. His occupation was also in elementary education, later in supervision of staff development. Our high school and college friends were mutual and we have always had many hobbies and interests involving people.

Raising our family and moving to another county changed our perspective, but it wasn't until my mother and retarded brother, Noel, passed away that I was reminded of the importance of memories. So I tried every way I could to learn more about my mother through her friends and family. Preserving her past provided me with such satisfaction that, instead of feeling her absence, I felt she was enjoying my success!

Before I knew it, I was drawing family trees, never dreaming that four years later I would become president of a 100-member genealogical society! My goal had nothing to do with the DAR or a coat-of-arms. I just wanted to thank all my ancestors for making it possible for me to be here, and to record the family history for future generations.

After ten years and seventy libraries, I have discovered even more about our family. By writing my memories, I feel my other brother, Gary, will be able to reflect on the view from **his** window.

I thought about all the homespun writings I've been drawn to read...those memories about special characters with gifts they share, memories that make us feel secure, loved and enriched as we count our blessings. And then I thought, that's genealogy, but it isn't MY granddad, or MY childhood...they were special too. I could tell you some similar stories, and if I don't, who will tell them for me?

Would they remember all the details, get them right, or will it get changed like so much gossip?

That was when I decided to write it down while it was still vivid in my memory. I found the more you remember, **the more you remember!** I wouldn't run the risk of misquoting others either. I'd tape them as they told me, assuring them I want to be accurate.

There are others in our family who don't feel any urgency to do this recording; why do I feel self-appointed? I think some of us do a lot of evaluating as we live our lives. There are many times that we have missed opportunities because we didn't think ahead. We learn from our past neglect and procrastination. Next time I'll be ready, we say.

So we decide to use some foresight and sort out what we want our family to be remembered for. We see some of our family passing away, and with them the memories they were storing up for us. Who will ever appreciate the person my mother was, if I don't write something down? If life is worth living and people worth remembering, we create memorials to all that it was!

By now, I have such a firm belief in the value of a recorded family history, that there isn't a topic that I can't relate to genealogy! (Did you notice that *genealogy* is spelled with an A for ah-h-h, not an O for oh-h-h?) Rather than risk being crossed off of everyone's guest list, I thought a book might give me a way to share what has become a journey into understanding and appreciating the past, and the many ways you may express it.

My main motive is to show you that you **can**, and **should**, preserve family memories in **many** ways in addition to charts. Charts are important proven documents to show our line of descent; but, like a report card, there was an awful lot that went on between gradings!

I hope you will sense my enthusiasm and find some activities that will work for each member of your family; for each person is on his **own** journey, making history while he's learning about past generations. I've included ideas for all ages so you can participate together, and your recording is just a natural activity to enjoy when you're *looking back.* We also learn that though experiences can happen to a whole family, each member perceives them in his own way. One person cannot speak for all. You may gain a new insight into your childhood, or siblings, by having them record their separate stories about the same episode.

I discovered that this beautiful song, once the theme of one of my programs of music, is now the theme of my genealogy.

TIMES OF YOUR LIFE
by Bill Lane & Roger Nichols used
with permission of Roger Nichols
Studios, Bend, Oregon

Good morning, Yesterday!
You wake up, and time has slipped away.
And suddenly it's hard to find the memories you left behind.
Remember...do you remember...

The laughter and the tears, the shadows of misty yesteryears,
The good times and the bad you've seen, and all the others in
between. Remember...do you remember the times of your life?

Reach back for the joy and the sorrow;
Put them away in your mind;
For memories are time that you borrow...to spend when you get
to tomorrow.

Here comes the setting sun. The seasons are passing one by one.
So gather moments while you may; collect the dreams you dream
today.
Remember, will you remember the times of your life?

Songs, poems, drawings, favorite sayings and stories created or chosen by our family reveal their "inner selves." Gather those along with the "outer selves."

My family anecdotes are liberally scattered throughout my book, serving to illustrate, to act as a record for my family, and to encourage you to insert your own in their place. So, I hope you enjoy my experiences as a genealogist enough to create some of your own. You'll be richer for it!

As for me, I'm late for my appointment with Madame Donna! She's staging a séance for us so we can contact Great-Grandpa Christian Smith. We're looking for his parents, and it's the only method left to try!

TABLE OF CONTENTS

This certificate

entitles you to

101 REWARDS

of

GENEALOGY

from

this day forward.

1

101 REWARDS TO BE GAINED FROM GENEALOGY

When I first became interested in genealogy, I couldn't get anyone to listen. It was as though I had become a religious convert and was trying to save the world. I felt as ignored as the mother of a teenager...which I managed to survive three times. Indeed my best friends of 40 years, Gloria, Lorraine, Doris, Shirley, and June would find other things to do if I mentioned the word "genealogy." This really challenged me; and I started to think of all the rewards I had gained that kept me so interested. Maybe they would want some of these rewards...maybe they thought it was just a lot of work to fill a lot of charts...so every time I thought of a reward, I went to my list and wrote it down. Here's what I feel are my rewards:

1. I want to *find* myself; know where I'm *coming from.*

2. I want our children to realize that they are a composite of many ancestors who came before them.

3. I want to appreciate my ethnic background by studying the qualities of those I represent.

4. I want to understand the lifestyle of the families my parents grew up in, as it related to their goals for me.

5. Genealogy makes me feel like a detective, tracing lost persons.

6. Research challenges me to stay mentally active and involved, knowing that *if you don't use it, you'll lose it!*

7. In seeing the diversity of my background, I better understand the complexity of the individual personality.

8. I appreciate what former generations went through to maintain their families through hardships of many kinds.

9. As I walk through graveyards, I develop more courage and sympathize with the loss of many children by epidemic.

10. I appreciate the evolution of highways from Indian trails, and see the streams and waterfalls as sources of power, food and transportation for my pioneer family.

11. I develop patience when I run out of groceries, have no car, or have the plumbing break down, and think of how the pioneers managed to survive...and I don't have to fight off any Indians!

12. I learn to be diplomatic as I approach a new library, and need assistance from the *busy* librarian.

13. Unlike skiers and golfers, genealogists need no special equipment...only a notebook and a pencil.

14. I rejoice when I find a new *cousin*—an instant relative—and hope he will be glad to meet me.

15. I am developing powers of persuasion as I attempt to interest the rest of the clan in my study.

16. I feel an urgency to visit the older folks, and suffer much regret when *death* gets there before I do.

17. I remember to guard the privacy of my informants, if this is their desire.

18. I become a reporter on assignment when I interview relatives, and feel that the interview tapes I have recorded will become more valuable as the years go by.

19. I enjoy assuring my older kin of the valuable contribution they are making. It comes at a time when they may be feeling useless and abandoned.

20. Vacations have a new meaning as we plan them around distant family homeplaces.

21. Suddenly all the family antiques and curios take on a genealogy of their own, and I am reminded that clutter can often become museum pieces.

22. I become a better record-keeper as I inventory and label everything for posterity.

23. I improve my calligraphy skills so my charts will look more personal.

24. My husband has become involved as my personal photographer who faithfully takes his camera and copy stand along.

25. We are always proud to give such a personal gift as a copy of a rare photo of our kin.

26. I am amazed at the hours I spend in libraries on this self-inflicted quest. No instructor ever inspired this kind of dedication...unfortunately.

27. I am persistent whenever I come to a *dead end*, and reassure myself, that, at least "now I know where they **aren't**."

28. I no longer dread rainy days, as they are perfect times to spend in the library.

29. I get my housework done faster, to earn *release time* for genealogy!

30. I become as excited over my 12-generation chart as a pirate with a treasure map.

31. I am creative as I make a table runner to be autographed by the family.

32. I am fun-loving with a motive—plan family dinners with a purpose—to update the charts, tell stories and bring us together.

33. I have become more aggressive as I phone strangers with the same surname, hoping they will be willing to speak to me.

34. I anticipate the mail, hoping it will bring me some new genealogy information, instead of just bills.

35. I can converse with new acquaintances immediately with "what's in a name?," instead of "what's your sign?"

36. I try to encourage everyone to donate files and tapes to the genealogical library if they have no need for them.

37. I can't sympathize with people who have nothing to do. They can read and clip old newspapers, make scrapbooks and collections, or make tapes of their own recollections.

38. I encourage the local paper to run a column of genealogical queries.

39. I honor the memory of my family by lovingly displaying their photos, books, curios as part of the decor in our home.

40. I prepared a Heritage Recipe Book by requesting samples and information from all our families.

41. I am trying to break down some of the barriers that separate the family, by concentrating on the things we have in common...especially when there's a Bible in their attic!

42. I feel more secure knowing I have re-established family ties that could become my support group, with the right communication.

43. I become more tolerant as I see that all families have a sampling of ancestors who became black sheep because of poor choices they made.

44. I will maintain my interest in genealogy because the study of people is always an intricate weaving of personalities, not just dates and names.

45. I cherish the photos and personal mementoes given me, knowing they can never be replaced. I try to think of ways to catalog and preserve them.

46. I remember how frustrating it is to identify old photos, so I try to label all in my collection.

47. I even invested in a computer and took classes, so I can discard my mountains of papers...if I dare!

48. When I speak of some of my relatives, I have broadened my vocabulary to include *unique and special*, instead of *weird and outrageous*!

49. I realize this is a hobby you can get *hooked* on; but there are worse things.

50. I think Medicare will cover me for eye strain from reading microfilm, or pneumonia from tramping through cemeteries in the rain.

51. I think I can claim our RV as a business expense, in that my husband needs a nap and coffee while I'm in the library.

52. I am grateful for all the genealogical societies that give us support and therapy, when all around us are shaking their heads.

53. I crusade with the slogan,"When in doubt, DON'T throw it out!" Old report cards, diaries, letters, and papers give valuable clues.

54. I am thinking of taking a speed-reading course; time is getting short!

55. I don't judge a book by its cover; search those old Bibles, page by page.

56. I encouraged children in my hometown to write a history of the town, as a way to remember local history.

57. I've found people in my past on whom I can blame my bad habits.

58. I am thrifty when I accompany my husband on business trips, because I spend the day in a free library instead of a shopping mall.

59. I try to maintain my composure in a library, even though I've just discovered an ancestor I've been looking for for five years.

60. I have mastered the ability to operate at least 15 kinds of microfilm readers.

61. I have been willed precious antiques because the family knows I will take care of them.

62. I feel like a link between the past and the present, and this has given a sense of importance to me and my family.

63. My prayers now include, "If I should die before I wake, The LDS my files will take."

64. Doctors find our family tree very useful for tracing our predisposition to medical problems.

65. Family stories could often provide good script material for the soap operas...no need to watch "All My Children" anymore.

66. I am devious as I twist conversation around to genealogy.

67. I link generations as I ask children to label Grandmother's photos.

68. Having been to over 70 libraries, I enjoy acting as a travel guide, sharing information and brochures.

69. I influence marketing when I ask the stationery store to consider selling charts and books.

70. I become an archaeologist when I look for early cemeteries to record and protect.

71. I become a political activist when I testify at a hearing for legislation to preserve graveyards and protect them from the bulldozer.

72. I become an art lover when I do a rubbing of a gravestone with folk art, or try a German scherenschnitte.

73. I have become an author with a desire to share my enthusiasm for genealogy with others.

74. I become an architect when I record a history of the homeplace, and try to ascertain its age from its style and materials.

75. I become a publicity agent for genealogy when I set up a registry at festivals, hand out brochures, and give directions to society meetings.

76. I quietly display my charts at family reunions to encourage interest.

77. I become a chauffeur for seniors and take them to childhood areas, so I can enjoy and record their comments.

78. I become a teacher each time I share new discoveries with my family, and give evidence to support it.

79. I have become an actor, of sorts, in videos produced for and by genealogists to be viewed on a local station.

80. I feel like a leader when I can network those with needs with those who can provide them, in the framework of a society.

81. I am grateful when offered a ride in a carpool to a city library.

82. I become a college student again when I work beside them in the campus library...but I don't have to pass an exam!

83. I am awestruck when allowed to handle the huge leather-bound ledgers from the 1600's found at the State Archives.

84. I am saddened when I see that many do not know, or even care, about the names of their great-great-grandparents.

85. I am glad that I found an old gravesite and encouraged the family to restore it; I hope someone will look after mine in the future.

86. I am elated when the family begins to send others to me for family information.

87. No research I do is wasted when nothing has been done before. Even **one** page is something.

88. I had no idea my husband and I had the same Uncle Charlie! I never knew he was married twice; first to Lee's aunt, then to mine!

89. I feel like a lawyer when I can provide evidence that proves family folk tales are really true.

90. I am relieved when I can finally put a name to the mystery portrait in my album.

91. I was amazed to find a thick lock of red hair in Grandmother Suella's Bible.

92. I feel like a scientist when I apply deductive reasoning to my theories in research.

93. I recommend genealogy to parents and teachers as a way to learn history and teach good research skills in doing a personal project.

94. I encourage each library to *open up* to genealogists by asking if they have special guides or collections like those I have used in other places.

95. I am encouraged by all the records which are being newly released or published by the Latter Day Saints and others.

96. I feel my research into the family tree is a legacy of love no one else may give.

97. I have more self-esteem when I realize that I am a unique individual, like no other, and yet a composite of all who have come before me.

98. I have become the eternal student, learning from all other genealogists with their creative methods of research.

99. I am amazed at the difference ONE person can make when I see personal collections and use research papers.

100. I am trying to learn enough foreign language to decipher the records I need.

101. I am so glad I have found an activity that allows me to use creative ways to make lasting contributions to my family, friends and community.

These rewards can all be yours, if you join me on a journey to discover our ancestors!

Will they have the lifestyles of the *rich and famous* or the *poor and pitiful* ? If you're like most of us, there will be some of both...so don't set your expectations too high. We all have our heroes and our black sheep, determined often by the choices they made at the time.

But when you think of these rewards, you can see genealogy is much more than charts. Charts act as an organized look at names and dates of succeeding generations. Behind each name is a lifetime of experiences which turn that name into a real person with a family to raise. Thank heaven he didn't give up, or you wouldn't be here!

A
CELEBRATION

OF
LIFE

2

GENEALOGY IS...A CELEBRATION OF LIFE!

To take a look at the family as a group of related individuals, each with his own purpose for being here, is to CELEBRATE LIFE! It's an opportunity to see just what we are capable of, and take advantage of it.

Like characters cast in a play, the members of a family relate to each of life's episodes in their own way. Often birth order, economics, and parental attitudes influence the roles we play, but basically we are different people. We spend an entire lifetime getting to know ourselves, physically and emotionally.

It is fascinating to realize that we are each so unique that our fingerprints, our genes and our DNA are our very own, thus giving credence to our special personality. That should give us all the self-esteem that we need.

But, alas, along comes that old pressure from our environment that may or may not nurture us, and we think we must fit in or perish. They tell us it is the balance we strike between nature **and** nurture that makes us a complete person. So let's celebrate the possibilities!

When we examine our genetic background, we realize that it has evolved from the generations that preceded us. We are a special combination of the genes of our ancestry. Look at all your characteristics...the talents, skills, coloring, walk, fingers, toes, allergies, etc...that you can credit or blame on your ancestors. But first, you have to identify them as the saint or sinner to whom you are in debt.

I looked for years for SOMEONE in my family who was left-handed. I enjoy this difference, and the *brain* talk that goes with it, but I needed to know *from whence it came.* Just last year, my 92-year old great-aunt recalled that my grandmother's brother had a left-handed ball mitt. So here's to you, Uncle Al, for making it a truth. Up to now, there was some talk about the milkman!

As you ponder the fact that you are a unique combination, why not choose one relative you feel very much akin to, and make certain he or she is never forgotten. Do what I'm doing, and write about her. There'll never be another person like her, so I want

you to know who she was. If she were here, she'd never allow
me to write such things...and, come to think of it, I wouldn't feel
I needed to. Her portrait...Madeline Moler...is on the front page
of this chapter.

I REMEMBER MAMA...
and I don't want to forget!

After all, she's the reason I got started on this quest
through genealogy, trying to find answers to all the questions it
was too late to ask. I thought I had plenty of time. Our three
children would soon be graduated and gone their respective ways.
I would no longer be working a job and I'd have lots of time.
Visits wouldn't have to be sandwiched in between other
obligations, and I could really get to know my mother. We sort of
forget that our parents really had a life before we came along. We
think all life began with us. But now that has changed. Mom had
a sudden heart attack, and I was reminded how fragile life is.
How could I ever find the answers to all the things I had planned
to ask her?

I sorted through her belongings thinking of the times I had
seen her use them, and the places we had been—the bargains she
had passed on to me, the piano duets we played together and raced
each other to the end, the trip to Europe she had finally gotten the
courage to take...and then I came to the photo box. This is what
really opened up her world to me. I was disappointed to find that
most of the pictures were not labeled, but I decided that someone
could tell me who these people were, and in doing so would tell
me about my mother.

That was ten years ago, and by now the photos all have
names, and I have learned a lot of things about Mom that would
not have been told had she been there with me. Many told me
wonderful compliments that they never shared with her. And oh,
how she needed to hear them! She hid so many of her talents
because she didn't want to risk criticism or be called conceited.

By the same token, she could not ever hug or kiss...it just
wasn't done. She came close...when my first baby was
born...but she stopped herself. You can't pass on what you never
received yourself. We children saw her love in other ways, and
we consoled ourselves that a hug had fleeting value and was only

16

done for show.

I could never decide if she was creative because she wanted to be, or because she had to be. Money was only provided for justifiable necessities, and sometimes the end didn't justify the trouble it made. So she sewed, knitted, crocheted, embroidered clothing, sewed drapes, garment bags, costumes, slipcovers, linens, coats, and hats. When money wasn't provided for my Girl Scout uniform, she made mine.

When Mom died she left so many unfinished projects waiting to be done, that I decided this was something I could do for her. So I worked every day, frantically filling the house with her pressed flowers as pictures, her money plant in vases, her beeswax candles in holders, her sheet music in frames over the piano, her doilies sewn into pillows, her quilt squares into a quilt bearing her name...so many things. I realized that more and more I was feeling her presence with me, and she was not gone at all.

I've since read in articles on counseling with the bereaved, that this is a very good way to work through your grief...to continue to feel their presence by creating a book, or acting in their behalf by serving in ways they might have served. It grew out of a natural need for me, and made me feel inspired. As we are to feel God's presence, I feel her presence...and actually I'm never alone.

You learn other things about yourself when your routines are interrupted, and you have to look inside for answers. I guess you have to be devastated to assess what you have left that you can salvage.

I am the oldest child and only girl, having two younger brothers. The older boy, Noel, was retarded and maintained an I.Q. of 75 (the mental age of seven), and was coordinated enough to participate in neighborhood games and ride his bike. He loved to draw, and you will see his art on the cover of Chapter 8. His inability to count money and read past a primer had him constantly trying to fit in.

When others went to school, got married and moved away, he became depressed. He wanted a job and some money like everyone else. No one in the community had the patience to help him, and sheltered workshops were not available at the time. He had to be institutionalized, where he starved himself to death.

Mom had never treated him differently, knowing we

children would make sure he wasn't in danger. But it was frustrating not to have answers. I guess he found his own solution. Ironically, in his last months, he did a lot of hugging and kissing us...but he would not eat.

At his funeral a beautiful thing happened! As we approached the gravesite, I was walking behind my mother when a blue and black butterfly flew down to her arm. She felt it and brushed it away. Hours later, our daughter, Teri Lee, told us that my mother had told her in secret about the butterfly, and how she thought it may have been my brother telling her that everything would be all right. (His burial clothes were blue and gray.) All this from someone covering her sentimentality. When I related this poignant story to my minister, he reminded me that the butterfly is the symbol of the resurrection.

When both my mother and brother were gone, I learned just how much I had been mentally involved looking after both of them. There was a big void in my life—it had lost a lot of its purpose. I never realized just how natural it had become to worry about them. I tried to find answers that weren't there. I know now what is meant by God closing a door, and opening a window. Genealogy has given me a window with a whole new view. So, find ways to "celebrate life," and it will lift you.

I needed to share those personal experiences so you would know why I value the life of my family...with all its struggles, and pain. To see how my mother stayed with it, found creative ways to enjoy her children, and was always there to help. Of course, I could never understand why she didn't know where my red shirt was, when she was home all day. She must have seen it somewhere.

But actually, I want to capture her on paper as a testimonial that it is only when you deal with life that you discover your potential. People today are running away from all the problems...sometimes with alcohol and drugs...maybe suicide. They seek to run things their way, planning and plotting as though they are always in control. Sooner or later you run into a roadblock, a dream that didn't come true and you have to settle for something else. If you don't know the recipe for lemonade when life deals you lemons, you may think YOU'RE the lemon! Then comes the time you need a good self-image, knowing you could

18

survive under any condition because you have talents you haven't discovered yet.

That's the neat thing about genealogy! By the time you dig into the patterns of each family, you begin to see that people relate to the same situation in many ways. I've heard it said, that *it's not what happens to you, but the way you react to it.* So it comes down to the choices people have made that determine their lives and make them interesting. Through genealogy you become less judgmental as you trace the lives of all your ancestors. Each has a story to tell; you have only to seek it out.

I guess I'll continue searching for clues as I want to feel I am a strong link between the past and our children. I want them to enjoy and pass on all the good feelings I have. My mom played the piano by ear. I always wanted to know her secret, as I had to practice to play. She liked cooking unusual foods so we would get used to eating everything. Now I ask you, have you ever eaten oyster plant and pork brains? And who made up the story about sending Mrs. Santa some fabric to make me some doll clothes?

I remember Mom was always singing...sometimes words, but mostly humming. It sort of kept her company as she worked. I find I do it too; almost lost my job at the soda fountain. It seemed that it indicated that I was not working, but just fooling around. (Now if I had waited for applause, I would have been guilty.) But it was an unconscious bit of pleasure that was a natural outlet. Makes you wonder if you inherit that too.

I didn't find out until college that no one had dessert at every dinner meal, but us. I remember asking, at home, what dessert was going to be, so I would know how much dinner to eat.

Mom was the one who said, "come look at the rainbow;... come see the wren." She was the one who only used two eggs when it said three, and wondered why the cake didn't rise.

She did things just to see if she could do them...turning "nothing" into "something." When her brother was going to give a nice glen plaid suit away, she took it and sewed it into a suit for me. It was very nice; but when I wore it, I thought everyone could see it was once my uncle's suit.

Mom always tended a flower and vegetable garden. In fact, I have tried to duplicate her garden in my back yard. I dug

19

some peonies, iris and daffodils from her yard. There are August lilies by the pump, and phlox and lily of the valley. In the spring we have pussy willow and forsythia; and later sunflowers for the birds, mint for the iced tea, and rose petals for potpourri. There was always lots of money plant and Chinese lanterns which were dried and taken to the fair.

I did an interview with my mother about fifteen years ago, thinking I might write a child's tour of Harpers Ferry, West Virginia in 1910. She used to spend every summer there helping her aunt. I tape-recorded it so I could remember the details. It was a few years before I could listen, but now, I enjoy imagining she's right there. She describes the whole town, and the people she remembered with their various duties. In fact, her Aunt Marie Shewbridge is still living there. She may enjoy hearing it. The last time I asked Aunt Marie to tell me about my mother, she said, "She always used to bring me a rose." I never knew my mother was sentimental...she who didn't hug and kiss.

And so, I remember Mama...celebrating the good and making excuses for the rest. Choose someone to honor with a record of your memories. Include the stories of all who knew her or him...maybe a scrapbook of letters. It is especially good therapy after a recent loss. Perhaps the cards of condolence have personal comments that could be entered into the book. I like the title the Mormons give to theirs...a "Book of Remembrance."

All of the writings on the subject of grief seem to say that you should lose yourself in activity, look for new direction, new purpose, closing the door on the past. You are supposed to realize that death is a part of life, and get on with what you have to do.

I have known young people who have lost a spouse who feel they must close that chapter and open a new one. They marry someone who lives a completely different lifestyle from their deceased spouse. I suppose they don't look for their former mate in this new setting.

But others need more time...to tend to unfinished business, and spend time making contributions that only they can make in this world. Again, believe that you were put here for a purpose, and that purpose was made more pleasant by having a spouse. But that same calling is still there waiting for you to respond.

Whenever one of our friends has a death in the family, we send a card of sympathy mentioning the many good things we know he/she did. We also relate what a help it was to prepare an album to honor and keep a loved one in the family's memory. Perhaps it will help them as well.

There is a short 12-minute film which was created to help a child understand death, titled, "The Day Grandpa Died," by BFA Educational Media. Contact your library to review it.

I also know that once one of your parents dies, you are reminded that you now have the responsibility to carry on in their place. To me, that represents the same feeling you must take about all of your heritage. Who else is going to do it for you? Who else would know and remember as vividly as you? This is something you would do the best and, believe me, you and your family will be the better for it.

A GARDEN OF MEMORIES

They say the flowers of tomorrow are in the seeds of the past. We in genealogy certainly can agree with that, as we attempt to give future generations an appreciation of the past. But saying that is not enough; we have to translate it into something visible, tangible.

With this in mind, I have been sending a living plant, or lily bulbs to be planted, when there has been a death in a family. If you know the person loved a particular flower, try to duplicate it as your gift. The family will appreciate the consolation in the present and the remembrance of the past. It's a gift that keeps on giving each time you see it.

This practice grew out of a genealogical experience, as we were researching the homeplace of Lee's great-grandfather, Christian. After following some sketchy directions about the *dirt road to the river*, we approached a boarded-up old brick structure, the last one before the road ran out. Everything was quiet and deserted and we tried to imagine the family at work. Upon closer examination, we discovered clumps and clumps of daffodils near the front door. Some evidence of life still exists there, as we imagined Sarah Jane planting and enjoying them in the garden. Lee's father, Gene, lay gravely ill with cancer so we decided to pick a big bunch and take them to him. We announced that this was a gift from his grandparents, and shared our experience. He was never certain which house was his grandfather's, and seemed quite surprised and pleased with our discovery.

I cannot tell you how rewarding that day was, and how it would never have happened had it not been for our searching for the past. You feel so much a part, a connection to bringing everything back together...like joining links in a chain that should never have been broken. When you and your spouse help each other, it also brings you together into each other's lives in a unique way. As I said earlier, it gives you tangible ways to react to a situation...often a poignant one such as this.

When Gene passed away a few weeks later, I related this story to our friend, Mary, and a few days after, she brought us a gift of daffodils in his memory, and even planted them in our new rock garden. To see those daffodils each year is to remember all of these people...and be glad.

I am reminded there was a second time when a daffodil played an important role in my life. Mom went through a period when she became depressed for two or three weeks. She wasn't even getting out of bed, and had no interest in anything. I decided to cut some daffodils from her garden to show her there was still beauty out there...beauty where she had been, where she had put them...just outside the door. She didn't say anything, but a few days later she began to join the world again. I'll never know just what helped—she never talked about it—but I'd like to think it may have been the beauty in little things that are all around, if we just seek them out. Let someone else worry about the **big** things.

To this day, I have no trouble meditating if I go out-of-doors...under the trees. It takes me away from all the affairs of man and into a world where seasons come and go, unaffected by judgments and stresses. Here you are not responsible...God is. I think of that verse many times that says, "You're nearer to God in a garden than anyplace else on earth."

Here is what Thoreau wrote in his journal on January 3, 1853; "If this world were all man, I could not stretch myself, I should lose all hope. He is constraint, she (Nature) is freedom to me. He makes me wish for another world, she makes me content with this."

To think of some of our friends and relatives is to see them tending and nurturing plants as though they were children. I can remember that before I had children, I felt the need to have something dependent on me, something I could see thriving under my care...be it a bird that rewarded me with a song, or a plant that managed a bloom.

We have enjoyed creating our gardens around focal points: a shade garden near the pump, an old plow in the flower garden, and a rusty metal wheelbarrow with its usual group of geraniums. A dinner bell, sundial, an old wagon wheel rim are other important accents.

When you're interviewing your family, find out what their favorite flowers, trees, and seasons are and why. It may open up a whole category you had not considered. The more you know about a person, the more you can respond in a personal way. At the time of a funeral, it has been sad to hear that the family doesn't always have some little personal quotes that the minister can relate. Just that they were "very sweet and kind" doesn't single them out.

Gardens are to be shared, and I think it's amazing that part of nature's plan is that flowers be picked to encourage new blooms to come. It keeps bulbs from putting out seed, and allows the bulb to store food for next year. The idea of pruning is promoted everytime we share branches of holly at Christmas, and forsythia in the spring. It truly is Nature's gift from you. It seems so fitting to put vases of flowers on altars at church, in memory of those who enjoyed them so much when they were here.

If you were to create a memory garden, what would you plant and why? Mine would have lots and lots of lilacs. They are my favorite, as my mother knew. She always presented me with a big bouquet when she came to visit in the spring, realizing I didn't have a bush.

I'd have old-fashioned larkspur in its pinks and blues, pointing out the little bunny that sits in the center of each bloom. Along the fence I'd have hollyhocks (that I seldom see anymore), and tall dahlias to remind me of my granddad who spent all his spare time in his garden. You'd never think a railroad engineer would raise dahlias, but he had rows and rows in his back yard.

I found this poem in an old magazine. It seems to speak for me:

HOMAGE

I'd paused, that autumn day, to see
Your garden, choked with weeds.
Each flower that knew your tender touch,
Spinning to wind its seeds.

I, who knew and loved you well,
Walked each tangled pathway there,
Gathering hands full of every seed,
Until each withered stalk lay bare.

Gaily my garden grows, and fair,
Color runs riot, brilliant and gay,
I tend each growing plant with care,
Paying respect, in my humble way...

by...Beulah Fenderson Smith

I love to read the Foxfire series of books, especially when the dialect of the mountain people is quoted. There are many true stories of the way our ancestors worked to grow their food, or knew ways to find it in the wild. I always have wanted to be resourceful, self-sufficient if I had to be. Necessity is truly the mother of invention, and we find we have the ability if we really have the need.

Those books, by Eliot Wigginson, even teach you ways to construct the tools that were used in farming. Especially interesting are the articles on the plants that were grown for their medicinal qualities. The methods of predicting weather had a great bearing on the time for planting. Investigate the customs in your families.

For the time my husband was in the army, we lived in Kentucky at Fort Knox. When we returned to Maryland, we decided we would take a black-eyed Susan plant as a gift for our friends when we visit. Since it is Maryland's state flower, we hoped it would remind them of us.

24

Climbing roses have been planted everywhere we've lived, and I've always blessed the first and the last that bloomed. Well, actually the teacher usually got the first one, as insurance for an "A" on the report card. I have found the easiest way to root a rose is to take a six-inch cutting, remove the bottom two leaves and dip the stem in Rootone powder. Place it gently in the ground where it will receive filtered sun, and leave it to grow. Put a large jar over it as a mini-greenhouse, water it, and the next summer you can remove the jar.

One old-fashioned pink rose makes the best potpourri, and it keeps giving pleasure even after it dies. Did you ever make sachets or beads of rose petals? Perhaps just a shallow bowl of rose petals on the lamp table will bring fragrance to the room. Remember, these were the first room deodorizers.

I decided sachets would be a perfect gift from my garden for *special friends* on surprise occasions. They can be fashioned in any shape and of lace and ribbon scraps. Filled with dried petals, your friend can *smell the roses* all winter. To save a rose from a special occasion, enclose it in a paperweight.

Another fragrant gift from nature's storehouse is a balsam pillow. We took the time to gather some balsam limbs when we were hiking in New England. Putting them in bags in the RV, they gave off a wonderful fragrance as they were drying. They continued to dry in the garage at home, and the following holiday we stitched up some green burlap pillows. We fringed the edges, and filled them with needles. On the top side we embroidered one yarn branch and tied on a red bow.

On a recent trip to Nova Scotia, we had been driving so long we needed a break. We had just entered the town of Calais, Maine, and there sitting among some lovely Victorian homes was a beautiful garden. Seeing a woman bending over some of the clumps of perennials, I inquired if I might look around. She was a lovely person, caretaker for Mrs. Burns, who enjoyed adding more and more plants every year. She gave me a tour, answering all my queries. When I apologized for the interruption, she said, "If no one stopped by, it would be like dressing up your children and no one notices!"

Back home, one elderly friend named Cerelia filled her whole backyard with all kinds of blooming bushes, and took very little credit for their success. She said, "I just go out every year and throw another bag of peat here and there." She's gone now, but the tiny pink rose she gave us hears a "Hi, Cerelia!" when I walk by. Marge's lavender mums are right beside. You can see why it's hard for me to move. I'd have to leave all these friends.

However, I read that seeds, bulbs, and roots were so important they were sewed into the hems of garments worn by the immigrants. This is how a lot of new plants were brought to this country. Today there are groups searching out these "heritage plants" near abandoned houses and farms. Some roses were named in the 1840's, and are considered more hardy, heavily scented, and easier to grow than the newer hybrids. Cabbage, sweet briar and moss rose are some of the older. (Americana magazine, May 1977)

Seeds are also being collected as "endangered species," and can be shared by sending a SASE (self addressed stamped envelope) for information to:
SEED SAVERS EXCHANGE
R.R.#3, BOX 239
DECORAH, IA 52101

For a catalog of unusual and heirloom seeds, send $3.00 to:
SEEDS BLUM
IDAHO CITY STAGE
BOISE, ID 83706

When I inherited Grandma's ironstone dishes, I was told they had a *moss rose* design. It was many years before I saw a real moss rose in a public garden, and it truly has a fringe-like calyx just like the design...another search rewarded!

One rose bush sacrificed every bloom to become a corsage from my boyfriend. He asked his mother's permission to cut them, and it must have had ten buds wired together. All through the dance, they kept dropping off, much to his disgust. To make it worth his while, I married the guy! Now all his flowers come from the florist.

GARDENS FOR CHILDREN

Some of our dates, and later walks with the children, were along the nature trails where I remember bluebells, lady slippers, hats from May apple leaves, pointing out Dutchman's breeches, and Jack-in-the-pulpit. Anytime we've tried to transplant them to our garden, they didn't root. It's as though they were begging to be left alone, so in the future, we'll go where they live.

When you see a patch of moss, get down close to see the miniature sprouts. Put your ear to the ground and listen to the little noises you hear. Become part of nature's world for a minute; take a magnifier and play detective. A lot of learning is in listening and looking, being tuned in to what has always been here waiting to be discovered.

That's what I like about genealogy...information waiting to be discovered. All we have to do is find the right key...the right direction...add up the clues...look in new places. If it's there, we can find it. I think they call it persistence.

How many of us would ever throw away the gift of a tiny bunch of violets, or a weed bouquet? Did you have a special little vase for these? Use doll dishes, toothpick holders, cruets, spice or perfume bottles, or a baby cup.

My friend, Doris, reminded me that May baskets were once a floral treat for the first of May. The children created baskets or cones of heavy paper, and filled them with flowers from the yard, woods, or fields. As they hung them on the doorknob of a friend's house, they rang the bell, and ran and hid so the friend would have to guess from whence the basket came. I'm going to make her one this year, just for *old-time's sake.*

I love camping; it's always a surprise, spontaneous and never boring; the weather will make sure of that! One of our fondest memories is of our four-week trip to California...a different location each day. While we set up camp, we sent one of the girls to pick flowers for the table. Along our journey over the roads, we picked one of every kind of wild flower we could get to, and faithfully looked them up in our guide. Did you know there is even a guide with scientific names for weeds? Everything has a family name, no matter how insignificant it seems.

Remember that, when you're *weeding out* your family tree! No pruning allowed!

What about disasters in the garden patch? I once found some ink berries which made an indelible mark on my memory AND on my dress, much to my mother's dismay! You must have had some run-ins with snakes, toads, and bees who have other ideas on how to use a garden. When our canary died, my mother told me I asked her if she was *planting* the canary! (Well, you don't bury the plants, do you?)

Did someone in your family dry or press flowers? After pressing in a big book, or flower press, have children mount samples in a magnetic photo album. On the accompanying page they could give the name and occasion when it was found.

Did they find uses for herbs? Growing and processing herbs in the past was the start of perfumes, insect control, cosmetics, condiments, soaps and drugs. And they had three kinds of gardens: the kitchen garden, flower and psychic gardens. They're rediscovering herbal powers again—one helps you sleep, one relaxes you in the bath, one even inspires conversation. The one I adhere to is to flavor food with herbs in place of salt. For others, read THE HERB BOOK by John Lust.

Herbs are great for sharing, and children can gather mint for the tea, oregano for the *pisghetti*, sage for the dressing, and chives for the cottage cheese. If they do the gathering and the snipping, they'll remember it. Grow some catnip for Kitty and watch her get intoxicated. I looked out one day and saw three cats having a little *nip*! Catnip comes up every year too. We send a sprig in the mail to our cousin Helen for her "Cinders."

Have you ever cut the top from an eggshell to make an egghead planter? Stand the big end in a holder and draw a face on the side. Fill the shell with soil and plant grass seed. Water it and sit it in the window. Grass hair will come up and you will have to give him a haircut!

Seeds are also something you can send through the mail when you can't be with your grandchildren. Tell a garden story about your childhood in an accompanying letter. Maybe there is a small child's book about planting that you can send along.

If a birthday is in the early spring, I have often given amaryllis or paper whites for children to watch, knowing that there is a bloom in there waiting to come out. I have a special green bowl with small stones that hold the bulbs.

If you want a child to grow something he can eat in three or four days, let him grow sprouts for salads. Here's the recipe:

Purchase mung beans from a health food store. Rinse 1/2 cup beans and cover with warm water to soak overnight. Drain in the morning and put in a wide mouth quart jar. Cover with cheesecloth held with a rubber band. Place on its side in a dark location. Twice a day, rinse with warm water and drain well, leaving the cheesecloth in place. Return the jar to the dark. In three to five days it will be filled with sprouts.

Almost everyone has grown at least one sunflower just to watch the birds enjoy it. And the red beebalm or monarda attracts both buzzing bees and humming birds. Were your families bird-watchers?

Some of the names of flowers are so amusing that I like to grow them for the fun of it...like Johnny Jump Ups, Bleeding Heart, Forget-me-nots, Queen Anne's Lace (Gloria put the stems in water with food coloring to tint), Buttercups, Honeysuckle to suck, Rabbit Ear to stroke. And the sight of a ladybug or a spider starts you off with a nursery rhyme or Eency Weency Spider. What about Mr. MacGregor's Garden and Peter Rabbit! Last year we had Bambi and a few friends eat the tops from our tomatoes, but we scared off the crows with a plastic Big Owl! Now I've got to find a different snack for moles and mice...evidently they LOVE tulip bulbs.

Perhaps your garden had places to hide, trees to climb,

secret places where you buried things, a willow for shelter, a tree house, deer and lots of squirrels. Maybe there were nut trees or fruit you picked...was there a swing?

Have you ever felt the sting of a nettle or the taste of spearmint or a blackberry along a stream? A garden tickles all your senses—you see the colors, hear the birds, smell the roses, press the herbs, and taste the berries.

If you have not grown up with some of these experiences, perhaps you can start creating a memory garden right now. If you cherish the moments, they're happening now! As the sun dial in the middle of my herb garden says,
> "Grow old along with me;
> The best is yet to be!"

House and Garden, June 1990—"Heritage Gardens"
Americana, March 1977—"Roses Of The Past"
New Choices, May 1990—"In My Grandmother's Garden"
McCall's, May 1990—"Romance Of Old Roses"

Ohrback, Barbara Milo. THE SCENTED ROOM. NY: Potter
    Publishers

COUSINS

BY THE

DOZENS

3

"REUNIONS...or COUSINS BY THE DOZENS"

Life is shared experiences that bind us together in many ways. We must get a lot of pleasure and security reliving those memories because seventy percent of us attend some kind of a reunion each year. Towns have heritage festivals, schools and colleges have class reunions, churches have homecomings, army units plan get-togethers, and families try to gather the clan. For school, it's a nostalgic return to the past to laugh at the trivial things we thought would make or break us. But for the family, besides good times, we also come to share what we have in common...our ancestry.

When you become a family historian, self-appointed of course, you try to think of ways to get the family together. After all, there will never be enough time to visit all those people in all those locations...to say nothing of finding them home, and agreeable to an interview. So you either plan a reunion or become part of one that is traditional. I like this approach as it gives you an opportunity to introduce yourself and your idea to everyone. It is far superior to doing it over the phone, or writing an endless pile of letters.

Though reunions have been going on for many years, you may be missing great opportunities for recording family history. I'd like to share some of the ways you can begin to focus on recording information that will involve ALL of the generations. This way you can not only record the past, but collect memories for the future. After all, that is one of the biggest rewards from a family reunion...to see yourself as a link between the past and future. It's there right before your eyes; a blood-line from infants to the elders that has become a mix of many ethnic groups, religions, and occupations from a wide geographic area. And they're all on the family tree. You could just sit and reminisce, or talk and eat...but let's look at some activities that will help us get to know each other better. Behind those faces lie all kinds of experiences from which we can learn.

FAMILY PARTIES IN THE HOME

Most families find themselves getting together periodically through the year for birthdays, Thanksgiving, religious holidays.

When they gather at your house, you can plan to add at least one of these activities to the celebration.

• Ask each cook to bring recipes that are traditional in their family, and you could create a Family Heritage Cookbook. Have them add the reason they chose them, and add their signature to personalize.

• Plan your menu of foods around an ethnic theme of the ancestors. Post a menu with the foreign names of the dishes, and/or stick a label on a floral pick into the dish. This is a time when you can use some of your antique serving dishes, on a buffet where they needn't be handled. I get tired of dusting things that I never use, yet I want them to be enjoyed.

• Ask guests to bring old photos of themselves or family members. You would especially like photos of ancestors and their wedding pictures, so you may camera-copy them while they are here. To keep photos from being handled and mislaid, display them on a large table covered by acetate plastic.

• Collect slides of past gatherings on similar occasions to be shown for entertainment. Seeing a slide helps us remember related events of that day, which stimulates conversation.

• Bring an artifact that has a story you can tell about your childhood...or perhaps a photo of it. (ex. Family Bible) When gathering in your own home you have an opportunity to show the way you display your artifacts and heirlooms. Why not give a tour, telling the stories behind them, and suggest that perhaps you should record an inventory in a card file or on video tape!

• Display the family tree on a surface where it can be spread out, and every person can find his own name and dates. Ask that everyone help complete it by making additions or corrections. If they seem to appreciate your research enough to want an individual chart, have copies available as we would like to feel we have partners in our efforts.

• If the celebration is a time for gifts, make yours one that focuses on genealogy: such as...a journal "Days Of Our Lives," an album with prints of the ancestors, a notebook with a family chart and a narrative to accompany it, with a promise to add more as it becomes available; a history book dealing with a local topic, an old map of the area, an artifact that you are ready to pass on, or a Grandmother's Memory book to be filled in. Though the gift is for one person, you are bringing attention to the importance of genealogy and records to the whole group.

• Choose a corner of a room adjacent to the gathering to take individual family group photos. A bench or chair gives seating while others stand behind and to the side. If Grandmother is the honored guest, you may want to make her the central figure to her related family. This then becomes a three or four generation photo for the children, which we have often presented for gifts We also have a record of EACH family that attended for our album. Large group photos are nice, but a bit jumbled when you try to point out relationships.

• Though small group conversations encourage mixing, there could be a time to come together so that different generations can get to know and appreciate each other. Here is a great way to get a response from each person present; ask a leading question to which everyone has a personal anecdote...such as:

What got you into the most trouble as a child?
What was the best news you ever received?
Who was the most famous person you ever met?
How did your life change during the depression, or the war?
What do you think you should get an award for? not always for the best, but the worst or the least likely or the most often...
Which holiday stands out in your memory and why?

This would be a good time to have the tape recorder on. We sometimes find ourselves seated around the ping-pong table, where we can have snacks while we watch slides and share activities. The recorder could just be placed in the center of the table, where it will eventually be ignored.

• Songs can be chosen where lines can be given out to individuals to add variety, and these make great recordings. My favorite is the Twelve Days of Christmas which we used ten years ago. Each voice had a different accent and timbre, and we found ourselves listening for them each time. It got funnier and funnier. The poignant thing about it is that at least half of those people have since passed away, but when we play that tape we remember them well.

• One year we even read a play...a shortened version of Dicken's Christmas Carol which I found in the library. After handing out copies and choosing a cast, we read it through aloud, taping it, thus putting a personal touch on a classic that is like no other. The unusual twist was that our daughter's new husband, Tim, had a natural part,...and he was relieved to find it very short!

• I have a huge hat collection, saved from all the character costumes I had for school and community musicals. So we ask each guest to choose a hat to wear for photos or when we sing. A good song to do as you sit in your circle is the Mexican Hand-Clapping Song (or Chiapanecas). Instead of clapping you trade hats, taking one from the head of the person to your right and placing it on your head. I always slow down the music so we have time to enjoy the new looks. Some hats are too big, some too small, and included are a few wigs...as if you didn't already have enough *characters* in your family. Don't overlook the fact that these activities can bring you closer and remind you of the time that...

• Since we never throw anything away, we have another cupboard filled with assorted rhythm instruments and noisemakers, including bicycle horns and washboards. You could probably form a kitchen band right now. Don't forget that upturned wastecans make terrific drums. These don't require lessons and experience...just discretion on when to make an entrance and when to be quiet. This is a great time for a director to "volunteer," and of course a long-hair wig would give him/her prestige.

I am pleased when years later someone who was there will say..."I wasn't going to come as I was so depressed, but it was such a good time,"..."I still have the picture of Raymond in that funny hat!"..."I didn't really feel like one of the family until that get-together at your house." Most of all, WE had a good time and that made all the planning worthwhile.

Now I'm sure you're feeling this is a far cry from record-keeping and charting your genealogy. Well, after you find yourself spending years researching, you realize this is YOUR life too, and you want to have something to say about how you spent your days with YOUR family, besides researching in the library. There are many ways to find out about your family, and I'm using them all!

LARGE FAMILY REUNIONS...
CLOSE ENCOUNTERS OF THE SAME KIND

Much has been written on planning a successful reunion to suit different needs. Using a general outline, I will cover the steps in planning the usual reunion, followed by suggestions for a genealogist to use this occasion to record a family's history. I'll add suggestions in *italics*.

1. Involve as many people in planning as you can. Different generations will point out the needs they will have to feel comfortable and have a good time. Choose a contact person for each branch of the ancestor's family to make sure you don't miss anybody.

Family charts are a good starting point as they provide a listing of names to contact. But a reunion card file could hold a growing record of each branch of the family. A 3x5 card could be sent, requesting full names and birthdates, of everyone in the family who will be attending. Ask for occupations, special interests, hobbies, and anything else that makes them special. Be sure they specify which branch they represent as married names could make it confusing. Add more cards if needed. These should be brought to the reunion and placed in a file box under the proper branch of the family. Additions may be made then. If you assign each branch a color, this color could be repeated on name tags and the large family tree on display.

2. Organize committees to take care of food, lodging, etc. *You would volunteer to help with program, and update or focus on genealogy...each year bringing new information and activities.*

3. Keep a notebook of all the arrangements, like minutes of a meeting, which then are evaluated in light of the next year. It may be considered a memory book of each reunion, and contain the roster of those who attended and signed it, and photos of highlights of the day. *You may want to get a group to help with a newsletter. This would not only report to those unable to come, but would keep all in touch during the year. The family historian would especially like to know when there is any event which should be added to the family genealogy, such as a death, birth, or marriage. An appropriate card could be sent in celebration of their life. Just seeing names in the newsletter keeps us aware of each other, and may encourage better reunion attendance.*

4. Set the date, notify all at least six months in advance. Try to stick to the same date. Sometimes, it is a birthday or anniversary date which is the excuse.

The program could take on the format of This Is Your Life, Elizabeth Wheeler, and each of her relatives could make some sort of presentation. Memory books could hold pages of items brought for an anniversary couple.

5. Choose a location...close for elderly; a park or group area with campgrounds available. Cabins or motels should be close by for those who don't care to camp. Those attending should indicate their choice. If the reunion will be extended over several days, sight-seeing brochures should be included or planned tours should be reserved in advance.

Genealogists could set up tours to ancestral points of interest in the area: the cemetery, school, homeplace, with the eldest or most knowledgeable acting as guide.

6. Designate a photographer with the expertise to take both single family and large group photos with a still camera, and take orders for prints. Take advantage of sliding boards, stairs, porches, picnic tables, or sloping grounds as natural risers.

Also try to find a video photographer to interview the elderly, providing an oral history as part of the genealogy. Do these two activities in a place set apart from noises and distractions, so you have control of the setting.

If you would like to video all the reunion highlights,

copies could be made and sold. Many unable to attend may like a copy, and one copy could go into the archives.

7. Think of something to autograph...a table runner with space saved for each year, (quilt squares perhaps, that later can be sewn together.)

8. Whole Group Activities—always seated in a circle or around the perimeter of the hall...usually after dinner.

It's best to start with a short business meeting to plan next year's reunion, collect any monies needed for the deficit, and perhaps discuss a project to honor the family or its members.

One project may be to mark the grave of an ancestor whose stone is no longer legible or to put up a post and chain around the site to show protection and concern for its preservation. If the cemetery is in need of care, perhaps monies could be donated to a local person to provide it in our absence. The teens could get a start that very day.

This is also a time to update the genealogy and encourage family to look at materials and assist in keeping the chart up-to-date and accurate.

A display of the large family tree should be put in a prominent place at the beginning of the reunion. Every person present should be able to locate his name on the color-coded chart. This way they can learn to use it and see how all are related to the past.

Any artifacts or albums you have asked to be brought can be displayed on the table below the chart. Some of the elderly, who do not move around much, could sit nearby and answer questions. If they know you need them, they will take responsibility for this, and will probably include many more stories than you had asked for.

9. There should be activities for all ages to choose, from the playground to volleyball and horseshoes. Hopefully there will be a lake or pool nearby for teens to use...all this before getting together later for a group program.

One time we brought all the yard games that hadn't been touched for years. We set up 12 games and handed out cards with the rules for age categories. You had to have a partner and you were allowed to skip some if you weren't successful. Prizes were given for the winner, and two 70-year-old women tied for 1st prize. They had been partners and wouldn't quit until they succeeded! (See sample score card.)

Choose 1 or 2 partners

Choose category you want

Record points if s<u>uccessful</u>

<u>AGE</u>
___ 0-30
___ 30-35
___ 55- ?

<u>GAME</u>	<u>MUST</u>	<u>EXTRA 1 PT.</u>
Horseshoes - make post ring twice (2)	___	Ringer ___ 1 more
Post Basketball - 1 basket (1)	___	Extra ___
Nerf Basketball - 2 baskets (2)	___	2 more ___
Ping Pong - hit 3 conservutive over net (3)	___	2 more ___
Croquet - hit ball thru 4 hoops (4)	___	2 more ___
Ring Toss - ring 2 posts (2)	___	2 more ___
Hop Scotch - toss to 7 + pick up hop to (7)	___	toss to 8 ___
Ball Bounce - bounce once into basket (1)	___	1 more time ___
Paddle Bounce - paddle 8 times into air (8)	___	10 more ___
Watergun - put out candle (1)	___	
Frisbee Toss - into ring 3 times (3)	___	1 more ___
Balloon Volleyball - 5 times over net (5)	___	

10. Contests create some rare moments if you team up dads and daughters against mothers and sons, in-laws against *outlaws* in a tug of war, or a horseshoe tournament. Small children can search for candy hidden in the grass or sandbox. Older kids can play kickball or go on a *People Scavenger Hunt.* (See sample, included with permission from Ellen Miller.)

---

the
PEOPLE SCAVENGER HUNT

DIRECTIONS: Find someone to autograph each space. You can only use any name one time. As soon as you are finished, jump up and down and touch your toes at the same time.

1. Find someone whose last name is Smith. _____

2. Find someone who lived at 728 Walnut St. in Catasauqua. _____

3. Fill in your name for your branch of the family tree. Then find people for two other branches.

Ellen & Titus _____   Marvin & Clara _____

Robert & Dorothy _____   Ruth and John _____

Fred and Catherine _____

4. Find, someone who traveled over 50 miles to be here. _____

5. Find someone from 3 generations on the tree.

Third _____   Fifth _____

Fourth _____   Sixth _____

6. Find someone born the same month as you (_____). _____
                                               Your Birthday

7. Find someone who is over six feet tall. _____

8. Find someone who is under four feet tall. _____

9. Find someone under 10 years old. _____

   Find someone who is between 10 and 19 years old. _____

   Find someone who is between 20 and 39 years old. _____

   Find someone who is between 40 and 59 years old. _____

   Find someone who is over 60 years old. _____

10. Find some one with a last name nowhere else on this list. _____

41

If you know of specific skills or areas which will help identify, include those. If not, just list someone who remembers the first radio, fought in W.W. II, hates to get up, sleeps with his feet uncovered...funny things just to get the group to circulate and get to know each other. As they sign, you will associate the face with the name.

11. Some other activities appropriate are:
—Variety Show of talent indicated on family 3x5 card. May include telling jokes, stories, juggling, magic tricks, monologues, mime, gymnastics, dancing, ear-wiggling, yodeling, puppets, and imitations, besides lip-sync with records, vocal and instrumental groups.

—Sing-alongs led by guitar or other instrument. Song lyrics can be projected on overhead with transparencies, but old songs are the best. Interject less familiar as special acts done by the Boone Sisters...the hams of the family.

—If grab bags have been brought, these can just be offered around the room...and time allowed to barter. If you want to take all evening, hand out numbers which indicate your turn at going up, choosing, unwrapping and showing your prize. If the person with the next number would rather have your prize than a wrapped one, he can demand it; and then you may choose a wrapped prize again. Each person whose number comes up can either choose a wrapped prize or demand another he saw earlier.

—Some reunion families bring items for a flea market sale, all proceeds going for committee expenses.

—Do your version of the Tonight Show and interview three or four of the oldest in the family. Ask questions about their past: what they consider the best thing ever invented, the hardest thing they ever had to do, what they didn't like about school, and their advice for staying out of trouble.
To balance, you may want to ask some six-year-olds some of the very same questions you asked the elders. Seat them in the same chairs to simulate a parallel.

12. Be sure to give teens a time to get together with their loud music, sodas, conversation and maybe some excursions to the pool or an amusement park. They'll be better company later in the day, if you let them plan at the beginning.

13. Another family project that we found very successful was a FAMILY CALENDAR. Display a large calendar requesting family members write their names on their birthdays and anniversaries if they would like to be remembered; and place money in a jar to cover cost of copying and mailing. You will also need to be sure their address is in the card file, so it may be included on the back of the calendar. One of our families wore theirs out and asked for a replacement.

14. To add interest and variety to each reunion, choose a different project, location, or encourage a far-away member to try to come for the first time. Keep popular activities, but vary the people involved. If you want to make copies of the reunion video, information and price could be made known and those unable to come will realize what they missed. Others may just want a record of the occasion.

Above all, once the plans are made, and you have a committee to back you up...just plan to go with the feeling that you are providing an opportunity for people to interact, get to know each other as a cross-section of humanity...who are growing older, changing, and trying to make the most out of life.

No reunion or program is ever the same, though the entire outline is repeated, because the weather will be different, some new songs will be sung, and some of the same people will not be there. Each year will have its unique memories...so don't miss a thing!

CHURCH HOMECOMINGS...AN EXTENDED FAMILY

Shortly after I met my husband's parents, I was invited to meet many, many more Spurriers at the church homecoming. If I were considering being part of his family, this would be a good time to look them over. That's just what they did to me also...but in such a pleasant way. All I had to do was follow Lee and do what he did, as I tried to remember all the names and relationships. When we talked on the way home, I could only say, "Was she the one in the green dress or the pink hat?"

I also learned that whether or not you are ready to eat a plateful of food, you'd better take some the first time through the line. And the sooner you get in line, the hotter the food. It's funny when you look back on it...but now that I do, I realize what an important place that day has in my memory.

How I sensed the warmth and importance of the day to everyone there, watched as they hugged, listened as they chatted, and then followed them as they walked through the graveyard. It had only been a year since Grandpop Spurrier had passed away—my husband's idol—and I felt as if I had been allowed to share some special moments with the family.

Now I realize how children perceive our emotions...when they do not understand the conversation, are not acquainted with all the people, they simply tune in on the emotions they observe and sense. I mention this because we have many children coming to *homecoming* and they're also picking up the respect we have for the elders, the church and everything about it.

A church homecoming is a different kind of reunion because it represents a family of God who have their beginnings in this place. There is a permanence about this location, an historic tie that binds these particular families. Often they represent the founding groups who may have inter-married and all lived nearby. They will always remember those emotional times when they have supported each other...the weddings, christenings, burials. Probably a lot of the conversation goes back to the church suppers, the summer picnics, strawberry festivals, the year they remodeled or built on the church hall...all at this location.

And now it's time to come home, partly to see old friends, partly to see if they have missed us. My hope as a genealogist is that someone is preserving these wonderful memories by recording them...so here are some activities you may not have thought of yet.

• Follow the same outline as any reunion, of course. You have the advantage of a good location where everyone knows the way. The program may include discussion on these types of activities:

• Create a file of the activities of the church each year. If the minutes of the church are not kept in the building, record the name of the person who has them. Include the names of every person who is a member, and the names of anyone who completes a project that helps the church to grow.

Even though a church is very small, and is only one of many that the minister serves, it is even more important that that congregation feel unique and special. Many of these records are kept combined with others and are hard to find when writing a history. Perhaps copies could be made and kept in the individual churches.

If families are encouraged to keep their ancestor's records in acid-free boxes, it seems appropriate that the church also be able to glory in its beginnings. In 1976, many churches were prompted to create booklets, some of which have been published. Consider choosing a year that you can do the same...and someone in those first families may find it a project that will add to their own genealogies.

Donate a copy to the local library so that others can see its value, and do likewise. Genealogists from all over the country may be looking for this information. By now descendants of those families are scattered all over.

• Collect and keep items that were used in the services long ago...altar cloths, hymnals, bulletins, cardboard fans usually available for hot, muggy days. Perhaps there are Cradle Roll lists and choir anthem music in the organ bench with names on them from the past. Old serving dishes may still be in the kitchen, and the minister's office may have papers that have never been claimed.

One church keeps these on display in a glass case for members to be reminded, and visitors to see that this church is proud of its heritage.

• Photographs are of great interest and may be found in albums of the founding families. If the elderly can remember anyone who took photos in their younger days, contact them. We had a minister who took many slides in our teen years. Though we enjoyed them then, we wondered what had become of them. Unfortunately, he had passed away, his wife remarried, and she was unable to find them. Express your interest in making copies before people move or pass away. Choose a committee to organize them into albums. Make them available to those interested.

• Have someone give a presentation on the history of the building, its changes from the early days of horse and buggy perhaps. Mention how the needs of the church affected the changes...for example, the use of two doors to separate men and women. Interview the oldest member about changes, or perhaps ask them to tell stories of "the way it was." Include any memorial windows or donations, using the names of families as much as possible. Some of the family may be there at homecoming.

Perhaps someone from the district office of the church could be invited to come and talk on the early history of the area. They may have suggestions on other sources of material.

• Prepare a Roster of Ministers and the years they served the church. Space should be allowed for additions.

• A worship service could be scheduled to coincide with other heritage festivals in the area. In Brunswick, Maryland, they did a re-creation, wore clothing of the Civil War days, and used music and order of worship from early records.

• Though church suppers may still be held with more modern appliances, menus might be printed up to represent one from an earlier time. I have two cookbooks that were sold containing recipes and names of the contributors beside them. These could be displayed, and some dishes prepared and served in their honor.

• On reunion day, competitions could be held and prizes awarded to the family with the most descendants present. It hearkens back to the banner they used to give to the class with the highest attendance.

• Though you will be using newer hymnals, you may have a family musician lead a hymn sing of the oldest ones. Ask an elderly member to help with the choice. Have younger members choose some as well, so they feel included...but it's important to sing some that all generations know and love. "Amazing Grace" is sure to fit that category.

• Walk with your own children through the cemetery, visiting each relative's grave, telling what you admired about them. Maybe take a bouquet of roses and let the children place one on each stone. Children remember what **THEY did** longer than what **YOU said.** If you want, take a small tape recorder so they can remember the day, and take their own walk some day.

Genealogists would make a diagram of the whole area, drawing and numbering the important stones and the location of the church building. Provide a key to the numbers on another sheet of paper..never on the back. Always prepare some kind of record in case you are not available to assist.

Homecomings are becoming fewer and fewer as our younger generations move out of the area. If their visits don't coincide with the gathering, they miss an opportunity to renew memories and ties. Then they feel no one will remember them.

Encourage any members of those once-active families to make an effort to attend, just as you would for any family or class reunion. In fact, you could plan a family reunion at the same time. The church and cemetery will always be there...waiting for you to "come home."

FOOD

FOR THOUGHT,

FAMILY

STYLE

4

FOOD FOR THOUGHT...FAMILY STYLE

The story of any family can be viewed through its relationship to food. Food seemed to bring everyone together routinely or in celebration...but together. I have facetiously said, "the only time everyone is here is mealtime." The comraderie of family reunions, the everyday gathering around the table, the gifts of food we accepted or prepared year after year have given us many memories. I guess you could say, we are **what** and **how** we eat...literally. Read the writings of Mary Frances Fisher, who feels we eat to satisfy hundreds of needs, and she is interested in all of them.

To provide a vehicle for oral history, I'd like to suggest a series of questions that center on food. I will answer the questions as they pertain to my experience, thereby showing you how varied the answers may be. You may want to use the information from many of your related families to create a HERITAGE COOKBOOK, interspersing recipes with these related stories. (More on this toward the end of this chapter.)

First of all, think of the kitchen of the past.
1. Describe it, along with the feelings you had when you were there.
The kitchen most vivid in our memory was at the home of our cousin Betty. Her mother, Aunt Helen, kept the room warm by making a good fire in the big iron cookstove. Many times, they opened the oven door, propped their feet up, and peeled and ate apples together. Her daddy had his favorite rocker by the end of the stove. The oak kitchen cabinet held the makings of noodles and potpie; and a closet under the stairs was filled with jackets, a shotgun, and a hunting coat. On winter nights, her mother banked the fire and closed the door, so the kitchen would stay warm until morning. The bedroom was so cold in the morning that Betty would run to the kitchen to finish dressing for school.

Besides the practical side of any kitchen, you could usually see collections that were dear to the heart of the cook. My mother had shelves for her pitcher and rooster collection. The window sill held many plant cuttings she hoped would take root, and looking outside she could keep a watchful eye on the wren house.

Though the large chalk-board was there for lists, I spent a lot of time using it as a drawing board.

To me the kitchen was a clearinghouse...where everything that came into the house was dropped: books, shoes, woes, hurts, excitement, news...sometimes all at the same time. At least we didn't all arrive together; so Mom took us on, one by one.

2. What utensils or dishes were used then that you no longer see today?

I remember green-painted, wooden-handled cookie cutters, mashers, ladles. Grandma made us snowballs with an ice shaver, and pancakes on a big oval iron griddle with hearts in the handles. The waffle iron had to sit on the stove since nothing had electricity or batteries. Cakes were mixed and potatoes were mashed by hand. You can see the spoons are worn off on one side.

Other utensils that now occupy a place on my shelf or wall are scales, crocks and candle molds that hold plants and flowers, a glass nut chopper, cookie and tea tins, and a covered pewter dish that got too close to the fire. Each one reminds me of a story I've heard or an experience I've had.

Dishes used in the past include curved bone dishes, salt dips, and bone-handled cutlery.

3. Are there any stories of mealtime disasters you can relate? How did you learn to cook?

Well, when my husband, as a seven-year-old, was called to dinner, he leaned his makeshift fishing pole up against the house. About ten minutes later they heard a chicken squawking and found it had swallowed the worm and pin on his rod. He wasn't fishing for chickens!

Then there was the coffeecake made with curry mistaken for cinnamon...and a lot of new bride fiascos...Tuna Surprise and all that!

I'd need another book to tell you about those concoctions in Home Ec. class, especially the details of pie dough stuck on the ceiling.

4. Just getting our food and preserving it has changed so much. Does anyone remember smoking, drying, pickling, or salting foods? How did you get your food other than the country store? trapping?

hunting mushrooms? clamdigging?

We lived near the river and when fishing was good we had enough for us and to sell to Wenner's Store. We especially love catfish. There's a special art to skinning them, and that method has been passed down in our family. Also hunting groundhogs, rabbits, and squirrels had its own ritual. The men got their own breakfast and left early in the morning. It was bad luck for the women to get up. Who wants to bring bad luck? The men cleaned all the game and it was ready for the skillet when the women entered the picture.

Butchering was a fall event that brought families and friends together to share the work and the food. I only went once, but it was like a carnival of sights to walk from one stage to the next of that hog being turned into sausage and pudding. I wish we would depend on each other like that again. So much work, but everyone was needed, and Jeanne even remembers getting off from school.

Did you ever go to a pea thrashing, corn husking, quilting or apple butter party? These jobs took so long that they were turned into a social, which then became a *date*.

Many foods were delivered so you seldom had to drive anywhere. Milk was delivered to the front door in glass bottles with little cardboard lids. In the winter the milk was there long enough to freeze, so the cream would push the lids up and they'd be sitting an inch above the bottle. My mother would take the cream from the top and save it to whip for dessert. (Now milk is homogenized.)

Ice was delivered to the back door and put into the icebox. We had to place a card in our front window to let the ice man know what size block we wanted. We kids would gather around the truck to see the pick carve the proper size. As the chips of ice flew, we gathered them up to suck.

Some farmers came into town twice a week with fresh vegetables. They would call out what they were selling that day, and weigh it up on scales that swung from the back of the wagon or truck.

As a family, we found a grove of black walnut trees and gathered the nuts regularly for holiday baking. We called it our *secret place* and guarded its identity like a fishing hole. In summer, we went for blackberries as well. They always seem to taste better when they've been waiting to be discovered.

53

5. Did you ever live on a farm and raise animals for food? Was it difficult? Did you have an orchard or raise vegetables? Describe or diagram the buildings and what you remember about your life there.

We raised chickens for eggs, and my mother used to say we only wanted eggs when the hens weren't laying. She tried to preserve the eggs in a solution called waterglass.

My father raised bees; called them hard workers, and very clean housekeepers. The only work he had to do twice a year was steal their honey and provide them with new comb to work on. After he extracted the honey from the wax, my mother began to make beeswax candles. (Like taking lemons and making lemonade, she finally accepted the bees and made candles.)

6. How has shopping for food changed? What is missing today? Perhaps you went to a market or country store.

Our grocery store was in town. Customers chatted as they stood in line to be waited on by Miss Elsie. She got each item from the shelf, using a *pincher affair* to reach the top shelves. The price was added to the others on a tablet of paper, and tallied when we completed our list.

We had to wait in a different line for the butcher to weigh meats, and he knew his reputation was also being weighed by the quality of his meat.

7. When it was mealtime, did you follow any set procedure? Did you have designated seats? Eat in the dining room? Who always said grace? Can you repeat it now?

We had a large kitchen so we ate there, sitting in the same place each time. Dad Smith always said grace but it was mumbled so we could hardly make it out...it went, "Our Heavenly Father, we thank you for this nourishment which we are about to receive. Pardon us for our sins, and bless our homes, we ask for Christ's sake. Amen."

8. Were mealtimes pleasant, or a time of reckoning?

In my house, they were the latter, so we ate as quickly as

possible.

9. Did you call your meals breakfast, lunch, dinner; or dinner, supper? How did the procedure change when company was there? Did you have assigned jobs, such as setting and clearing the table, washing and drying the dishes?

We only had lunch at school...it was dinner and supper at home. When other than family were there, we ate in the dining room, opened up the drop-leaf table, put on the nice cloth and better dishes.

My brothers and I were expected to help on call, but had no regular chores. Mom was too particular; it had to be done right.

10. Were Sunday dinners different from other days? How?

11. Were there foods you had a bad experience with, and have not eaten since?

I think we all have, and it's interesting to see why. We children were given everything under the sun to eat, as though everyone does...foods like oyster plant, pork brains, tongue, and once in a while, bear and deer meat. Mom wanted us to learn to eat everything. When we didn't see her eating it, she told us she was on a diet...which she tried every other week. I found out years later, she didn't like some of the foods either, but wanted us to learn to eat everything!

My husband's grandmother died when his father was twelve, and the cook who helped care for them served roast beef every Sunday. He would never eat roast beef again.

I cannot tolerate the taste and texture of rhubarb, but I have forced it down. When the old timers say,"Do you think the rain'll hurt the rhubarb?" I say, "I hope it kills every bit of it."

12. Are there foods you can never get enough of?

Of course, and Santa puts a lot of it in our stockings every Christmas: licorice, peanuts, swiss cheese, M & Ms, animal crackers and Gummy Bears for the appropriate *child*.

13. Can you remember ever being very, very hungry? Explain.

55

14. Did your children ever call their food by some funny name? What foods did they first learn to prepare?

We had to stifle our laughter when our daughter called all meats *ham*, all fruit *apples*...and the day she asked us to pass the *sauercrap*, we nearly fell off our chairs. We all know about *pisghetti* and *hamburglar*; what can you add?

Of course, my brothers thought for years that a few spoons of dirt were necessary to their diet, and they would come in from play with a black ring around their mouths. As for me, I went in for mudpies, properly molded in spoon shapes, and topped with some grass coconut. I had a readymade market right in the family!

We continued the tradition of making homemade root beer, and formed an assembly line of bottles being filled from the lard can in the sink, to the bottle capper, to the box, where they would ripen on their sides until the holidays.

When I was a teenager I proved my culinary prowess by fixing my date many grilled cheese sandwiches served with tomato soup. (He must have been impressed; we've been married 39 years!) We still get out the brown-handled soup bowls for tomato soup...keeping those memories alive!

15. What other foods did you make for children?

I hope they remember the animal shaped pancakes I tried to make. After falling short of perfect bears, I played *rorschach* and named them AFTER they baked. Also, I made doughnuts by poking holes in refrigerated biscuits and frying, as well as stocking cookies with goodies inside.

16. Do you remember regular trips to buy sweets?

Mrs. Parker and Mrs. Larue had penny candy stores in part of their houses, and we'd stop by after school. It's fun just listing all the kinds: "I'll have two of those, and one of those, and...;" it was so hard to decide. Also when I went to the *pictures* with my Grandma, we would stop at Mills' for a drink called *lemon phosphate* after the show.

Usually on a summer Sunday we would take a ride to Main's Homemade Ice Cream store to cool off. It was about fifteen miles away, but well worth the trip!

17. Did you take pride in growing your own produce? Ever win any prizes for your foods or receive a special compliment?

My sister-in-law, Pat, and I used to try making original birthday cakes in all shapes and sizes. No molded pans for us...and we have the photos to prove it! Everything from booties to treasure chests to pianos, and recently computers and teddy bears. For the latter, just make two round layers, one slightly smaller for the head. Add seven cupcakes for ears, feet, and nose, checkers for buttons and eyes, and a real ribbon bow at the neck. Easy to serve too; just disassemble. Also, don't forget to use fresh flowers on a plain iced cake when you can't make those beautiful frosting roses. It's cut up so quickly and gone!

I once received a compliment I've never forgotten. It was the first time after we were married that I was asked to bring something for the church picnic. Being inexperienced, but determined, I slaved for three hours baking a special chocolate chip cake, checking and double-checking. When one of the men bellowed to my husband, "I see why you married her," I just beamed.

18. Were there church socials, strawberry festivals, block parties, carnivals, where you helped with food?

19. Who ran the local restaurants? When did you eat there?

Mrs. Himes', when my mother was ill; Foster's for hot dogs on the way home from the movie.

20. Do you have special traditional foods that MUST be served at holidays, special birthdays?

Oyster stew is a Christmas morning special here, as is a cup of eggnog the night before. Then I found out our daughter really doesn't like eggnog, so we give her cider instead. Tradition is supposed to keep us together, not drive us apart!

For Thanksgiving, I always add mincemeat to my bread stuffing. It tones down the strong flavor of the mincemeat while giving interest to the bread cubes. I had success with making my own fortune cookies, so we throw a Chinese New Year's party just so I have a reason.

One of my brothers always wanted an angel food cake, the other a devil's food. I wonder if that was a character analysis? My mother always made her father some sugar cookies for his birthday, no matter how busy she was.

21. Did you ever send food out to someone or contribute to a potluck dinner? What was your specialty?

Sending food to the home of a bereaved family is traditional. In the old days they sometimes sent a funeral pie.

I usually send chicken-corn chowder or, in the summer I fix marinated broccoli. We used to have luncheons or cake sales at church. Everything my mother fixed never turned out as well as when it was for home...the shells of deviled eggs always decided to stick and really looked like the *devil*!

Mom made up for it at Hallowe'en when she made decorated cupcakes for the poor children down the street who never got anything like that.

Food is the greatest gift when it is given as a bit of yourself. When it presents a problem, maybe chips or rolls would be better.

22. Were you ever given unusual gifts of food? When?

The kitchen staff at the school where Lee was principal, sent us a baked ham every Christmas...a wonderful gift at a busy time.

When the teenage cast wanted to thank me for my direction of a musical, each family took a Saturday and brought me a homebaked goodie. It was a wonderful idea, and for fourteen weeks I felt *special*...and I never forgot it.

23. Were you ever asked to give some food to a *tramp* at your door or send food to a disaster victim or the homeless?

During the depression and all during the 1930's many people were out of work, hungry and traveling from place to place. Since we lived in a railroad town, "hobos" (as they were called) would come to the door and nicely ask if you could spare them a sandwich or anything. They usually offered to do some work in return. I remember my mother giving more than one a sandwich to eat out in the yard. She was afraid to let a stranger in the house.

My husband's mother invited them in for pancakes, trying to give them something filling. They say that the "hobos" would mark the houses where they were fed, so the next ones would know where to try. Sounds like the underground railway, doesn't it?

24. Do you remember when food was rationed? How did that work?

We were given books of stamps each month, limiting us to amounts of food, gas, shoes, etc., so that more energy and supplies could be given on behalf of our soldiers and the war effort. If you want to get the drama of the moment, just go to the library and read a newspaper from the early 1940's. The headlines, the ads, the obituaries and the editorials all show what patriotism was all about. It involved everyone including the homemaker and the people at home, and what they could do to help. The war effort unified the country and everyone wept and rejoiced together.

Those were the days we saw recipes for sugarless, eggless, butterless cake, and Poorman's Cake took on a new meaning. Today it would say low calorie, no cholesterol, lowfat cake containing fiber and served with diet soda.

25. Can you tell us anything about food in the army...K-Rations, USO Canteen during W.W.II, doughnuts during W.W. I.?

26. Did anyone in your family work with food as a livelihood?

My husband and I ran a Humpty Dumpty ice cream truck to save money for college...but on rainy days, we ate more than we sold. Who among us has not sold Girl Scout cookies, subs to buy band uniforms, and held bake sales for PTA? Even with a college degree, teachers were not paid in the summers in the 1950's, so Lee worked in a corn canning factory.

27. What is the most unusual food you ever ate?

Frog legs! Lee told me that his father took him at night to catch frogs. His dad would wade in the water and shine a flashlight along the bank of a small stream and grab the frog with his bare hand. He would then take the frog to the bank and put it into the burlap bag that Lee was holding.

28. Did you carry a lunch to school or work? Describe.

Most of us lived close enough to school to walk home for lunch. I remember listening to Kate Smith sing on the radio while I ate at home. After school, I hurried home to hear the serial "Jack Armstrong, the All American Boy." However, one of the teachers, Mrs. Deener, decided to bring in her hot plate and fix soup to sell to any who couldn't go home. It wasn't approved by the school board yet, but she decided to do it anyway.

My husband's father walked to his job on the railroad, carrying his lunchbox and coffee bucket. The aluminum bucket was not insulated, but the coffee stayed hot on the radiator at the shops where he repaired the engines. The bucket now hangs on the wall with my other kitchen items.

29. Have you ever had the experience of cooking food out-of-doors? Was it out of necessity or on a camping trip?

My very first attempt at campfire cooking was with baking potatoes. While exploring with my knowledgeable Girl Scout friend, we wrapped some in foil and threw them into the fire. After what seemed like eons, we dug them out half-burned, but good when you're starved!

My husband grew up camping and living by the river every summer. Water for cooking was carried down from town in large clean 30-gallon cans. One was filled with river water for clean-ups and washing a few clothes. I always got them mixed up when I tried to help, as they weren't marked...a constant concern to one trying to make a good impression.

Cooking was done in a screened summer kitchen, and appetites were always keen. Lots of fish and pancakes were consumed. Tomatoes and corn from the fertile garden were in daily supply. Living that close to nature, the weather determined our activity. On rainy evenings, we played cards and ate cookies; on dry ones, we fished and counted stars.

Later, when we camped in a tent, I enjoyed cooking on my

two-burner stove set up on the end of the picnic table. All the smoke and grease went up in the air, and anything I accidentally spilled was absorbed into the soil. I sent one child for a bucket of water, another for some flowers for the table, and the third to set the table. As I cooked, I had a constantly changing scene from a beautiful butterfly to a flock of Canada geese floating by on the river.

One-pot dishes were the usual, and Squaw Corn was a breakfast favorite. This mixture of scrambled eggs and creamed corn, I say, was passed down from my husband's Indian ancestors. Not really...but it's a good reason to introduce ethnic foods into your menus.

The chuckbox we used for those camping days has now been made into a dollhouse. We put a peak on it for a roof and attic, and made most of the furniture from things around the house.

30. Have you ever used certain foods as medicines, to help your health in any way?

Yes; honey and lemon juice as cough syrup; the membrane from an egg shell as a poultice; and warm cigarette smoke blown into the ear when it ached. I'll never forget seeing my mother light a cigarette and puff the smoke into my brother's ear, the first time in the twelve years I'd known her. (Who was this worldly person?)

I was told many times, "if it tasted good, it wouldn't be medicine." So you got well to avoid repeating it!

31. Do you have your tastebuds trained in such a way that if I say, "pork chops," you associate sweet potatoes and corn?

It's a sort of word association game you can play with food. You may get out of your rut when you hear what others say to the same. Try a few...fried potatoes and...; roast beef and...; chicken and...; then throw one in like pig's feet and... Maybe you'd like some new sandwich ideas. Peanut butter doesn't always have to marry jelly. Try marshmallow cream, chopped dates or bananas!

In other words, tradition can get dull if we don't explore a few new ideas. Don't serve all first-time foods at the same meal. Try a new bread one time, a new salad dressing another. Use every possibility in those books that come with appliances that we seem to promptly lose. I decided to see what else my blender will do besides make crumbs, and found the quickest best way to make potato pancakes, is by grating the potatoes, adding the rest of the ingredients, and pouring the batter out on the griddle from the blender. Terrific with sausage and applesauce!

32. Since Thanksgiving Day is our biggest celebration to honor food, describe a typical visit "over the river and through the woods to Grandmother's house."

In our case, we walked to her house as we all lived in town. My mother was one of six children so we looked forward to seeing our cousins. Grandma was bustling around in the kitchen, assigning tasks to her three daughters. She was wearing her apron pinned on at the shoulders, but then that was part of her daily apparel at home. Flour was everywhere as she rolled out the pastry for the pies, but she'd smile and greet us as though she hadn't just seen us the day before.

It was too crowded to stay in her small kitchen, so we were shooed into the dining room to play. Since I was four years older than the other children, I became the game planner. Early in the day, we went outside to play dodgeball, but inside it seems we mostly played follow the leader, circling in and out of the rooms. Many times we made a path of pillows taken from all the chairs, and proceeded to somersault all around.

The grown-ups tried to talk over our noise and giggling, but when it got too much for them, they called a *time-out*. When I heard a lot of laughter from the kitchen, I would hurry out, hoping the women would share a joke with me, but they would say I wasn't old enough!

Granddaddy sat in the living room smoking his smelly cigar until he was called to carve the turkey. Then we all gathered around the table. I don't remember the food, except it was good and plentiful. Just the odor of sage and turkey and candied yams made us hungry. (I wonder if anyone has put that in an aerosol yet?) I'm sure it was traditional, as I didn't see a recipe book open anywhere, and the menu was always the same. After all, it was Grandma's gift to us, and we didn't want it to change any more than Grandma.

Just a word of caution, (and I speak for more than one tired Grandma out there): keeping up with tradition and the work accompanying it may become too big a job for Grandma to continue. Maybe this year is the time she hopes you will say, "Let's each bring a dish next year so that all Grandma has to do is fix the turkey." Convince her that yours may not taste as good, but it will be served with love and concern for her. Too many families I know assume that Grandma wants it this way, and she doesn't know how to shift the responsibility without appearing old and lazy.

In the old days, most everything they ate that day was grown or raised by the family; however, today most of the feast is *store-bought*. When I taught vocal music in the schools, I made up this little rhyme for my class, later sending it in my greeting cards:

"Over the highway and through the pollution
    to Grandperson's house we go.
We've filled the car from near and far with everyone we
    know.
Spent all our money on gasoline, vacation without pay!
O lucky me, it BETTER be a happy Thanksgiving Day!

Instant potatoes, Green Giant peas and Mash's salt-free
    ham,
Campbell's soup, Del Monte corn and cranberry sauce
    that's canned,
Stovetop dressing, Pillsbury cake, and butter that's
    Parkay,
A bucket of chicken that's finger-lickin',
A modern Thanksgiving Day!"

...L. Duane Smith

33. Did your family store food to eat over the winter? How?

Though there is work to canning, and freezing, the biggest problem is the urgency of it all. When the produce is ripe and sitting in your kitchen, it's now or never. Everything else is put aside until this mountain of tomatoes, corn or whatever is safely put on the shelf. Though I blanch my vegetables and fill plastic bags for the freezer, I have several blue Mason jars and a jar lifter sitting in my window sill for flowers, as a reminder of the past.

34. Do you associate certain foods with certain places? Have you created memories of moments you've enjoyed with friends or on vacations? Foods seem to taste better when prepared by local cooks in areas right where they're grown. We hope the foods are fresher, the cooks more experienced with how to cook and prepare than we. Do you ever ask for the recipe or a hint at least? What do you recommend when I go there to eat?

We were surprised, as we've traveled, to find out that a sub, hero, grinder, po'boy, hoagie, and torpedo were all the same...just depended on what area you were in. We've traditionally eaten at some of the same restaurants: Santa Maria's in St. Augustine, where the catfish fall over each other to eat what you throw them. We go back to check on our memories!

When we went to Chinatown, we bought a package of five fortune teas, each of which had special powers—good luck, long life, fertility, prosperity, and good health. I invited all my girl friends to visit, bring a teapot, and we'd sample the teas; but, no one wanted to try the "fertility tea."

35. Name some places where you've eaten and the food came second to the scenery.
At the foot of the Grand Tetons where we dangled our feet in the water of Jenny Lake; along a hiking trail while we chilled our sodas in the creek; at Peggy's Cove where we ate a sandwich on the rocks beside the lighthouse.

This concludes my series of questions to assist you in producing an oral history involving food. I'm sure you can think of many more pertinent to your family.

APRON STRINGS MAKE FAMILY TIES

When you have a family reunion, do you look forward to Aunt Mamie's chicken salad and Mary's blueberry dessert? Then you're starting to associate certain people with special foods. Would you like a project that will bring your family together, one that only they can create?

Then this is the time to start compiling a family cookbook! There are cookbooks on every conceivable type of food, representing geographic areas, historic periods, ethnic groups, age groups, as well as the use of various appliances and methods of preparation. You could include all of those categories in a unique collection of a family's treasured recipes.

The "Heritage Cookbook" I put together was an outgrowth of genealogy, when I was looking for a project to help the family to become aware of each other and our heritage. I figured if **lovin' can come from the oven**, then why not a cookbook from and about those most dear to us! It would be a gift **from** the family to the family!

When I visited relatives for interviews I asked if they might share some old recipes and cookbooks. I found out that these books tell us the lifestyles of the times, and were even used as places to record news, store lists and other clippings. So in addition to foods, you may find many other unexpected rewards which you can mention in your cookbook.

The earlier portion of this chapter suggests many of the experiences we have with food. Now this project will let you share the foods that have come out of those experiences. You can make your cookbook more interesting by interspersing the recipes with the stories behind them.

When you ask your family to contribute their traditional recipes, ask them to also relate the origin of the food, and why it has become so special. To encourage them to respond, you may want to include two recipe cards. Then you could just photocopy the cards onto the pages, and it will take on a "scrapbook" appearance. The designs on the cards will add visual interest.

Ask each person to write longhand or sign a typed version to make it more personal. You want your cookbook to reflect the uniqueness of each individual...a sort of autograph book of foods.

As I received the recipes, I set about putting them in the

categories of Main Dish, Salad, Dessert, Bread, Fish, Ethnic, Fun Foods, Beverage, Crafts, Kid Stuff, and Food For Thought. Later, we printed each category on different colored paper, on one side only. This defined the sections, and the blank sides allowed for new recipes to be added. After all, I knew I would be finding new cousins, and they would be asked to contribute to the book.

Try out as many recipes as you can before printing, to see if any ingredient has been left out. What was called "Best Ever Cake" turned out to be the Worst Ever...so I had to print a correction!

Well, after a time, I had received lots of recipes, but very few stories. I don't think they realized how meaningful this would make it...or that I really would create a book. So I decided to mention things about them that I knew they had in common—hunters, fishermen, teachers, Methodists, children, new brides, elderly, and crafty.

I included information in the preface to the recipe about the person; i.e., "Nancy serves this dessert to the Baptist Fellowship when they meet at her house." Or, "Jeanne always takes this to potluck dinners at the Senior Center where she is program chairman." Use anything that will describe the person in a unique way that relates to his food. If they wanted a particular thing said, they should have sent it to you. They won't forget the next time you ask!

When my cookbook turned out to be so satisfying, I wrote the local paper and suggested the topic to the food editor. When Beth Bohac contacted me requesting an interview, I was very pleased to share my project. She is the one who thought of such a clever title for the full page article, "Apron Strings Make Family Ties." She gave genealogy a boost and even included one of my recipes...Black Walnut Cookies. To thank her I baked her a batch!

Below, I will list suggestions, in random order, that may give you ideas of ways you can introduce the family and the food at the same time. Though the stories will be varied, I would still stick to the basic sections I mentioned before, to eliminate indexing.

At the holidays, I plan to send any new recipes I have received along with the Christmas card. I feel this will encourage the family to look at this little book as something that will always be growing, and one day be an heirloom!

IDEAS FOR A HERITAGE COOKBOOK

• A COLORFUL COVER AND TITLE—on heavier card stock for durability. You hope these recipes will be enjoyed by all. The title may include the family name...like "Fisher Family Fare"...you'll think of something.

• INTRODUCTION—"This cookbook is an attempt to pass on some of the mouth-watering traditions we have been enjoying all these years...with due respect to the cooks who have contributed them. If we have left some important recipes out, please feel free to send them to the printer. The management wants to express appreciation to...for typing, compiling, publishing, etc." Your name and address.

• YEAR OF PUBLICATION—Without it, it has no heirloom value.

• KITCHEN HUMOR—such as Rules Of The Kitchen: "Don't criticize the coffee—you may be old and weak yourself some day."

• GRACE BEFORE DINNER—(1st serious, 2nd humorous)

"We thank you, Lord, for this food.
Bless and keep us from above.
May this family and our friends
Always grow and live in love."

"God of goodness, bless our food.
Keep us in a pleasant mood.
Bless the cook and all who serve us.
From indigestion, Lord, preserve us."

• ETHNIC RECIPES REPRESENTING YOUR FAMILY HERITAGE—if you have none you regularly use, you may involve some neighbors who have lived in some of these lands to give you some easy favorites that represent your heritage. It makes them feel accepted in the American community and they will be pleased to be acknowledged. Learning a little of the language and the customs of cooking and eating makes us aware

67

of our ancestry. Maybe tack up a menu with the foreign name and the translation the next time you serve an ethnic meal. Here are the ones we share preceded by, "In respect to the Indian blood in the Twigg, Weaver, Kain, and Spurrier families," we include: Indian Pudding, Corn bread, etc.

> German—Schnitz Und Knepp..apples and dumplings with ham...Hot Potato Salad. (name German family surnames).

> Irish—Corned Beef and Cabbage...Soda Bread Dublin Potato Salad, cubed beef & cabbage added. (These to honor ancestors and Pat's St.Patrick birthday).

> Jewish—Chicken Soup (cure-all), Kugel, Latkes, Jewish Apple Cake...(to include son-in-law Jeff into the family).

• WORKING WIVES...mention the work and include quick dishes.

• 1850 COOKBOOK...given to Eleanor by her mother-in-law, (feeling sorry for her son, no doubt!). Recipes I chose are Green Turtle Soup, Fried Eels, Pickled Pig's Feet.

• CAMPERS, SCOUTS..."eating out!"

• HUNTERS, FISHERMEN..."the providers."

• TRAVELERS..."try this when you go there"...or to represent cousins in that state.

• FOOD AS THE FAMILY BUSINESS...farm, family restaurant, advice.

• PIONEER RECIPES...Journey Cake, Bean Bread, and Short'nin' Bread. Include some background on living in the Appalachians...nearest store a week away, trips to town for supplies were few. Cooking in an open fireplace more of an art than a science...directions included "pinch of salt, lump of butter the size of an egg, beat while you sing two stanzas of a hymn."

I included some recipes from the "mountain humor" of mountain folk for fun. I used those for "Nebriated Catfish" and "Stewed Squirrel" because a lot of the kin like to hunt and fish. The book gives the ingredients in dialect, followed by the correct words. Similar books are sold at tourist attractions as souvenirs...not found in libraries.

Include individual's favorites for:

• BIRTHDAYS...Lee's Valentine Day Red Velvet Cake

• FOURTH OF JULY PICNICS OR REUNIONS...i.e., Aunt Mary's speciality. This is also when you can ask them to bring recipes for you to add to your book.

• BUTCHERINGS...include the methods, by whom, where, when.

• FOODS WHEN CHILDREN WERE ILL...to make it all better. Aunt Clara always sent a bowl of tapioca.

• FOODS FOR A SNOWY EVENING around the fire, name the time.

• FIRST ANNIVERSARY DINNER...or fiasco.

• PREACHER DINNER...special for right after church.

• POT LUCK DINNER CHURCH SOCIAL FAVORITES

• FORTUNE COOKIES for Chinese New Year...no, we haven't Chinese ancestors...just for good luck.

• BLACK WALNUT COOKIES...we gather and pick the nuts every fall.

• ROOT BEER...made in a family assembly line for Christ-mas.

• ARMY FOOD/COOK MEMORIES...recipes for 500.

• BOARDING HOUSE memories of food.

• FAVORITE SMELLS from the kitchen were of...

• MENTION THE CHURCH if person is an active member, preparing dinners or hosting house meetings.

• RE-NAME SOME RECIPES to use the town of birth... "We could call these Engle's Switch Sugar Cookies as they were a favorite of Fred Moler. His daughter baked them every year for his birthday."

• PHOTOCOPY FOOD ADS from old papers, and add them for interest.

• FOOD HISTORY ITEMS...Coca Cola created in 1886; Hot Dogs introduced at World's Fair 1904. (See list at end of this chapter.)

• WORLD WAR II VICTORY MEALS...Eggless, Milk less, Sugarless Cake...photocopy ads to "Keep the U.S. Strong"...from the 1940's.

• HOMEMADE MIXES..."never buy if you can make your own!"

• CHRISTMAS MORNING FARE...Oyster Stew in this family. Books on celebrating the holidays would also be a source of ethnic ways.

• THANKSGIVING TREAT...Mincemeat Stuffing.

• FOOD GIVEN AS GIFTS...Spiced Tea Mix, Fruit Butters with muffins.

• FOOD SENT IN TIME OF NEED...funeral, flood, fire, homesick college student.

• DANDELION WINE...made secretly by my father and hidden up over the door.

• HONEY RECIPES...when my father kept bees, my mother made candy and cakes and vinegar. I added a label from his honey jars to this page.

70

• CRAFT RECIPES included beeswax candles, soap, pot pourri, coal crystal plant, salt beads, play dough.

• KID STUFF...I mentioned all the teachers in the family, then quoted some kid's version of recipes, also a sampling of misnomers the kids gave foods. For our granddaughter, Heather, I included some mud pie recipes I had kept from an old McCall's.

• FUN FOODS...Pickled Pink Eggs, Strawberry Sun Preserves, Fruit Leather, Fastnachts from tube biscuits, Snow Cream, Ritz Apple Pie, Poor Man's Crab Cakes from zucchini.

• PARTY IDEAS—SPECIAL TOUCHES...Mom used to serve Kool Aid in a punchbowl with lemon slices, just for a summer meal. *Company* unnerved her, so she treated us like "company."

• FOOD FIRST AID...Folk medicines and concoctions used in past by family. May want to include superstitions concerning foods...sauerkraut, black-eyed peas for good luck in new year.

• FOOD FOR THOUGHT...Philosophy dealing with foods...the way to a man's heart...marriage is like a stew...with the right ingredients. May include cooking hints from the past, (Advice for brides or bachelors.)

The important times of our lives were made more so by the sharing of food...as the cook or the guest...it was a gift! Indeed, some family cooks feel if you don't ask for three helpings, you must not like their gift. Whenever an empty space appears on your plate, they want to fill it up! To this day, that's why I love buffets...I can take what I want and go back when I want.

Often it was where you were, how old you were, who was with you, or all of the above, that made a meal so special! So go back over the fellowship times, imagine yourself there, and see those around the table, and include them in your cookbook. Prepare those foods again, tell those stories to the children. Mine are starting to supply the endings, so I know they won't be forgotten!

These are only suggestions, and will reflect your family only if you strive to represent things dear to them. Your traditions are your own, and make your family *special* . YOUR "Heritage Cookbook" will be one-of-a-kind, but I hope you get lots of requests from your family. Maybe you'd like to trade one with me...I'd love to see it!

Mine is a standard shower gift to new brides in our family. It is something both practical and sentimental. I was proud to present mine as a holiday gift a few years ago, and we're still adding family contributions every year. Food brings people together to celebrate...so "apron strings really do make family ties!"

"100 YEARS OF FOOD HISTORY"

by
Helen Huber
Marketing Specialist, Maryland Department of Agriculture

Do any of us ever take the time to remember that the items being offered today were not always available in retail food stores? No one ever existed without frozen foods, sliced breads, tomatoes and other salad fixings the year around or turkey being available any month of the year!! How fast some of us forget. For others, it has been a fact of life during their shopping existence.

I thought it might be interesting to look back over the past 100 years and see how long some of our marketed foods have been available to us. Most of the things listed here came from a listing in the "Produce Merchandiser" of August 1984.

1886 — Coca-Cola was created in syrup form to be used at an Atlanta, Georgia soda fountain.

1895 — Milton S. Hershey invented the Hershey bar.

1902 — The Pepsi-Cola Company was founded.

1903 — A scoop for ice cream cones was patented by an Italian immigrant living in New Jersey.

1904 — Hot dogs were introduced at the St. Louis World's Fair. George J. French introduced prepared mustard the same year. Could it be this is why we look at these two foods as being complimentary?

1915 — Processed cheese, first made in Switzerland, was launched in the U.S. by Kraft. It was very popular from the beginning because it stayed fresh in the sealed packet.

1919 — Food chemist Joseph Cohen developed gelatin.

1921 — Wonder Bread began nationwide marketing.

1923 — Skippy Peanut Butter began nationwide marketing.

1925 — Automatic potato-peeling machines were introduced and the production of potato chips boomed.

1928 — Will Kellogg introduced Rice Krispies in his continuing effort to change the breakfast habits of the nation.

1929 — Grocery stores began marketing prepared baby foods.

1930 — Sliced bread was introduced which was considered the "niftiest" thing.

1930 — Poultry farmers constructed the first year-around rearing sheds, making spring chicken a thing of the past.

1931 — Miles Laboratories introduced Alka-Seltzer.

1933 — There were 516 grocery stores in the nation equipped to carry frozen foods.

1937 — Spam luncheon meat was introduced by George A. Hormel & Co.

1939 — Birds Eye introduced precooked frozen foods.

1940 — Swanson frozen dinners were introduced.

1942 — H. J. Heinz sent processed foods in tins to the war front which was capable of being heated with enclosed sterno cans.

1945 — Minutemaid Company developed a powdered orange juice that soldiers could reconstitute in the field. Within a month, the war ended and the company turned to frozen juice concentrate.

1947 — The first microwave cooker was placed on the market.

1948 — General Mills introduced prepared cake mixes. The first McDonald's hamburgers were sold by Maurice and Richard McDonald.

1949 — Cyclamate-based artificial sweeteners were introduced for the weight conscious.

1954 — TV dinners made their debut.

1955 — Electric deep freezers arrived.

1956 — Colonel Sanders franchises his method of frying chicken in vegetable shortening with eleven herbs and spices.

1958 — Instant mashed potatoes arrived.

1969 — Yogurt makers for the home were introduced.

1980 — A U.S. government survey found out that french-fried potatoes were the nation's most consumed vegetable.

1980's — Irradiation began to have big place in marketing foods.

Wasn't it fun following through from the time you first remember a new marketing breakthrough. Recalling these events can also make for some good conversation with your customers. I wonder what new things will be talked about in the year 2000?

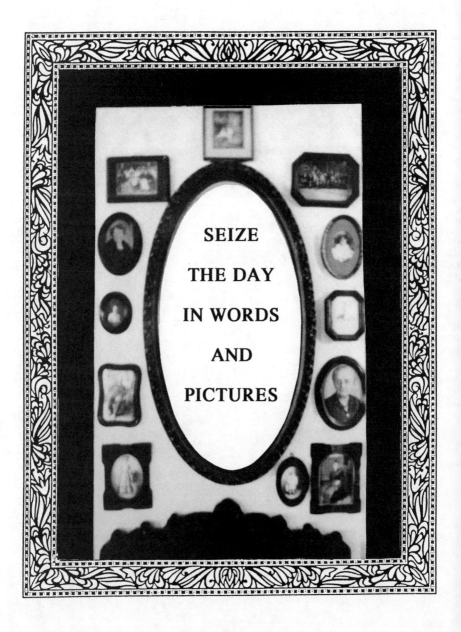

SEIZE

THE DAY

IN WORDS

AND

PICTURES

5

CARPE DIEM! SEIZE THE DAY OR MOMENT!

A recent movie featured a highly motivated teacher who wanted his students to *seize the moment* while you see its possibilities. So I feel it fitting to say to genealogists "Carpe diem," in fact "freeze the moment" with photos and sound!

We should consider the ways our history is enriched with photographs. They are the easiest to share with one another, as they can be printed, used in books, and can be viewed privately. We can rearrange them into albums, or choose certain ones to copy and share with others. And they were the first way known to record a person's actual image. Before that time, portraits were commissioned and appropriate backgrounds added. Artists felt threatened by the invention of the camera, because the public would no longer depend on them.

The person who said, "A picture is worth a thousand words," must have been a genealogist. Nothing sparks more interest than an old picture. You can have pages and pages of narrative, but it will be the pictures that make it come alive. As we have visited cousins, hoping to gain new insight into the family, some are reluctant and feel they have no photos to contribute. "I don't know where my old pictures have gotten to...probably lost when we moved; that was too long ago," are some of the comments we hear. But again, a genealogist is persistent...don't stop there.

WHERE TO FIND THEM

We were visiting Lucy Spurrier, a cousin who was in her eighties. It was an interview we had been looking forward to for quite some time. She lived in the same town as we, and we both knew that she was related, but family history gave us a special reason for visiting. You make time for visits that you should have made all along. She was very sweet, but insisted she couldn't remember much from the early days.

Then we thought of asking if she had her wedding picture. She was only gone a minute, into her bedroom where it must have been displayed. Not only did she let us camera-copy it, but she spent the next hour telling us all about the wedding day, and the few years after. Her husband had been called to fight in World

War I, and came close to dying in the flu epidemic. She continued her story up to the birth of the first son...all from the sight of that one picture. So remember always to ask about the wedding picture first, and you will have a record of both sides of the family to illustrate your chart.

Other sources of old photos are high school and college graduation pictures and yearbooks. The added plus is the many organizations your relative may be pictured in. Also the fashions and activities you will see give you a sample of the times.

Libraries often have photo collections or albums donated by individuals. In our community of Brunswick, one man went about taking photos of buildings, people and activities for his own enjoyment. Thanks to Myer Kaplon, we have an irreplaceable remnant of the past. Since these collections are unique to each community, it would be worthwhile checking out.

Ask about the library's newspaper collection; there may be issues from the time period you are seeking. Obituaries are often accompanied by a photo.

See if there are any books on the photographic history of your area, or local history books which may contain photos to illustrate an industry or certain time period. These will add interesting facets to your research.

Community organizations, such as lodges, may have photos of their members and officers. Inquire whether they maintain a history of their group.

It is difficult to locate the families who possess photo collections. We have learned from experience that they are probably in the hands of the daughters...women being the sentimental savers; the ones who send the cards, clip the newspapers, decorate the home. We need the names of the men they married, so we may locate them and their children, and when we do—beg, borrow, but don't steal.

My husband and I are from the same town, and know many of the same people. But we were too young to know that Mr. Norman Thompson's mother was on the Smith family tree. When we finally figured that out, we called to visit. As we talked about our common heritage, he related that he had a portrait in his basement of Lee's great-grandfather, Christian Smith. Christian had died in 1904 before Lee's dad got to know him, so we were excited to see it. When Norman found out how interested we were in saving the family records, he told us we could have the portrait. You will find that others in the family will feel secure in leaving some items with you, knowing you will appreciate and take care of them. I have heard it said that no one owns artifacts; they are just given to us as caretakers for the next generation.

If you are given an old framed photo, you may find, as we did, a clipping or obituary behind the photo, inside the frame. It isn't worth damaging the frame to get inside, so weigh the value. In our case, the owner, John Peacher, was apologizing for the broken frame, when out dropped the obituary as though to introduce the man in the photo with his wife. All the children were named, and we were able to complete the whole family record.

We were removing the contents of a large old blanket chest, preparing it for sale. Out came the linens, one by one, until we were down to the old newspaper liner. I became excited at the thought of old headlines...but the reward was **under** the paper...two charcoal portraits of a man and woman! When I showed them to my father, (he never knew they were there,) he surmised they must be his grandfather Virts and his wife, Julia Frye. Nothing beats the thrill of discovery!

LABEL THEM

Once you find these valuable photos, you should promptly label them. With the photo on a hard surface, label the back using a very soft lead pencil or ballpoint—never a felt pen. Try to find out the correct name, date, place or activity. This would be a good activity for older children and their grandparents. As the child hears and writes the names, he will begin to notice similarities, and become familiar with the family. If some photos have *mystery people*, you can keep them separate and quiz others in the family.

If you have some group pictures of teams or school classes, it may be profitable to ask the local paper to run them, asking for identification. Use your name and phone number as a contact.

COPY THEM

But wouldn't it be nice to have copies to share, to preserve the original, and to have a negative for the future? It also provides each member of the family with his own copy. There are many reasons why this is a good idea:

     a. There are no future arguments over who gets the ONLY copy.

     b. Each child has an opportunity to learn the names.

     c. It may develop an interest in collecting more photos.

     d. Additions may become a regular gift.

I have tried to share copies of all the photos I have with my brother, Gary. At first I had a small portrait of our mother copied at a copy shop, where they can reproduce the color. I had the copy in my hands two minutes later, and it was remarkably clear. Framing it in a shadow box, I added dried flowers Mom had saved from her garden, and never used.

Five years ago, I started an album for Gary, and added a four-generation chart in the front. Each Christmas I get copies of any new photos and wrap them as a gift. They are always enjoyed by everyone, and are circulated around the room. Because there are only a few each year, we have an opportunity to relate the new stories and research that brought the photos to us. This reminds everyone that this is a growing study with lots of unfolding secrets.

There are many ways you might organize an album:
Chronologically—from birth to adulthood.
One Family—separate albums for each surname.
Pictorial Research—charts, maps, narrative with photos.

An album can be enjoyed more if a small notebook is prepared as a key to the photos. Number the pages in the album to correspond to pages in the key, and list the subjects in order. For safe-keeping, keep the key in an envelope which you have glued to the back cover. This same envelope could hold the negatives that accompany those photos. It's good to keep things close together. Initially, I prepared albums with charts on the left-hand pages and photos on the right opposite. I kept an album for each of the four main surnames, Smith, Virts (Wertz), Moler, Spurrier. By now I have such an assortment of documents that I am starting three-ring notebooks, which hold mylar pages for documents, photo holders, maps, charts, background material, and family narratives to tie it all together. There are three-ring albums that have removable magnetic plastic pages, which will hold a variety of sizes and shapes of material. Although these magnetic pages make mounting easy, they may damage the photo if you try to remove it later. I prefer mylar pages and pockets for each photo for a three-ring binder. These can be put into another regular large notebook. See what your photo shop suggests and make your own choice.

IMPORTANT FAMILY PHOTO OPPORTUNITIES

Our sister-in-law, Pat, has been adding to albums she began at the birth of each of their three children. She says her photos may not be the best, but it will help them remember the occasion. Those moments are gone so quickly. You should become familiar with your camera so you can operate it on the spur of the moment. This means having it handy so you don't miss a thing..."seize the moment!"

Perhaps it would be good to make a tradition of taking photos at the same time every year: the toast to the new year, measuring the height on birthdays, sitting the children with a display of their gifts each holiday. These make good gifts later in life.

Here's a long list of *firsts* you won't want to miss!

First day of birth
    visitors presenting gifts
    solid food
    haircut
    crawling
    walking...in new shoes
    school or day care

Typical day's activities: bath time, napping, Daddy changing
      diaper, swinging, enjoying a variety of toys and areas
Family in front of home on moving day, either in or out
Neighborhood friends and babysitters
Each new pet, pet shows, tricks
Birthday cake, circle of friends at party, measuring up
Favorite gifts at birthday or holidays
Hallowe'en: knocking at Grandma's door
Spending quality time with each relative; choose activity
First train and/or bus trip
Teacher each year of public and church school
Graduation from same with principal and award
Teachers of gymnastics, music, band, chorus, with student and
      instrument, music or equipment; being in uniform adds
      another feature.
Whole team, cast of play in make up, recital, performance group
      around piano
Class social activities in addition to yearbook
First roller skates, ice skates
First big wheels, bicycle, motorcycle, car
Pet show
Art Exhibit
Yard Sale
Talent show
Day teen received driver's license
Car wash group, sub sales group, making the float
Parade marching unit
Prom finery plus date
College: moving in, roommate, buddies
Graduation with diploma and family
Annual picnic at the beach, swim suits, bathing beauties
Holiday rituals: hanging stockings, reading the stories
Reunions, get-togethers, family group photos
Anniversaries: wedding party 25 years later, all the children
First fish, or deer from the hunt
First plane trip
First job, at desk or location in proper attire for work
First apartment
Moving day
Family doctor, nurse
Home from the service, in uniform for first time
Part-time jobs to pad allowance, on-the-job look

82

We made a gift of *the first day of school* photo to Mindy when she graduated from college....signing it "You've come a long way, Baby!" (She's on the left with cousin Chris.)

I realize that those of us who use cameras a lot don't need a list, but a reminder when the time comes. But the trouble comes when we get caught up in the moment and are so involved that we haven't planned ahead. My husband says **he's too busy living to write about it.** But you must capture the moment or it will be gone.

All of these occasions emphasize the pride you have in your family, so set them up to show **all** to advantage. Though posed, the attitude can be light and informal. For large groups choose hats, dramatic poses, angles, making sure that each can be

83

seen by the use of ladders, stairs, porches and steps, farm wagons, cars (from bumper, roof, hood, tailgate), pyramids, swing sets, fences, sliding boards, jungle gyms, picnic tables. Maybe add a title board with date on some occasions...a slate will do.

Sure you're going to get moans and groans from those feigning embarrassment and boredom with the whole idea...I know, I did it as a teenager...but tell them to humor an older person and do him/her a favor. Or wear an old hat and stick a PRESS card in the front of it, and tell them you need copy for the EVENING NEWS. Believe me, they're going to be glad you saved the moments and will be begging you for copies years later.

HOW TO COPY

I have mentioned we camera-copy. In truth, it is my husband who camera-copies. He enjoys the challenge of new skills, but reading and research are not two of them. Our marriage has been one of complementing each other, respecting the freedom of one to enter into a project in his own way. When there is something we can do for each other that helps without taking over, we feel we are making a needed contribution. I research his family with the same fervor as my own, since it is the ancestry of our children. He does appreciate it, and handles the many logistical challenges that present themselves.

On many of our visits to interview cousins, we wished we could borrow old photos to copy, but their owners were reluctant to let them out of their sight. So it was plain that we were going to have to bring the camera to them. Lee got some very good advice from a photographer who recommended the following:

1. Use 400 ASA black and white film.

2. Have a macro lens on a 35mm SLR camera, for close-up.

3. An adjustable stand which can be raised or lowered easily. This stand allows him to keep the camera still as he focuses, crops, or singles out figures.

4. Work with strong daylight, but out of direct sun. This eliminates the glare of floodlights, and gives good overall balance of light.

5. A polarizing filter to use on glass that is curved or seems to reflect images.

6. Blue filter to provide more contrast to faded photos.

7. Yellow filter to neutralize stains.

8. Keep black right angle matting to frame ragged edges.

It is a good idea to purchase your camera, macro lens, and filters at the same time. That way you will know that they fit properly.

Lee has copied some large framed portraits and gotten them to a size that can be shared in an album. In contrast, some tiny locket portraits have been enlarged to show many details. For those large group photos, such as graduation and reunions, he focuses on just one person, if that is our desire. These really need to be enlarged to be able to recognize the individuals within the group. Incidentally, don't try to write all those names on the back...put them on a separate sheet.

If you were preparing a book, all photos to be included on the same page should be of uniform size for a professional look. So all could be taken with the same camera in preparation.

Whether or not you publish, all valuable photos should be copied, and the originals may then be stored in an acid-free box, away from excessive heat or moisture. With the negatives also stored, you don't have to be as careful with the copies. However, I enjoy living with these photos, and do my best to display them in sensible places.

Lee offers to copy genealogical society members' photos about four times a year. Since this is only available to members, it is another incentive to join. He says he learns a lot from the variety of photos they present him with, everything from tintypes, ambrotypes, with tears, stains—each with new challenges. Nothing beats experience!

Another great advantage to making your own camera copies is that valuable photos do not run the risk of being lost or damaged in the mail. Also, when you are doing the focusing yourself, you do not have to communicate your needs. We send our film away for processing, and even then have to closely examine the negatives. At times, the photos show that tops of heads have been cut off, indicating machine-centering problems. If the negative is fine, then we have them done over. Still the valuable photograph is with its owner.

Speaking of irreplaceable photographs, I must tell you of a foolish deed that I will regret the rest of my genealogical life. I remember vividly the huge portrait of my great-grandfather, peering down from a very ornate gilded frame...not a very pleasant countenance, to be sure. In addition, because he was my grandmother's father, from the wrong side of the family, my mother kept it on the wall in a storage room. Later, when the house was rented, a decision had to be made about who was going to keep the portrait. Neither my brother nor I had the wall space, so we left it there. We discovered later that it had been stolen when the renters moved out. We should have thought to take a photo of it; bringing it to a size to put in an album or small frame. And secondly, we should have realized the worth of the frame, for I'm sure it has been sold for a tidy sum.

Though I suppose Great-Grandfather Boger has been added to someone's landfill, if you see a blonde-haired, bushy-browed German facing to the right, please write me. I do remember reading about people who buy these portraits to give visitors a good impression. When asked, "Is that an ancestor?," they reply proudly, "Yes." They just don't say **whose** ancestor.

When you copy a photo, you are also going to have a negative whereby additional copies may be made to share. We have found this a good way to reward cousins who are generous with their help. At the beginning of our quest I was very generous with charts and photos, but I found that people were just putting them in a drawer, and had no further interest. Now I only share with those who are involved and have a genuine appreciation for our research.

Cameras copy many other records than portraits of ancestors. Taken to the library (with permission) you may take pictures of documents, church records and rare fragile books. These cannot be borrowed and sometimes are very costly to have copied by the repository. Family Bibles, tombstones, houses, churches, all the places that were part of the family's life need to be photographed. Write that part of your story and take any photos needed to illustrate your story. Concentrate on one family area at a time, and get a real feeling of accomplishment!

PHOTOCOPY

Another way to copy photos to share is by photocopying. This is available to everyone inexpensively. The copies can be sent through the mail without fear of loss, and several may be copied on the same sheet of paper. You may want to experiment with a collage, or turn a portrait into notepaper. A wedding picture may become the invitation to an anniversary party. Some faded photos can be improved and darkened by photocopying. It's worth a try!

Other tricks can be tried on the copier. My friend, Peter, showed us how he copied a large group photo onto the center of the paper, leaving a margin around it. This may require reduction. He then used it as a key to the original, drawing lines out from the heads and labeling names. This is far superior to having to keep turning over the photo to read the names on the back. There is usually not enough room there anyway.

DISPLAY

But let's think of other ways to share photos. Albums get put on shelves and in drawers. People would have to ask if you have any albums of old photos they can look at...never happen! Let's display them right out in the open...proudly...as though our ancestors came over on the Mayflower or invented champagne!

We have an old washstand in the entry hall, with an oval mirror above it. We purchased frames of similar color but varied shapes, and placed photos on the wall around the mirror. It's the first thing you see when you come in the door. A few of the frames are the original wine velvet so I put them opposite each other at the bottom. You may want to look for some antique frames at auctions or flea markets. They would add to the value of your photo display. (See chapter cover.)

Another friend of mine painted a huge tree that extended from her basement floor up the stairwell wall. On it she hung framed portraits of the family on the appropriate limb. I felt this was good use of a very large space, while at the same time visitors could get close enough to see them.

Photos can be mounted in those small oval miniature frames and hung on the Christmas tree. Or for year round decor, they could be attached to a wide ribbon in a vertical row.

You should always be careful to keep photos out of direct sunlight or sources of heat in your house. If you want to spotlight them, use a low wattage and only turn it on for short periods of time. Photos fade very quickly.

I was especially proud of the large portrait of my mother at the age of five with her two brothers. For years, I thought one of them was her sister in her dress and hair bow. I think the theory of putting boys in dresses was that boys were easier to diaper...can't think of any other! Anyway, I decided to make a padded fabric frame for this portrait, using some of the rose brocade from Mom's living room drapes. She had made them and I foolishly gave them to the thrift shop. I console myself that that makes this piece I saved even more valuable. There may be meaningful pieces of fabric from your ancestry to use as matting or padded frames. Directions are available at fabric stores.

My father worked with wood and created frames with acetate instead of glass to cover. It's much lighter and safer to work with. The popular collage frames are perfect for a variety of shapes and sizes. We have a grouping of each daughter's yearly school photos.

CARE OF

One of our oldest portraits is beginning to deteriorate. We haven't decided whether we can afford to have it restored. In the meantime we took a picture of it before it became any worse. This is the same reasoning behind the photos of tombstones. Weathering and vandalism may destroy the stones over the years, and you have a record which can be sent to cousins who cannot visit the site themselves.

When you see a portrait deteriorating, you wonder what you could have done to prevent it, and whether there are ways of protecting what you have so carefully collected. After speaking with several archivists, I felt I should include a few guidelines:

1. Treat photographs as you would precious art pieces.

2. Never touch photo with fingers, metal paper clips or staples, which rust, or rubber bands which eventually rot and stick to surface.

3. The best home for them is stacked between acid-free bond in acid-free boxes. If they stand on end, they may curl.

4. The best atmosphere is neither basement nor attic, but where temperature is between 65-70°F, and humidity is no higher than 60% to prevent mildew and mold.

5. Never display or store in sunlight or near heat source.

6. To repair a torn photo, use only Ph neutral document repair tape on the back.

7. For best protection of valuable photos, encapsulate in mylar, leaving one corner open for breathing.

8. To frame, use only mat of 100% rag content, four-ply weight, and synthetic glues made for mounting.

Techniques for restoring photos depends on how the print was processed. This may lead you into a study of the history of photography, in an attempt to determine the age and materials used.

Knowing the history of photography gives a historian a way of dating a photo. The earliest photographs were usually done in a studio because there was a lack of knowledge of the art of photography. The equipment was expensive and quite cumbersome. If you see more candid photos of the early period, they were probably taken by one of the few persons who decided to document the history of the day. These collections are now very valuable, and are chosen for exhibition at fine art museums.

When you start collecting your family photos, you will probably come up with a variety of types. This may lead you to study the difference between tintypes and ambrotypes, and all the others between the 1839 Daguerreotype and the 1960's Polaroid. Genealogy is constantly educating you as it takes you in new directions. In each family's background are new experiences just waiting to be discovered.

OBTAINING GENEALOGICAL CLUES FROM PHOTOS

Most obvious clues are the writing on the back, and the name of any studio or photographer on the front. The city and state may also be mentioned. Some historical works have been written on photographers of certain periods. (i.e. DIRECTORY OF MARYLAND PHOTOGRAPHERS 1839-1900 by Ross J. Kelbaugh, Anchor Press, Garden City, NY, 1973.)

The background may indicate a location, a work place, or a vacation spot. Furniture on which the subject is sitting, or standing beside represents the time period. Check some antique guides for approximate styles. Hair styles and clothing will provide clues as well. Others in the photos may have facial similarities that place them in the same family, and begin to look like those you have in other photos. It was quite a while before we discovered that one of the ladies in a family group photo was a neighbor who helped with the children.

Do you wish you had photos of the past, a certain area? They're out there—someone has a few. Get to know someone who can introduce your idea to others and you can bring together a collection that is unique...irreplaceable.

Check the county and state historical societies for photos of your area. One motivated person with the right equipment may have made a series on a certain industry, ethnic group, or city that interests him or her. If it included a cross section of all the people, or covered many decades, the collection makes a significant contribution to history...what ONE PERSON can do.

Film of remote areas (Yosemite) or endangered species (seals) or crises of the homeless or starving have led to legislation by bringing evidence to the people at large. In these cases, a picture **SAVES** a thousand words of explanation.

RECORD THE PAST WITH PHOTOS OF TODAY

Up to this point we have been thinking about photos that already exist. Let's look at some subjects we should consider adding to our collection. As you retrace those country roads, take photos of family homes, schools and churches where the family attended, and places of business where they worked, or the empty or renovated building.

How many people think of taking a picture of Dad or Mother at work, sometimes a little dirty or weary, but with their *tools of the trade*? While these subjects may seem so ordinary, we genealogists know this is what makes us REAL people. In the old days, people had portraits done with objects important to their image. Why not catch family as they go about their hobbies of quilting, sewing, carving, building, working crossword puzzles, or enjoying card games with their best friends?

How about including the family pets, be they ever so small and short-lived. And what about a picture of you with some of the handmade clothing or gifts you give away?

Above all, don't forget those old cars or new cars. They will only be one of a series throughout a lifetime. They represent a lot of highs and lows in the game of life. Hardly a year goes by without us having some life experience centered around a car...the first car, old jalopy, one you borrowed for the prom, the one that broke down when you moved, the getaway car when you married. Listen when people are looking at old photos; the women see the fashions, the men see the cars! They had a lot of money and time invested in those cars. It's hard to let go!

It is also a good idea to take pictures of your most valuable artifacts. This provides a record for insurance claims. The photos act as an accurate reference when trying to trace the value of a certain piece to an antique appraiser. I don't plan to sell any of my artifacts, but I want to know what the design is called, and the background of their manufacture. It makes me value them even more, and I'm grateful to be the caretaker. When the pieces are passed on, the photo and the background information will go with them.

When we had family get-togethers, I wanted to see what old photos they might bring to share. So we bought two sheets of heavy acetate the size of the dining table. We placed them on top of a plain colored cloth. As relatives came, we asked them to place their photos under the acetate in a certain area. This protects the photos from handling and being misplaced. Soon the cloth was filled and everyone walked around and around the table, bending over to see photos of themselves that they didn't know existed. Everyone was chattering; it was great! The acetate is strong enough that some guests were able to have their snack while they enjoyed the photos.

I used the same device later in the year when I displayed antique Valentines under the plastic. Of course we seized this opportunity to sing the praises of genealogy...and to tell how many pictures we still want to find. After all, we hosted the party...so they're our captive audience. Later, Lee made camera copies of some photos we needed, to show that technique.

While everyone is visiting, this is a perfect opportunity to create some new photo memories. You may want to set up a corner with families choosing character hats to wear. We've had a lot of fun and gotten a lot of unusual photos that we're sure won't be duplicated anywhere.

Have family groups gather on the stairs, seated or standing; they make perfect risers. If it's a summer gathering use the porch steps, if you have them. Another good setting is straddling a bench, or on and around a porch swing. I wish someone had thought of this the first time I met my husband's family. I came away from that reunion remembering little more than *all the ladies had gray hair and glasses, and all the men were smoking pipes.*. If only I could have sat down with family photos and organized the pipes and glasses into names and relationships.

A word about angles and lighting: our nicest graveyard photos are when we could compose the setting with the stone in the foreground so the epitaph could be read, but with the church in the background. This is not always possible, but worth consideration.

Anytime your subject has the sun behind it, be it stone or person, use your flash. A white card or book can reflect light into the subject. Use of the flash indoors can wash out some set-ups and cause unattractive reflections. Sue uses a clamp-on floodlight to give depth and cast shadows. We have all read that the best photos are taken in the morning or late afternoon for the same reason. I can still remember how flat and uninteresting my first paintings were until I added shading. Then they began to jump out at me with a new importance.

UNUSUAL TECHNIQUES

They said it couldn't be done, but Lee even tried taking photos of my uncle's home movies. First we had to locate an 8mm projector we could borrow to even review them. There I was, ten years old, playing dodgeball in the front yard with my cousins. After deciding which views we'd like to have, I took my place at the projector, stopping it at precisely the right moment. Lee had borrowed a tripod which he set at a slight angle to the screen, and we were in business. Again, he used the 400 ASA film, but set the shutter at a slower speed. The pictures were priceless to us; a bit blurred from a beaded screen, but they said it couldn't be done! We are going to have the movies transferred to a videotape, however. My left-handed dodgeball throw is the only one in my family...want to preserve that action!

There is another technique that my husband discovered, and was so excited about. It seems that even the large film processing houses do not want to give personal attention to photographic problems, when they did not cause them. One of the society members, Jeanne, brought three of her old glass 4x4 slides which showed members of her family in Sweden. She had been told that there was no way they could be printed because all the projectors from that day were in a museum. Lee asked all the professionals he knew, and they had no solution. Suddenly he remembered our light box for sorting slides. He thought if he put the slides on the box, one at a time, and covered the rest of the light, he would try taking pictures of the lighted slide. He could hardly wait for the film to be processed. They were perfect! We love it when we find solutions to challenges. You can't stop a genealogist!

Photographs are so important for the memory to have a picture of the past. Lee's mother suffers from Alzheimer's Disease and she has lost her sense of identity. She does not talk except in grunts and murmurs, and sometimes not at all for a whole visit. We show pictures to help her to remember. I suppose they give us something to talk to when she doesn't respond. We had one printed that shows her as a pretty young wife, and another shows her fishing on the river...a link to a better day, an active person. We tacked them to her board so the nurses have something to ask her about, times when she was young and healthy and independent. We show her the photos; she looks and shakes her head. We hope she remembers and knows who we are.

I have always wished that more nursing homes would ask the family to provide photos and background on topics in which the patient took pride. This would stimulate conversation between visitors, nurses, and the patient. These residents were once leading exciting lives and making meaningful contributions. They

94

are still meeting new faces through the staff and visitors. When you look into those eyes, you try not to see the frail person, but what they may take pride in from the past. Don't wait for the nursing home to do it; set an example, be a catalyst!

We are doing too many things to specialize in just one facet of genealogy. We hope this plants some seeds that will grow and give you the satisfaction that we have gained. Listed at the end of this chapter are several references that are practical for the novice.

TELLING A STORY WITH VIDEO

Genealogy presents you with many opportunities to use your camera, to preserve your memories on film. Photos punctuate the verbal or printed words, and give meaning to your story. Movies bring action into play and may add sound, but the reels had to be developed and were very short.

The video camera, or camcorder, has given us a new freedom toward photography. We can view our results immediately, rewind and tape over; no waiting to get the film processed. We have all the advantages of color reproduction, automatic focusing, added light in low-light situations, zoom capabilities and playback for an audience. You also have the advantage of recording your narration, adding the sound effects, the accents of people in the area, or city noises to add interest to your story.

Our favorite video so far is one of our granddaughter, Heather, looking out the window for Santa on Christmas Eve. She kept trying to find him and then, jumping up and down, she pointed him out. Bedtime came easy that night.

After much reading on the topic, I would like to help you compose a good genealogy story by setting up a series of pictures. Let's suppose you have chosen to make a video memory story of the family reunion. Think of yourself as the director of a movie, and analyze the variety of ideas they use.

1. As an introduction, take a shot of a sign bearing the name of the homestead, or church...maybe a road sign with the name of your destination. This gives the setting of what is to come...such as that shown at the beginning of a movie before the narrative starts.

2. Next comes the perspective of the winding road leading into the gathering; a view of the overall layout of the property.

3. Years from now the cars will be different, so why not a shot of the parking area with some of your friends waving hello.

4. Time for a close-up of someone carrying a covered dish, or some food to share. Some may be bringing sports equipment.

5. Now is the time to show the number of people who have congregated...perhaps around the table. This gets across the joy of seeing each other after a year's separation.

6. Focus on some of the youngest to attend, maybe for the first time. Contrast these with some of the oldest as they show off a new dress or something they brought.

7. A long shot will show the continuous parade of food being placed on the table from the kitchen area, giving credit to those who have organized the reunion each year. If there is a buffet where all are lined up to make their choices, you can get the whole lineup by calling to them as they hold their plates. We want faces as unposed as possible.

8. Now all are seated at the table, and as is the custom, Granddad is asking the blessing...get a picture of him from the opposite end of the table; then zoom in on his face for the entire blessing.

9. There are usually some boys who sit together to avoid the girls, who are giggling from the other side. Won't that make a statement several years later? Sound like a Norman Rockwell photo? You know he did all his painting from photos he had posed in just those *down-home* activities.

10. After dinner, most of the men and boys are getting away from the clean-up to play ball. Single out a few you haven't pictured before, especially the ones who have received some sports honors. Get them in action, or about to hit or catch the ball.

11. This is another good time to get a group shot of the spectators...at an angle, semi-profile.

12. Find the old-timers who wish they were out there showing the others a thing or two. Chances are, they'll be sitting together, talking about the *good old days*. Get a close-up of those character-building wrinkles!

13. Meanwhile back with the food...the women are lingering over their empty plates, sharing recipes and gossip. New mothers are getting advice, and new girlfriends and wives are being introduced to the family. (I know, I was one of the new wives once, meeting about 25 families at once.) Take a sampling of pictures of these informal groupings, from tablecloth up, as they chat and use their hands.

14. No one needs to see dirty dishes, so just like the movies, we'll leave that out. Perhaps the young single girls have taken the babies to hold and walk, gearing themselves up for motherhood someday. Have the girls sit on a bench, holding the babies for a group picture. Or maybe they could straddle the bench with the babies on their knee.

15. The conversation may go back to the days when others were still living. In missing them, a few families may wander over to the adjoining graveyard. Take a picture of them from a distance as they stand gazing at the tombstones. Try to position yourself so the church, or house, is in the background, with a few readable stones in the foreground. If you avoid straight rows, you will pick up more shadows, which add texture and depth.

16. You will certainly have some of your ancestors in this cemetery. Don't miss an opportunity not only to take photos of the stones so they are legible...again at a slight angle to encourage shadows to emphasize the inscriptions...but have the oldest member of your family reminisce about the persons buried there.

This is when a camcorder is especially nice, because their voice will be with the picture.

17. If this is a gathering at the ancestral home, you can accompany your elder relative around the grounds. Take a view of the overall scene, and then zoom in on the individual buildings. Let the narrative guide what you picture, rather than the other way around. You are literally doing an oral history with pictures.

18. At times when your relative is pointing or using his/her hands to describe, step back a little to include them in the shot. You need to picture who is with you, and a gesture gives them life and emotion.

19. Animals and pets may interact with your group, and you may have some charming close-ups with the children. If Grandma remarks how she used to slide down the cellar door, re-create the scene with her granddaughter. Or perhaps there will be an old pump where you can get a drink. Children need to experience the activity to remember it, not just hear about it.

20. Perhaps Grandma will remember a photo she has of herself in this same yard as a child. Get a pose of her along the same fence or porch so you can compare them later. There may be an old tree she used to climb that she has a story about.

21. Granddad may still have the old plow or rake that he can demonstrate. Mine got up on the tractor for a familiar pose. He may gesture out over the fields, retelling the hours he spent planting, or the time the cattle got *out of fence.*

22. If it is convenient, have them take you on a tour of the house room by room, pointing out things they feel are precious memories. You are fortunate in these days to live in a house long enough to store up memories. Keep them alive with pictures.

23. There will certainly be a time for a total group picture for the archives. I have seen some grand settings using the big porch, steps and yard to create several levels. One unique photo of Dan's family was taken **under** the family tree with a few people sitting on the lower limbs. In a church gathering, the choir loft

and steps leading up to the pulpit are great. If an outdoor setting seems more feasible, use the picnic tables end-to-end as risers...some folks kneeling on the table, some standing on the bench behind, children sitting on the ground.

24. This is also a perfect time to take family group photos. Choose a corner of the grounds where you have an evergreen backdrop, and announce at the start of the day that you will be taking family group photos at certain times. Besides giving you a record of the family for your genealogy, you may offer prints or a negative to the family. Of course these and the total group photo will have to be taken with print film. Each type of photography serves a unique purpose.

25. If this is a church homecoming, tour the church with one of the elders and have them point out the way services used to be held. There may be a memorial window in the name of one of your ancestors. Slides of this window may later be printed as a greeting card.

If there is an actual service held, picture some of the people as they lend their talents of speaking, singing, and playing instruments. But please, do all of your camera work from the back, using a zoom lens. Nothing angers me more than to have a service of devotions turned into a Hollywood production, by having a photographer darting around the church.

26. If the gathering is over before sunset, try to get some long shots of the people going to their cars, backlighted by the setting sun.

27. A close-up of Grandma and Grandpa hugging your family goodbye, or perhaps waving to some.

28. A lone car going down the road silhouetted against the evening sky. As the song says,"Memories are time that you borrow, to spend when you get to tomorrow."

Now granted, we rarely get exactly what we want in the way of weather, poses, angles, settings, cooperative subjects, etc. But on the other hand, if we don't know what we want and don't plan at all, we come back with a hodge-podge, wishing we had thought of this and that. Any good result usually comes from a lot of pre-planning. It's good to take advantage of the unexpected, but not when the occasion only comes once a year.

You could add a "fun" element by following one particular person eating a lot, and keep going back to see if he's still eating—or the toddler, with you speaking his thoughts.

Remember some of these people will not be at the next reunion, for one reason or another. Reunions are never the same, although they seemed that way when we were children. Time was forever and a lifetime was a long time.

You can take slides or photos in **any** order and put them in story sequence later. With camcorder, you **must** take them in sequence, but you can rewind and do some segments over. For most of us who aren't pros, we are satisfied to have tried to capture the precious moments before they got away.

Our biggest problem was always being so involved talking and having a good time, that we forgot to take pictures of others doing the same. It is a perfect job for someone who likes to tune in and circulate like a roving reporter.

Now, my husband and I work together; one talking to the subject, the other operating the camera. We have planned our sequence ahead of time. But the major advantage is that the subject does not have to be aware of the camera. The camera is just eavesdropping. The end result is a view from a reporter's angle with a personal touch.

COLOR SLIDES

When our first baby was born, we could see ourselves going into *show business*. No more passing a few photos around; we were going into big screen productions. After all, ours was the first grandchild on both sides; so it was something to celebrate with slides!

I laugh when I think now, how we called all the family to "come over this Friday night; we've just gotten another roll of film developed." Now we had taken a few of the rest of the family, so they just *might* see themselves...but all that for 20 slides, and a

100

little cake and ice cream. We have continued with slides for 30 years because we enjoy looking at them together, sometimes just the two of us...but we're able to see more detail as we relive the moments. It's interesting to hear what different ones of us will see in the picture, and remember what happened AFTER it was taken. As we said before, a picture is worth a thousand words because it reminds us of things other than what we actually see.

I suppose sharing is a great part of the enjoyment I have with all of living. When I am alone will be soon enough to sit with the albums. They serve their purpose, those albums, and I have many of them. You can incorporate other paper materials and clippings with them, and keep related items altogether. But I always get a lot from other's perspective, and I like to hear from everyone.

Slides do require additional equipment: **screen, projector,** and storage in metal or plastic boxes. But they can be rearranged and organized for special needs.

As teachers, Lee and I have found ourselves presenting programs and workshops. We enjoy planning which slides we can use, or take, to illustrate a point. Often we have put recorded music as a background with them. You may pause and discuss one slide longer than another; or you may put the whole show on a timer and let it click away in sequence.

I have created programs many times by asking all involved to contribute some of their personal slides. This way it was a shared program where everyone had input.

We created a slide show with title slides to tell the public what a genealogical society is all about. This time we used a rear projector screen on a table.

My favorite program was when my children's chorus was going to sing "Bless The Beasts and the Children." I asked them to bring in slides of their pets, labeled for their return. I wanted to show the slides to illustrate the lines of the song, as we sang them. Of course, some didn't have slides, so I went to their homes and took the pictures in advance. I had to let the chorus look at the slides in advance, so they wouldn't forget to sing at the program.

Now our school system presents programs using eight projectors aimed at different parts of a huge screen to produce a multimedia show. Slides were collected from all the schools in our county, and shown at the opening meeting of the year, accompanied by some upbeat jazz...an exciting pep rally! Slides unify groups at church, reunions, or any time people can bring a little sample of their lives to share with others.

If most of your family photos are slides and you would like to make copies for others, prints can be made and put into albums. And the photographs can also be made into slides by being camera-copied and developed into slides.

For years we had taken all our pictures as slides. Being in color, they require storage in a dark, dry area. We like bringing people together to look at them, and find ourselves reorganizing them according to our audience. The longer we keep them, the more they are enjoyed.

With slides you have the advantage of having them printed, or viewing them with an audience on a screen. In showing them, you can pause between slides to add as much commentary from you or your audience as you like. We used this idea at a school reunion when we asked each person to bring photos of their children. As each slide photo was projected, the person to whom it belonged narrated information about it. We felt this involved everyone and allowed the more timid to speak in the darkness about their proudest possessions. Of course our classes were only 65 students so this was a feasible activity.

We have made a point to label our slides before we forget the location. Thank heaven the year is stamped on them. Since we are elementary teachers we have many of school activities 35 years ago. We are planning to show these at reunions and offer them to the students. If items are important to you, make plans for their ownership after you.

You may want to put all your slides of a certain child on video tape for a gift. Narrate as a key to the occasions.

TAPE RECORDING

As we look at the old photographs, we wish we could hear the stories those people would tell. We read their diaries, cookbooks and letters, which are terrific in themselves, but we wish we could hear their voices. Then we could catch another side of their personality as they describe their memories and how they felt at the time.

It was at the time of Alex Haley's, "Roots" that we learned to appreciate the practice of oral history in Africa as the chosen way to carry on their traditions. It was no accident that at least one member of the tribe was respected for his title as story-teller or griot. The stories of many succeeding generations were repeated and remembered, and this helped Alex to find his beginnings. Now I ask you, when are we genealogists going to get some of this respect?

Well, hindsight is good, in that we learn to seize the moments from now on...carpe diem!...and keep audio records as well as photos. In fact, one of the very easiest ways to start is to take an album of old photos and ask one of your elders to describe who and what he sees. Tell him you need to know and don't want to remove the photos unless necessary. You would like to tape record his *labeling* to keep with the album. Number the pages so you can mention each page he is describing. You may use an old 1900 catalogue reproduction or Time-Life photo book to spark memories.

I feel this project doesn't involve quite as much preparation as a sitting for the express purpose of doing an oral history. Your subject has something to focus on besides a series of questions. She will not take as much notice of the tape recorder itself, and you will have time to get acquainted with the photos yourself, and how this relative views them. I feel that better prepares you for a return visit for more personal information.

Use this same album with others in the family for a more complete record. There may be certain *mystery people* you all have been unable to identify...and like a crossword puzzle, it fills in a few more blanks, you know...a few more clues to finish 15 **down and 6 across!**

WHAT TO REMEMBER WHEN DOING AN
ORAL HISTORY

First recognize that no one **starts** his research with a taped session with a family member. Research with books, Bibles, documents, and paper records is usually organized and charted for easy reference. Then when you see where the blanks are, or the uncertain areas, you have a specific need to mention when you contact and visit these subjects. Their information, and sometimes photos, will complement your other material and start giving it firsthand validity.

1. Assess the information you would like to have on a certain family line, and prepare a series of questions that are organized into certain periods of time. A good reporter asks questions beginning with "who, what, where, why, when" to avoid answers of "yes and no."

Then choose the persons who could provide the most information. Never just ask a person to tell you all he remembers about his early life. You will come out with an unstructured mass of information, which at times **may** hit on what you need. If you have an outline, you will be able to guide the topics in the right direction. When I have come across some valuable information from a relative, and inquired why they hadn't told me that before, their answer has been, "You never asked!" So make it a point to ask!

2. Send a letter with somewhat of an outline of questions you would like to have answered on a visit. The manner in which you introduce yourself will have everything to do with how cooperative they will be. Mention how you are related and why you have become interested now. Put yourself in their place to establish some trust.

Ask permission to tape record so you have a record to refer to later. Suggest a date and time period of one and a half hours. Emphasize how important you consider their contribution is to having a better understanding, as you were not living in the area at the time, and would just have to imagine how things happened.

3. Enclose a SASE (Self-addressed, stamped envelope) or your phone number to confirm the date and time, to be certain they are agreeable.

4. Become familiar with your equipment...a **recorder** with a **pause button** and a built-in **microphone**, that runs on electricity. Always take an **extension cord** so you can set up where you are closest to the subject. I like to leave the recorder on the floor where the subject isn't constantly reminded of its presence. Use a **medium volume** that can be increased on playback if necessary. Using **C-90 audio cassette tapes** seem the best with 45 minutes on each side, as they are more durable. Know how to flip them over without a lot of ceremony. Practice this as well as the whole recording process, so you may give all your attention to your subject. Know well which button is the *pause,* so you may eliminate any noise or unrelated interruptions as they occur.

5. Take along a **pad of paper** to hold your outline, and also any notations of special names, places, or related topics that are new to you. After your taping, get the spelling of these correct before you leave.

6. When starting the interview, try to eliminate noise by closing windows or doors. Set up your recorder before the subject enters if you can. Take time to get acquainted and tell about the help Aunt Mary or Grandpa have been, so they know others have been willing to participate. You wouldn't want to leave them out!

7. Be sensitive as to when to structure the interview and when to let your subject take new directions. Suggest a break after the first 45 minutes, and talk about others in the family and where they are today. So as not to slight others who may feel left out, mention you would like to return another time, and hear from

them. Perhaps, then you can do a group interview of things they did together, and their general lifestyle as a family in the early days.

8. Never argue a point of information you differ about, unless you blame it on a book you read. I always remind myself that I'm collecting records to bring the family closer together, not drive them apart. There is no pleasure in recording a *gossip sheet.*

Occasionally, a cousin of the female sex will ask you how old Cousin Mae told you she was. I reply by saying, "If I told you, I would have to tell her yours." That usually ends the discussion. I had already gotten both of them from the family Bible.

9. Make friends with your cousins to the point where they become *partners* in your research. Hopefully they will want it to be as complete a record as you ALL can make it. Treat it like a *reunion feeling* and not a *business meeting*. You are becoming better acquainted, but in a different way, than over a pot-luck dinner.

10. Always keep in mind, that while you're scrutinizing relatives in the most personal way, they will be scrutinizing you. This is a favor they are doing you, and you must respect their wishes. If they don't care to answer some of your questions, you must leave that portion out.

Remember the rights of the Fifth Amendment!

11. As you proceed with the interview, watch for signs of fatigue and stop before you overdo. You hope to be welcomed back in the future. Tell them what a help they've been, and ask if you may contact them again if you have more questions. If they have photos, they may allow you to copy them on your next visit. If so, you could add them to the printed transcript to create a booklet or eventually a book.

12. As soon as possible after your visit, transcribe the interview on paper. This will provide an easier reference to certain facts you need for your charts. You may want to share the information with all the family, and some will not own a tape recorder.

If you do plan to publish or print in quantity, send a copy of the transcript to the subject for their consent, just as you would a copyrighted article. Ask them to make any changes they feel necessary. Have a release statement ready for their signature. Explain that it is to give them credit for such a great contribution! You could present yourself as their agent or editor, ready to make them famous as a great story-teller. I know I would be extremely flattered to know that anyone cared.

TAPING YOURSELF

There are many people who may prefer to talk their memories into a recorder, than to have to sit down and write them. They have things they want to say...don't need to be interviewed. With a personal tape recorder, they can choose the most convenient time to sit and tell stories. I've thought it would make a good gift...the tape and the recorder.

Consider doing a chronology of your life, touching on the milestones and outstanding times of your life. Even though you are relaxed and conversational, jot down somewhat of an outline so you don't end up having to go back and mention the things you left out. And make a few notes of what you **did** include, so you won't repeat yourself if you don't finish in one sitting...and you won't!

This would be a good activity for someone who has to go through a recuperation period of any kind. It's a time to think...perchance to dream...and dreams and hopes and goals are nice to share. You're human to have failed at some, but gloried in others. What were they?

Want to make a tape for your grandchildren to listen to at bedtime? Our friend, Doris, used to tell stories to the children at the library, and subsequently, on the radio. Our daughter plays tapes for one and a half-year-old, Christine, on auto trips.

Want to sing all the crazy songs you ever heard...as our friend, Ed is going to do? No accompaniment...just like he's out with the boys!

Give some thought to your chosen life work, and how it has changed over your lifetime. Certainly some of it has been made easier with change...but then there is something to be said for the quality of the product. Describe a typical workday, how it changed, the names of people who were there, and the way you felt when you retired, if you have. You spend so much time on the job that it should be appreciated by your family.

Tape record your visits as guides to those who want to trace your steps...to the cemetery to locate gravestones, through the streets of town, past all the haunts of your childhood, or walking around the home property. You can play the tape as you are taking the tour, much as a driving tour/tape guides you. You note the left and right turns, and mention markers to look for. Be sure to put it on PAUSE when you stop to investigate something.

SPECIAL MOMENTS TO RECORD

• When children are rehearsing their recitations at home.

• When they want to read **you** a story.

• When Grandpa reads **them** a story.

• Record when they are practicing an instrument. Grandma would appreciate a tape of the repertoire.
Do this periodically to show progress. Hopefully, there will **be** some.

• If there is a piano accompaniment, make a tape of the piano part for the student to rehearse with. It makes practice a lot more interesting. Don't forget to play a tuning note first...and set the tempo so you can come in together.

• When you need to memorize lines in a play, or a choral selection, make a tape **with** the script (music) and play it on the car tape player as you drive around, or wait in traffic. Later, the tape can become a memento of the occasion done in your voice.

• When you're singing, give lines to each person to sing alone so each stands out, ever so briefly...such as the numbered items in Twelve Days of Christmas. Let them change the items for a surprise. We have the voices of a group of relatives including six over 70 years old!

• We used to have talent shows using the hearth as a stage

108

and the children (and cousins) would each perform. We'll never forget the year they paraded with instruments, and Paul called his paper bag, the *sacks*!

• New Year's Day is a perfect time for everyone to enumerate why they will remember the old year, and what they're hoping to accomplish in the new one. Then the next New Year's Day, you can play the tape and see how many reached their goals. That might teach me to write shorter lists...but I doubt it!

• Send audio tapes instead of letters, which can be answered on the same tape and returned. When filled, save them as records instead of taping over them. They're like diaries, only filled with the emotion of the moment. Again, make notes before beginning...but never read from your notes...it will sound like it. Just imagine the person is sitting across from you and talk away! You can have a lot more fun adding special effects to your conversation...a little song, the *meow* of the cat, the sound of the lawnmower, a little Hi! when the neighbor drops by, a favorite poem or joke you saw and it doesn't matter if the clock strikes in the middle.

• I play the piano, but rarely have someone around to play duets, so I tape recorded the Primo page and played the Secondo with it. I did the same thing with a two-piano selection, which was a lot easier than trying to get two pianos together again...and we were already in tune.

• My brother, Noel, used to pretend he was a D.J., announcing and playing records. Luckily, I thought to turn on the tape recorder.

• Ask for each in the group to tell which period in history they would go back to in a time machine, and why...or any other query that would include all ages...(time they were most frightened, hungry, poor, proud, embarrassed).

• Record community ceremonies marking milestones in its history. My father went to every function to record speeches by the town leaders, and enclosed a program with the tape. Since reel-to-reel tape is inconvenient now, they should be transferred to cassette, and placed in the town archives.

• Interview the centenarians of the community to get an idea of the history that each has lived to see. Grants are available for projects of this kind. Call your state Humanities Council or Cultural Alliance for information.

• Tapes are souvenirs of occasions when you could not be there or hear speakers. The most unique example of this was the tape my girl friends made of MY baby shower, when I had the baby the same day as the shower, and it was too late to call it off. One of them, who was pregnant, sat in for me, and they opened all the gifts, and then wrapped them up again. Periodically, they would call out to the recorder telling me how nice everything was, and that I really should be there. They decided to freeze part of the cake for me, and stopped by the recorder to tell me how glad they were that the baby was here. I had the shower all over again when I came home! I plan to get them all together some day, and we can listen and laugh and I can thank them again.

This group has been getting together every year since high school when we named ourselves, "The Hags." It seemed funny then, but somehow it's beginning to get us down. I can't imagine why!

• Just turning the recorder on for the Christmas gift-opening turned out to be a hodge-podge of everyone giggling and talking, but it sounded so nostalgic years later. The focus was spontaneity, not perfection.

The ultimate use of any of these tapes would be to find slides to illustrate them, and present your own multimedia program. Each would complement the other, as the video tape does...but this is before camcorders. A lot of the people in our early slides and tapes are no longer living, and this makes us very glad we have this record. This is what it's all about..."CARPE DIEM"...for the future!

ORAL HISTORY
Shumway, Gary L., ORAL HISTORY PRIMER
Nichols, Evelyn and Anne Lowenkopf, LIFELINES. VA:
Betterway Publications, Inc., 1989

PHOTOGRAPHERS OF NOTE
William Edward Booth—Richmond,VA
William Henry Jackson—The Western Frontier, 1843-1942
Margaret Bourke-White
Edward Steichen—World War II
Alexander Alland 1902-1989—New York City
Wallace Nutting
Peter Palmquist—Humboldt Co, CA
Lewis Hine—Immigrants 1900's in Ellis Island, and the east
J. Harry Shannon—Washington DC 1912-1928, in Wagner
Collection, Columbia Historical Society

PHOTOGRAPH ANALYSIS
Lichtman, Allan—Your Family History—NY: Vintage Books
1978
Davies, Thos.L—Shoots, a Guide to Your Family's Photographic
Heritage—NH: Addison House 1977
Eakle, Arlene—Photograph Analysis—UT: Family Hist.World
1976
Family Heritage periodical, No.1,2,3, 1978, "Hidden Stories
in your Photographs"—May D. Hill
Akeret, Robert A.—Photoanalysis—NY: Simon & Schuster 1973
Taft, Robert—Photography and the American Scene—NY: Dover
1964
Welling, William—Collector's Guide to Nineteenth Century
Photographs—NY: Colliers 1976
Newhall, Beaumont—The History of Photography from 1839 to
the Present Day—NY: Museum of Modern Art 1964
Kelbaugh, Ross J.—Directory of Maryland Photographers 1839-
1900, Garden City, NY: Anchor Press 1973

VIDEO
Sturm, Duane and Pat, VIDEO YOUR FAMILY HISTORY. UT:
Ancestry Publishers 1989

MAKING COPIES
Shull, Wilmer Sadler—Photographing Your Heritage—UT:
Ancestry Publishers 1988
Shafran, Alexander—Restoration and Photographic Copying. NY:
Amphoto, 1967
Weitzman, David—Underfoot, An Everyday Guide To Exploring
The American Past—NY: Scribner 1976
Branch, Tom—Photographer's Build It Yourself Book
Grill, Tom—25 Projects To Improve Your Photography

COLLECTION AND CARE
Weinstein, Robert & Booth, Larry—Collection, Use and Care
of Historical Photographs—Nashville: Amer. Asso.for
State and Local History 1977
Time-Life Library—Caring For Photographs—NY: Time-Life,
1972
Reilly, James—Care and Identification of 19th Century Photo-
grapic Prints—NY: Eastman Kodak Co, 1986

POST CARD

Mr. & Mrs. Lee Smith
10360 Cullen Ter.
Columbia, Md. 21044

April

23 Monday

24 Tuesday

25 Wednesday

26 Thursday

27 Friday

Knox, Kentucky

Sept. 15, 1953
47 today oh me

DO THE WRITE THING!

My School-day Chums
My friends so dear
Your Autograph —
Please sign it here

6

GENEALOGY IS...DOING THE "WRITE" THING

Wouldn't it be exciting to find some old letters written by your great-grandpa to your great-grandma when he went west to look for gold? And what about the journal she kept when she went to join him...what a find! How wonderful that they have been saved all these years! Now you can see that they were real people, not just names on a chart.

Are you saving some similar writings so your children or nieces and nephews will understand how you lived and learned? Or will you go without a trace, a clue, a reminder that you were living here? If you choose to record the life of your family, you will become the family historian. Just as an artist looks for shades of color, you will begin noticing all the little details to include. Here are some of the ways you may choose to do the **write thing**.

Keep a diary or a journal, entering not only personal events but those that happen at school and in the community. Note disasters and job-related news; times when changes occurred that affected the town, you, and your family. Include decisions, births and deaths, any experience that brings your emotions to the surface. These are the times that shape our lives and form our character.

Somewhere in your journal describe a typical week, day by day. I often ask this of my letter friends when I've been out of touch. It tells what their priorities are at the moment. Use the names of friends, neighbors and those you work with, so you reveal your social life as well.

There is a wonderful and unique set of books on daily life in Frederick, Maryland in the mid-1800's. Written by an average citizen, later mayor, named Jacob Engelbrecht, it is a diary of opinions on what he sees from his window and in his travels around the county. The charm lies in the verbal pictures he paints of the little and big items of each day. Since he uses many names of friends and political figures, it has been indexed. Starting today, why don't you do the same, saving family secrets for another record?

This would be a good project for a very opinionated relative. Then you could say, "Why don't you put **that** in your book, Aunt Mary?"

Here is a quote in support of diaries from the writing of Eileen, a past president of our genealogical society. (It appeared in the Family Tree newsletter, January 1981.)

"Because my father was a great storyteller and knew many of the people who frequent Gussie's diaries, reading about them after hearing his stories was like meeting old friends for me. My father knew them as old people; Gussie knew them when they were young. When the diaries were sketchy, Father was able to fill in the details, which leads me to wonder how many other good tales are hidden in some of Gussie's short, matter-of-fact sentences. A case in point: 'May 29, 1904—Noah found dead in bed.' A lengthy explanation by Eileen's father revealed a court case involving foul play after a whole night of reveling, but no charges were filed."

She ends her article with this advice, "To really get to know your ancestors, not just names and dates and places, but to really know them and their friends and neighbors, and to feel for a while what they felt as they lived their lives, believe me...there's nothing like a set of old diaries."

Read DOMESTICK BEINGS by June Sprigg, which quotes diaries of seven 18th century women—a midwife, schoolgirl, invalid, spinster, farmer's daughter, and the wives of a farmer and a president.

As I have mentioned elsewhere, a journal affords you more space than a diary, as you date it only when you make a new entry. It has been suggested that a plain cover will discourage others from asking or reading about your private thoughts.

My husband purposely used a "journal" format when he wrote three books covering changes in education. He wanted to show the day-by-day steps he took to change from traditional graded schools to an open non-graded curriculum.

Some diaries become observations on a person's outlook as they pass through a crisis. They are even requested by some doctors as a window on the patient's thoughts that helps him verbalize and work through a problem, a step at a time. It seems therapeutic just to get it out, and it's there to read when the patient is better. Anne Frank's diary was powerful because we followed her innermost meditations, as though she were talking to the only friend she had.

Lee's pocket calendars were kept religiously for at least ten years. Each one went everywhere he went, and though meant for business appointments, he kept notes as well. When he recently retired, I made sure he kept them as mementoes. He'll wonder how he ever kept that pace!

Diaries or journals kept over a long period of time can help you see how your own thinking has changed, your friendships have matured or been replaced by involvement with responsibilities. It is written proof that our attitudes evolve and our understanding deepens, so be liberal with your opinions and observations. That's what a journal is all about!

Make a scrapbook, including items along with your story. As a teenager, I kept movie folders, ticket stubs, corsage ribbons, prom decorations, and photos of old boyfriends. I think I printed on one of the pages, "there's many a beau that I let go, because I wanted you." I wrote a narrative to go with it that is pretty silly...so it keeps me humble.

At this stage of my life, I remember all the pen pal letters, written in different color inks, in circles, upside down with pin-up photos enclosed. I didn't keep any letters, but often wonder about the people. Now my pen pals are *genealogy cousins* helping each other with research.

As your children grow I'm sure you will keep mementoes of their school days. I have three boxes, labeled for each child, that hold items I had hoped to get into scrapbooks. I also put in greeting cards, programs, all manner of paper memorabilia. Quickly add a date, if not already noted. The later sorting-out is part of the fun of discovery. For better preservation, use acid-free file boxes.

Our friend, Jackie, put a lot of cartoons, notes, and mementoes in a scrapbook about her life with her husband, Bill, and gave it to him as a Valentine. After her example, I created one for my husband as a tribute on his Valentine birthday. It included photos, clippings, jokes, awards, notes, poems, souvenirs from favorite trips, even a bill for the first furniture we bought! I left a few blank pages as "the best is yet to be."

A chronology is concise but meaningful, as it puts your life in perspective. Because it is just a line or two for each date, you are more liable to keep it current. Trying to go back after 40 years and make one is so difficult, but from then on you will be glad you recorded the milestones.

When my father passed away, we found a one-page chronology he had typed with the heading "The Life Of Orion Jacob Virts." As we gathered at the house after the funeral, a hush came over the room as we told everyone to read what he had chosen to record. Not only the births of his three children, but date and price of the houses we had moved to, the year of his parents' divorce, and later their deaths. His last entry was his retirement from the postal service; he had carried mail 38 years, twice a day in those days. I don't think it was what he said, but the timing that made us realize there would be no more entries. It also gave us time to reflect on what he considered the milestones of his life.

Keep a trip journal...or let the children fill the pages. Include each day's highlights, cost of meals, mileage, gas prices, funny incidents, opinion of motel or campground, names of new friends, etc. Use paper or a book that can be kept with the photos from the same trip.

I have one our daughter kept at the age of nine, and she mentioned every bridge we went over, and every state line. We don't realize how unique these family trips are until our children are married. Then there is little time to spend a day together, let alone a whole vacation!

My mother kept a journal when she and my father went to Europe, with prices and opinions of everything. I like the part where the Italian man asked her for a date...she thinks!

Perhaps a **post card collection** would be a good idea! Purchase picture post cards at each stop, and record your experiences there on the back. Maybe include the fees, and whether you enjoyed it or felt it was over-rated. Hotels, motels and campgrounds always have cards, so include them on your evaluation...makes a good reference in many ways. Keep them in a three-ring binder with mylar pages you can purchase at a camera shop. It will be another sample of your or your children's handwriting, and a record of the time you spent, not just a picture. No worry about taking photos in bad weather; and the children can help you make choices of cards to purchase.

When going to a museum, our young friend, Heather, buys her three-year-old Morgan post cards of art work at the gift shop. As they tour, Morgan tries to find the treasure.

118

As a *keeper*, I have also been corraling post cards into one big box. Recently, I went through them, sorting as I enjoyed them, deciding their value to the next generation. Some were of buildings, motels, and scenes from the years when they had the linen finish. I must record them as more antique.

One was handmade by my father from a slice of wood in his workshop. He had addressed it and mailed it to me. It then occurred to me that those postmarked were already documented. Perhaps we should always mail the ones for our collections so they would have a date and place. We could ask the same relative to save them for us when we return.

Some were sent from our vacations, and were mini-journals of our trip. As I suggested, they could be written and kept on purpose by the children for just that reason. These should be put in the pages with four sleeves, so they can be read from both sides...or taken out and read. Between the pages of cards, you can place a narrative with additional information.

Many of the cards were from family members and neighbors who have since passed away. I will share them with the families, perhaps make a copy of the message and give the card to them as a favor.

Some were mailed to us in thanks for recommending these places when we had traveled there. We often share our slides and brochures, as I'm sure others do, but we had forgotten about it.

At least a dozen cards were sent to our daughters when they sent their names into a pen pal column, asking for cards. I'm giving them back to them so they may suggest their children do the same. Most children, even boys, can manage a few lines on a post card, and it assures them a steady stream of mail. A lot of us adults only send post cards when on vacation, but it makes sense to send them all the time. The children not only get a photo, but you would do it more often as events occur.

We have some cards of places and activities that tell a lot about our lifestyle...covered bridges, historic houses, parks, boats, crabbing, beach hotels, lighthouses, and the like. So Lee and I decided to choose a sampling that we would enter into a notebook. We decided to go through the notebook and tape record our memories of these spots and activities together. While your children are still at home, it would be a way to get all their voices on tape, so they would be less inhibited. In fact, you don't have to tell them you have the recorder on until it's over. The tape would act as a key to the collection and the experiences.

Some of the post cards I found were purchased by my parents when they went to Europe. Then I remembered that I have the log my mother kept of the trip, and stored the two together. When you keep such a variety of things all over the house, others never realize they are related. As your possessions are disbursed they may be put in separate boxes, and taken to "who knows where"...so as a good genealogist, I'm trying to keep them together.

My postal worker father enjoyed saving post cards of other postoffices around the United States. We would usually send him one when we traveled. I am considering selling those that have no personal message on them, as there is no one else in the family who is interested. But take a look at the next antique show you go to, and you can find all kinds of categories that others do collect.

Did you ever write out your **budget**...when you were in college, or first married...or lately? Well, keep it for a sign of the times...recession, inflation, depression, whatever. I found the one we used when Lee was in the army in the 1950's. It seemed like the car broke down every other month so we had to do without something else. We only had $3.00 for birthday gifts for our parents, (can't imagine what we got with that!) Old newspapers would give you the current prices, but a budget shows what **you** had to manage on, and what you chose to spend it on.

Of course, the army delivered our baby, Teri Lee, for $8.50 so I guess we can't complain. In those days you could only spend what you had...and the army knew what you had!

And **lists, lists, lists**...grocery store lists, Honey Do lists, and Christmas shopping lists, card lists, address books...all reminding me of the past. I guess lists gave me a false sense of being organized...I didn't have to try to remember what I had to do...and it would feel so good to be able to cross them off. Just like setting up my goals and shooting them down. But my lists look like the duty roster for an army company, not just one person with an impossible dream. So once in a while I run across one, and I laugh as I realize I survived in spite of falling short of ALL my goals.

And **notes** scribbled in a hurry by or for the family are sometimes hilarious...such as where you've gone, what jobs you wish they'd do, or why they won't be home on time; the apologies, the love notes in the lunch bag are what families are all about. Our favorite one is "Mom, I'm out soliciting; I'll be home at 5:00."...translated to "selling Girl Scout cookies."

Did you keep **letters** from your parents when you were in college? I only had the money to come home three times a year, so those letters are like journals themselves.

Or did your husband write you sweet nothings while in the army? I crossed out the mushy parts with a black marker, but those accounts of typical days are collector's items.

Letters are such character sketches that a recently popular play was staged with just a man and woman writing their letters to each other. The plot concerning their relationship unfolded with each reply. Got any old courtship letters?

And how about those letters from the kids at camp? Maybe they were just post cards, but they are still a little touch of home to read them again.

I was able to allow my daughters to read letters my mother-in-law had written when we announced that we were engaged, and again when we wrote we were expecting her first grandchild. If she had just verbally told us, we would have nothing to re-read and share with others. Think about it! Sometimes being apart is an opportunity to say things we couldn't or wouldn't otherwise. My mother was never able to say she loved us, but seeing her first letter to me signed with "love" really choked me up!

There are many kinds of letters that reveal who we are; those written to the editor and published in complaint, those with congratulations, letters of reference, some of support through difficult times. They show the closeness of friends, by being there to be read and re-read, to be savored, and treasured whenever we need them. Though phone calls are quicker, letters are lasting. Take the time to do the **write** thing...(not fair to type).

Though I don't run holiday letters off in quantity for my friends, I find myself chronicling the year to many. It's a good idea to make a copy for yourself to keep as the year in review, if you haven't thought of another way.

However, Mary uses the holidays to create **"Christmas Newsletters."** Around October, she invites all of the families to send her an update of the year's events...deadline being Thanksgiving. Mary then combines them into one chronicle, gives it a festive cover, makes copies, and sends to all.

I reserve one drawer of my desk for **souvenirs of happenings** throughout the year...and I drop in memorial cards, programs, greetings, cartoons, letters, all manner of remembrances. When the drawer is full, I put them in a box, and start all over again. I imagine whole years are layered like an archaeological dig, and I should probably throw in a dated sheet at the end of each year as a marker.

I especially treasure the creative, one-of-a-kind tributes I have. For about ten years I worked with a talented group called the Village Voices who wrote and participated in original musicals. They were basically a choral group; some could also write, act, draw, and dance. While I played the music, dancer Grace Nelson kept us on our toes. Their work was created for one or two performances, but I would like you to see them "one more time." Eleanor Mayer's **program design** is the cover of Chapter 10, and here are Bob Kramer's inspiring **song lyrics**, printed with his permission.

START ALL OVER AGAIN

When you walk through a rainstorm, and you're wet as you can be; When you've climbed every mountain, and a cramp is in your knee; Then it's time to stop and think about tomorrow, and START ALL OVER AGAIN!

When you looked to the rainbow 'til your eyes are getting weak; When you ford every stream you see, and you're still up the creek; When your throat is sore from singing in the rain, then you must START ALL OVER AGAIN!

Mountain high, valley low, every place you've had to go; You have been and come back; Now face the sober fact that ...

When you've followed every highway and you still
can't fold a map; Touched each tree along the by-
way, and your hands are full of sap; Then it's time,
my friend, to call it quits, surrender, and start all
over, you'll be in clover, if you START ALL
OVER AGAIN!
........*Robert Kramer 1978*

These lyrics are perfect for anyone who's just a wee bit discouraged.

Hang on to those **resumes**...for they quickly tell your family and friends who you are professionally, without you saying a word. Also, you may return to work after a hiatus, and you won't have to "try to remember."

Glance through **old recipe books, Bibles, books and ledgers** for scraps of paper and notes that your ancestors may have put there. Sometimes important information was written or kept in these as though they were the *safe deposit boxes* of the times. Curiously enough, one Bible I saw must have been an extra in the household, for it had literally been used as a scrapbook. Newspaper articles and obituaries had been pasted right on top of the scriptures, page after page. In fact, our society transcribed the information so it could be filed in the library.

On special occasions, instead of buying a card, you may want to write a letter or **create a card.** If you just mention some personal remembrance you have from the past, how you watched the person climb the ladder of success, or perform many kindnesses, or go out of their way to help an organization. On a student's graduation day you may recount a time when he made a reckless comment about dropping out, or becoming a professional *bum.*

I wouldn't trade some of our girl's cards, especially the one to the two best parents on their *annivirshary*. Some people just spell phonetically, right?

Once as a *thank you* for my years as their director, my choir gave me a Friendship Chain of Notes. Each person had written a tribute on a separate notecard; these were then tied into a four-foot chain. To me its worth more than gold.

For some of us, writing is like "mental housecleaning," leaving space for new ideas and thoughts. As we write we organize, digest and encourage dialogue with others who share similar feelings. That is certainly my goal in writing this book...a way to share my enthusiasm with others.

What I've been pointing out in all these samples of writing is the fact that anything created by each person reveals something about them. Anything in a person's handwriting gives it authenticity and makes it personal, the same as a voice on a tape. That is another dimension to help us identify them.

When we go into this search, we value everything that can give us a true picture. Without these clues, we just have to imagine who they are, and what they were like. So consider yourself and your family important enough to be remembered for all that they were, not just what a few cold, lifeless documents can tell us second-hand. It doesn't matter whether they were your favorite people; they affected your life in some way. Tell us about it; **do the write thing!**

Here are some of the forms your story can take:

• Narrative about one family...THE BRADLEY BUNCH.

• Narrative about ONE relative whom you admired and who influenced your life.

• Booklet of charts plus narrative and background material on as many generations of one surname as you have completed. Many of us do a different booklet for each family line we represent.

• Write letters to each of your ancestors as though telling them how you found out about them. They are hiding out in so many obscure places that it is a thrill to finally flush them out! They move about so much that it's difficult to catch up with them. I found a genealogy written entirely with letters to each of the writer's ancestors.

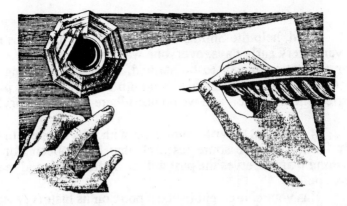

• Write a child's version...beginning with "Once upon a time there were three brothers who emigrated together"...or whatever you've heard in your family. It is a joke in genealogy circles that everybody seemed to have three brothers who came together. Whatever the story, pass it along...but identify it as family folklore. There isn't anything wrong with folklore, as long as you don't pass it off as truth. I guess its place is somewhere with the tall story epic. I always say, "It is thought to be..." or "Some say that..."

• True stories about your own life and the good old days as a child would be both entertaining and historical. One of our friends, Ed, chronicled all the mischief he got into and called it "Only In Canadaigua." Now he's working on a tape of all the songs he used to sing.

Perhaps you would like to send your stories as letters to your grandchild, suggesting they be kept in a notebook called "When Grandma (or Grandpa) Was Young."

• If you want to seriously learn to write, consider taking a college course in creative writing. It teaches you to turn your genealogy into different story forms with ready made subjects...your family characters! They would show up in essays, anecdotes, themes, short stories, novels, plays and even poetry! Why some of those plots would rival television scripts.

• Some people research to prove "what's in a name," THEIR name. They try to document everyone past and present who have that same name. They print newsletters, they have reunions and celebrate their fame. At least they don't have trouble remembering names.

Lord, help the Smiths...please! The old joke goes that in the very, very early days, everyone was known as Smith. But as their reputation began to be stained, those not wanting to be disgraced chose other names. Enough said? I'm very proud I married one, however, and we do not adhere to such a story!

If you want to write something with wider appeal than just your family, choose some research that hasn't been done yet. Anything that preserves the past will be appreciated, and may sell many copies.

Has your church published a book on its history?

Start interviewing residents, do some historical background and turn out a history of your town. For a bigger project, organize a commission on history and divide the content into chapters, which may then be assigned to different organizations..

Choose a topic or two and get residents to comment on the old days. It's just like sitting on a park bench and talking about the past when they knew it best. Give it a title like "I Remember The Time When..." or "Have You Heard The One About...?"

Write on the history of the industry that is responsible for the life of the town, and changes that have occurred. Include a lot of the people who assumed leadership.

Focus on the early families, many of whom intermarried and are still there though in smaller numbers. Perhaps include a collection of wedding photos...the one picture everyone seems to have.

Choose a decade or a particular year, and tell what it was like to be alive at that particular time, in your particular role. The drama depended on where you were when it happened.

If you would like to earn some money abstracting and copying old records, contact a genealogical publishing company near you and ask if they need any assistance.

But the story you can put the most into is the one about YOURSELF! There isn't anyone who knows more about that subject than YOU. The material will be documented, filled with detail and drama because YOU were there! If you feel that your experiences can help someone else to understand the times, find a way to record them. Or if you never had an opportunity to share

126

them with your children and grandchildren, the story of your life will keep you ever in their memory.

For suggestions on organizing and publishing your own family story, see Chapter 14.

A WINDOW ON YOUR MEMORY
—Use Diagrams—

If you could go back to your childhood home, what would you look for? Perhaps the door where you marked your height each birthday, the bedroom where you could watch the birds in the tree nearby, or feel the pain of falling on the floor register as you raced through the hall. The kitchen table where you did your homework or played Bingo with homemade prizes wrapped in newspaper. We can see it in our mind's eye; why not put it on paper?

I recently took my father and his cousin, Jeanne, back to the house where they were raised, thinking it would provide some new insight as it sparked their memories. But the house had been remodeled, and they were confused. It was hard to reconstruct the past with all the rooms rearranged. However, the yard and trees did echo parties they had had on the lawn with lighted lanterns hanging from the branches. They glanced down the roads and fields and recalled walking to school with nearby family children.

Later, I thought I would ask him to diagram the layout of the house and tell me about it. Besides describing his daily routine as he went about the house, I thought he could tell me if it had *secret places* , back stairs, a *company parlor* . Were there any accidents, fires, remodeling, regular meetings or entertainments? Was anyone ever buried from this house?...the body always lay in state in the home in those days. Picture the family as you lived there...what were they usually doing and where?

This could be part of an oral history, provided the drawing was kept with the tape. Still I think it a good idea to add notes on the same paper or key it to another sheet.

Though I felt I knew my husband of 38 years very well, I learned so many more things when I had him diagram the river cabin and surrounding area. (I use the word **diagram** because it does not indicate artistic talent, just includes necessary items as they relate to each other.)

Lee spent every summer for ten years living at the cabin. He, in fact, helped his father and grandfather build it from "found" items, and it took on its personality from the type of materials they found. Starting at age seven, he helped the family move from town to the river, and new routines were created for living in three large rooms and the great outdoors. Visitors, like me, quickly became acquainted, and most of our dates were out fishing on the river, or playing cards with the family.

I even had him diagram the river with its favorite fishing rocks, grasses and worm-digging islands. The rocks were named for the relatives who preferred fishing from them, rather than a boat. As Lee drew the river, he talked about the people and the experiences he remembered. It was remarkable how well he knew that river.

When Lee was ten, he delivered a huge bundle of papers before he went to school. I asked him to trace the route and the names of the people he delivered to. He recalled the temperament of most, and even remembered whether they got one or two daily papers. When he was 14 he even came to my house selling church calendars. You may not have married a person from your hometown, but to record the many ways a young person made his money gives you a look at their values and insight into early choices.

Though his father was not much of a conversationalist, he did possess a remarkable memory. Many times he mentioned the early days of our hometown of Brunswick when the town was between the tracks. All those early businesses, the opera house, and markets have been washed away by floods and replaced on higher ground. How I wish I had thought to make a diagram of those!

I did get my mother to tell me about early Harpers Ferry when she was spending so much time at her grandmother's house around 1919. (I know now that my grandmother Shewbridge was born on Virginius Island, and her early home was washed away also by the floods.) The Park Service is doing restoration to make it look as it did in 1865, 40 years earlier, but I wanted to see it through my mother's eyes. She didn't just tell me whose store and house was where, but how they reacted to her as a child, or played an important role in the town. Mr. Dittmyer, the druggist, always pulled her hair, Mr. Jones kept his horse and carriage here and always met the trains to provide taxi service, the 5¢ movies were accompanied by Miss Anna Marmion at the piano. Mom bought Hershey kisses to eat while they changed the movie reels.

With the tape recorder on, I did the diagram, but she had to keep telling me where to put the buildings. It is much better if the story-teller is also making the lines. You also have their handwriting and personal touches that give it more value.

As you interview your relatives, perhaps they could diagram the operation of their business, and their important place in that operation. It would be like a field trip to their workplace. If they are retired, it would be an opportunity to record the process and the workers of bygone days. No one wants to be forgotten, and many years were spent in that operation sharing experiences with those special people. There is rarely even a photo of the group.

I learned a lot about the operation of the railroad yards when the elementary students interviewed Jim Shriver, a recently retired worker. His description of the work of the switches and the trainmen was perfect for their book about the town. Adults may feel more at ease and take more time with a child than with another adult. So perhaps we should ask more young persons to do the interviews. It also gives the children an opportunity to be with their grandparents and add to the genealogy of the family.

If most of your history takes place in the same town, you may want to diagram the streets enough to show the locations of certain events. Of course you may be able to find a map of the town and mark it, but you could diagram the location of the streets and areas that figure into your family story. This way, it is truly your own and will only have the "important" places on it.

It seems a diagram provides a focus to evoke memories and story-telling. The teller paints a mental picture in the direction he wants it to go. It's a visual aid that sets the stage for the action. As a matter of fact, I used to do similar things with my orange-crate dollhouse.

We have a blueprint of the house where our children spent five years, as my husband built the house himself. So that diagram is already drawn...to scale. I suppose we should have copies reduced from the original to add to our collection.

Maybe a diagram is better than trying to go back to your home or workplace again. Too much is changed and going on without you...in fact, it seems that the minute you are gone, the next owner deliberately tries to give it a new personality that shows that it is now theirs! Whatever ties you have are mental, not physical, anyway. You can close the door just like the day you left—but open a window of your memory and peep in anytime you want.

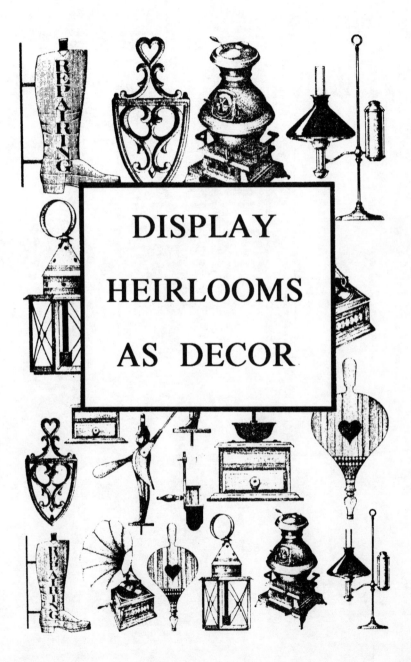

DISPLAY
HEIRLOOMS
AS DECOR

7

HEIRLOOMS BECOME DECOR

Heirloom is defined as *a possession that is handed down from generation to generation.* As long as the owner is taking care and using the item you don't imagine it as your own, but when the owner passes away, you feel a responsibility to continue the care as part of your family history.

Well, don't just dust your artifacts or store them away. Find new uses and live with them as an extension of your family...a link in a chain of caretakers. This way the young will remember the past and appreciate its special contributions.

You don't have to lose someone to start searching out the heirlooms. While Mom and Dad, Grandpa and Grandma are still around, start to ask questions about the origin of the old dishes, furniture, especially anything handmade. If manufactured, ask how they came to have it, how much it cost, and what the design or style is called. You don't usually go plundering through the attic, as though you're greedily looking for your inheritance. But sometime when all your brothers and sisters are together, you might ask parents to show you what's in that big old trunk. They may have left it just as it was when they inherited it...filled with paper items that look like a lot of crumbling trash. It may turn out to be immigration and naturalization papers or letters from the first American in your family.

I wish I could claim ancestry in the Snowden family, for they donated a most unusual heirloom to a local museum—a "hairbarium." It is a collection of locks of hair, each tied to a ribbon, dated, and glued to a framed background. It can be seen at the Howard County Historical Society Museum, Ellicott City, Maryland.

As part of our family history, my husband and I have turned many heirlooms into items that we see and live with every day. Hardly anything is still in the boxes and trunks where no one can see and enjoy. We seem to be arranging and rotating all the time.

In trying to find the stories to go with the articles, we began to meet new cousins and hence, genealogy became a way to tie it all together. It all has to do with an awareness and appreciation for all that came before, so that you take up your

133

meaningful role in the family line. If you don't, YOUR family could become an endangered species..."Peachers? Who are they?...never heard of 'em!"

Where else might you look for heirlooms besides the obvious trunk and strongbox? The book "Once Upon A Memory" by Alessi and Miller suggests going through the house, room by room, where collections of various types exist. The tool box, fishing tackle box, address book, family Bible, old recipe books, sewing cabinet, jewelry box, book shelf, desk, garage, and kitchen utensil drawer all hold items that have never been cleaned out, (thank heaven!).

Now here is where pack rats get appreciated! Where would museums be without pack rats? It seems to me that a membership in the *High Order of Revered Preservationist* should be awarded to all those who have cared enough to hang onto those last remnants of long gone civilization. I tell myself that my day will arrive when all things shall pass away, except the ones I have so lovingly cared for. Then it will no longer be trash, but a treasure!

So what can we do with these treasures to make them come alive again and be appreciated? We have found ways to display them, enjoy them, and be reminded of the past. It also evokes conversation from visitors about things they may have grown up with. But they must be *arranged with a plan,* or they'll just look like a lot of clutter. I will try to list some of them by types with suggested areas of use. At the end of this chapter I've listed methods of preservation.

IMPLEMENTS

Since many are made of cast iron, we fastened them to the white painted wall of our family room. So far we have an assortment of tools from our past. We are only interested in the items that have meaning to us, not just any antique.

The rest of the wall holds kitchenware, consisting of various griddles, muffin pans, cooky molds and cutters, rolling pin, and hanging scales. A meat hook could hold a hanging plant. For variety, I have interspersed some replica tavern signs, but framed copies of kitchen ads would be colorful.

134

Items having a base we placed in the bow window, including Mom's collection of antique candle molds, some of which hold dried flowers. Also in the window is an ice shaver my Grandma used for snowballs, a glass ice crusher, standing scales which hold a potted plant, and a Mason jar sitting in a canning holder.

There is also a telegrapher's key, which I purchased at a flea market. My grandmother Shewbridge had five brothers, all of whom worked as telegraphers on the B&O Railroad, and I wanted to have a reminder.

An old colander or bowl could hold fruit, and a bread or cutting board could support a grouping of blue Mason jars. These jars can be used as vases, canisters and even candleholders with sand in the bottom. Calico covers can be added to the lids for color, held on by ribbons over rubber bands.

Small items, such as cookie cutters, can be hung on a calico covered board with cup hooks and framed. Small things need to be placed together for impact. I used the open aluminum cutters as napkin rings.

Old milk bottles can act as vases, but I want to have a cardboard lid for mine, so I can demonstrate how it used to pop up when the cream froze. Now the cream is homogenized.

A small crock holds the wooden spoons I use every day.

A rack by the door could hold an apron or bonnets.

Use an old muffin tin as a tray to serve drinks.

A round dining table invites a lazy Susan which holds a centerpiece in the round. Perhaps a teakettle of flowers in the center and small items around.

I keep books on kitchen antiques nearby on the coffee table for easy reference. Old recipe books and mail order catalogues are entertaining as well. They would be great in an old wooden box with a food label.

The soffit above the wall cabinets was the space I chose for my trivet collection. There's a name for each of the antique designs. This would be a good place for copper salad molds as well. I have seen a basket collection atop cabinets without a soffit. A trailing plant adds softness to the corners.

My friend, Eunice, has implements hanging from a Shaker peg board against a white wall. If you prefer wallpapered walls, choose a small print or check. To coordinate my painted pantry doors, I added the Ohio Star quilt design cut from scraps of the wallpaper. Now if I just had the chair cushions done...

In the house where we lived before, we wanted shutters for a kitchen pass-through. Luckily the old postoffice was remodeling and we obtained the ones from the patron window. Keep your eyes open for those valuable additions when old

136

buildings are torn down.

My father has even removed decorative trim from wooden furniture and used it on other pieces...scrolls, leaves etc.

MANTLE

If your fireplace wall tends to be dark, you can place pewter pieces here to reflect the light. It is also the perfect place for the clock that Lee and I put together with an embroidered face. On the hearth we have the usual tools and broom. Propped against the screen, I placed Mom's two aluminum cake pans shaped like a lamb and rabbit. Opened up, they face each other, and also reflect light. If pewter is the poor man's silver, then aluminum must be the **very** poor man's pewter.

Actually, in the summer, the fireplace opening is another frame for an arrangement of large-scaled items. This is also when we use the coal hod for magazines instead of wood.

TOOLS OF TRADE

The wall of the stairwell is often wasted space. We thought it was a good display area for larger, heavier items. Covered with gold burlap to coordinate with the wallpaper, a sheet of pegboard provided a display area which supported tools...and still had a rustic background.

Here, we hung Lee's shotgun, presented to him when old enough to accompany the men when they hunted rabbit and squirrel. Nearby we placed some kitchen tools and a flint sparker.

To represent his time working for the railroad, we hung Lee's dad's lantern and cap, and one of the coffee buckets he carried to keep heated on the radiator. My father's ice skates are there to testify to lack of interest, after falling down the first time. Smaller squares of pegboard could be covered with fabric and used with pegs to hold smaller items.

The old woodworking tools can be grouped on stained pine boards, and hung in the basement hall near the workshop. They could be handled if kept in the old open toolchest.

If you would like a collection of 20 types of cut nails, write for a brochure to:

Tremont Nail Company
P. O. Box 111
Warsham, MA 02571

They come with a printed history from 500 A.D. to 1819.

Fishing tackle should be kept in the old tackle box. If you only have one or two pieces, you may want to put them with Dad's old hat or a cross-stitched fishing motto.

In displaying items, define the area for emphasis: use wallpaper borders, wood molding, boards for unity. Or select corners, alcoves, cupboards, walls that are reserved for related items.

Use the sill of the bay windows for stick birds or decoys. It's as though the sill is the stage, complete with curtains and spotlight to feature. Birds would go very well with plants in winter, and shells in the summer. The shore birds make a variety of profiles against the light and the driftwood complements all year.

I have seen them sitting in sawdust curls with the carving tools beside, as though the carver were still working on them. Maybe some things should be left that way...the half-knitted sweater and yarn, the quilt square and needle in a hoop. I'm afraid my house looks like that much of the time.

INSTRUMENTS

Both our families were quite musical, and our daughters are continuing to play woodwind instruments and sing. Our daughter Mindy is presently teaching oboe and bassoon. Lee and I met in the high school band, and I have spent 35 years in vocal music work.

The grand piano provides a focal point in our living room, so we mounted white pegboard on the corner walls to hang the family instruments and the metronome. I needed a place to store the music stand, so decided to leave it beside the piano with a sheet of music and a recorder resting on it.

In between the instruments we have framed some of the antique sheet music that was my mother's. We chose some of the more ridiculous titles, such as "Where Did Robinson Crusoe Go With Friday On Saturday Night?" and "Come After Breakfast, Bring 'Long Your Lunch, and Leave 'Fore Suppertime." I was willed a collection of sheet music from Elizabeth Hovermale who played for a lot of community functions. Since she only played by ear, she would call me to come and play any song she had a request for but had never heard. After a couple of times through, she would tell me she *had it down,* and she went on to her engagement. We had a good working relationship, and there were many times I wished for her ability to play from memory. I guess the music was her way of thanking me.

It's always good to add a shelf and a plant to soften the arrangement. It's also a perfect place for the pitchpipe, and a piano jewelry box, which holds a charm bracelet for all the shows I have been part of.

Record album covers may replace the sheet music if you desire. These are often works of art. Even the space under the piano is shared by the guitar, a large plant, and a ceramic cat.

Speaking of cats, I think it adds a nice homey touch to include animals and birds in your decor. Mom sat small ceramic birds in with plants and I have ceramic and cloth cats sitting on stools or peeping out of baskets. No animal upkeep, and Christine still gives them a pat and a kiss.

FLOOR GROUPINGS

Large heirlooms may be grouped together to soften the corners of a room, or tie in other pieces of furniture. Crocks and baskets of various sizes now hold potted plants. My friend, Gloria, had a nice bouquet of Black-eyed Susans in hers.

Lee's grandfather's copper minnow bucket is a unique holder for a fern. If you look closely you can see his initials pressed into the lid. A flour sack still bearing the name of the company is stuffed and tied and leaning along the side of the corner cupboard.

An idea we used on the unpainted cupboard was to hammer a dogwood blossom design into the wood with leather stamps. Do this before staining. When you add the stain the design will be darker since the fibers absorb more stain. It gives a hand-carved look to the otherwise plain corner molding.

A large basket makes a good holder for magazines or dried flowers, stuffed toys, or wood. My picnic basket has yarn and needles showing under an open lid. Smaller interesting baskets are often hung from beams, or paraded down the staircase along the wall. Perhaps you can use them in the bathroom to hold towels. I have seen them with the bottoms fastened to the wall, creating shadowbox containers. Grace uses

140

baskets all over her house to hold plants, mail, towels, napkins, and the like.

Since smoking has been discouraged, our floor model ash tray has become a plant stand. Now if I had only kept the old birdcage, it could hold a hanging plant too. Our canary always sang whenever Mom played Brahm's Waltz on the piano; they did many impromptu concerts.

DOORWAY

In the entry hall we have a milkcan painted flat black to hold umbrellas. It still bears the imprinted name of the local milk company from the 1930's. We have a friend, Judy, who uses hers as a plant stand outside the door.

Beside our milkcan we have the shoe last on its stand that my father used to repair our shoes. A stuffed goose sits on the foot. A small child's last is now a paperweight in the study. On the wall inside the door is a "welcome sampler" made by my mother and framed by my father. He cut out wooden maple leaves for the corners to copy Victorian frames.

The hall is a perfect place for a bench or washstand, using the wall behind to display framed photos or a mirror.

BOOKENDS—DOORSTOPS

Bookshelves are decorative when filled with the many colorful bindings of books, but more so when the books are punctuated with artifacts! A breakfront in the living room gives us adjustable shelving—some open, some with sliding doors—so we have many choices. That is the luxury of living...choices!

Many heavy items can add variety to shelves as bookends. Would you believe that we use a handmade brick from the homeplace of Lee's great-grandfather, and on another shelf we have two iron snowbirds from the roof? Some townspeople kept bricks when our old high school was torn down. We should paint a section white on the bottom and print the source of these in our log. My father's rock and mineral collection yielded some choice specimens we can use in the same way. The rest of the collection occupies a print box.

Acting as doorstops for each of the bedrooms are the small and large flat irons. I prefer to leave them plain, devoid of cutesy folk art. To me, they are items of work, not mere decoration. I leave that to fabric and needlework. Another doorstop is an anvil that our railroader created from a piece of iron rail filed into a point.

A spittoon makes an attractive doorstop if weighted, or may hold a potted plant. I have also seen one in Eleanor's house as a hanging planter, where the brass picks up the light.

PORCH

First impressions begin here and we want everyone to be forewarned that we appreciate our past. We have set up a half barrel under a hand pump through which a trickle of water is constantly flowing. This same water is being recirculated by an immersible pump. An enameled dipper lets me water plants that sit on an old water bench. We love the rustic, cooling effect; and as a matter of fact, two of our ancestral families were coopers and barrel-makers. We've circled the porch posts with plants whose plastic pots are sitting in crocks.

Over the deacon's bench we mounted a large crosscut saw and a scythe stands in the corner. Father Time has been known to borrow this for New Year celebrations. We purchased a firemark iron plaque to display as they did in the old days, that shows this house is covered by fire insurance. Alexandria, Virginia has many of these by the doors; also *busy-body* mirrors by second floor windows to allow you to see who's at the door.

Two hickory rockers from Lee's grandfather's home are places to *sit a spell* and read the paper. And a school desk by the door holds a slate and chalk for messages should we not be home. Actually, the desk was saved from an abandoned three -room school where both Lee and I taught at Burkittsville, Maryland.

I thought I would give the entry an air of antiquity by painting a tavern sign to read "HISTORIC SMITH INN, 1980," which was the year we moved in.

FURNITURE

I am fortunate to have had creative parents who were always pursuing some new skill or activity. They were both Virgos as am I; do you suppose that has anything to do with it? My father taught himself to cane chairs and we have several of his chairs and rockers. He built a maple cobbler's bench for us, and numerous small candlesticks and wooden articles. At one time he was making reed hampers and bread boards. My husband has also done some pieces of furniture, playhouses, and table and chairs for the children.

The oldest piece we have is a handmade single bed that was made by my great-great-grandfather Hood. We removed about five coats of paint to discover a rose and leaves carved in the headboard. For a while it was the bed our girls used when they graduated out of the crib. Now we use it in the guest room.

Our friends, Roy and Carla, have a beautiful head and footboard that they incorporated into a sideboard server by adding a wooden counter between.

A wooden sewing cabinet holds a darning egg, needle case, stork scissors, and a jar of buttons; and sitting on top are a toy machine and a mannequin. Some of the 15-cent patterns are also collectibles now.

Years ago we had guests autograph our door to the basement family room. When we moved, we took the door with us and made it into a table by attaching four screw-in legs. (We DID replace the door!)

FAMILY ROOM

Our friends, Carol and Jesse, have turned their family room into a vintage working soda fountain with an old cash register. On the shelves around the room are lots of interesting artifacts and colorful advertisements. Game boards are attractive on the wall.

LAUNDRY

If I had a neater laundry, it would be the perfect place to hang the washboard, wash tub, a roller towel, drying rack, and some homemade soap. Don't forget a clothes pin bag filled with wooden pins. I have all the items, but no proper space...maybe you do!

TOYS

The guest room is the room where we have put the children's old toys and dollhouse. The latter was once our camping chuckbox and we didn't want to throw it away. Since Lee built it with four compartments, it was perfect for a dollhouse. We decided to remodel it and make some furnishings a month before Christmas. Rooms could be furnished to represent your own childhood home, and be the setting for many a story from the past.

The rag dolls are each sitting on one of the steps to the basement, with legs dangling over the edge, like mischievous children peering through the bannisters.

Shelves hold my old doll and blue cup, tiny bank, and animals that used to be part of the Christmas yard. We purchased a small curio wall cabinet for my doll dishes.

A good place for outgrown toys is on a shelf around the room above the windows. It acts as a three-dimensional border. I sewed a ruffle for this shelf that matched the bed spread of pink and white checked cotton, and stapled it on.

DISHES—GLASSWARE

Though too fragile for general use, I have found occasions when I can use a few dishes at a time. At family gatherings I serve buffet style, so I use the beautiful handpainted bowls for serving dishes. This way they do not get handled a lot, but are still admired.

The one-of-a-kind teacups have held small bouquets, and the one pewter teapot I am using for dried flowers. The Jefferson cups make small holders for mints or pot pourri.

Our girls remember the green cracker jar that my mother kept filled with candy. Why don't you buy an assortment of *penny candy* to share the next time the *kids* come to visit? Besides dressing up the table, it's an education in itself...root beer barrel, watermelon slices, Mary Janes, jaw breakers, wax bottles...remember?

I wish I were more knowledgeable about the origin of these dishes. I heard my mother mention some were wedding gifts, some belonging to grandparents, but I didn't pay attention. Now I'm asking her sisters about them, but even they aren't sure. What we can do is at least learn the name of the company, design, and approximate age. This will attach more value and will aid in passing them on.

There are a couple of pieces that are so unusual that I am very curious to research, so we are taking photos of them with us as we travel. (It isn't enough we are looking for ancestors; now we're looking for dishes as well.) A good antique price guide would be a help. We owe it to our ancestors to realize the value of things. At the sale of my mother's belongings, I told a woman I had no depression glass; that the only dishes I had were in a group for $.50. She came back with two pieces and told me they were indeed depression glass, offering me a slightly higher price. Had I known the value I would probably still have them.

Small cups or saucers could hold pins or pot pourri on the dressing table. They make attractive place card holders. To hold miniature bouquets of real or dried flowers, use spice bottles, cruets, condiment sets, little gelatin molds, or Lotus cups.

Plates can be displayed on a plate rack, on the wall in groups, or in a window if they are translucent. Decanters and bottles also dress up a window. Use the ledge as well as the sill. If you want a jeweled look, fill them with water tinted with food coloring. Voila, collector's items!

PERSONAL GROOMING ITEMS

If you're lucky enough to have your Dad's shaving mug and brush, razor, or mustache brush, find a place for them in the bath. Shelves on either side of the mirror, or a tray could hold them.

Mirrored trays are perfect for a lady's dresser set, and could include nail buffer, perfume atomizer, kid curlers, and marcel iron. Hat and stick pins could be stuck into an old pincushion.

145

Fans, decorative combs, beaded purses would make an interesting wall arrangement in the bedroom. I display Mom's crocheted gloves on a wooden hand that came from an old dress shop. During the winter, Benita is proud to show the handknit mittens with Latvian designs that her mother made.

Antique clothing, dresses, hats, etc. could hang on a Shaker peg board or clothes rack, provided it was not in strong light. Head scarves can be tied on a pillow or tied around a hat. Hats are sometimes just placed randomly on the foot of the bed or the back of a chair...the idea, of course, to be *at home* instead of a museum.

CHILDREN'S ROOM

We all wish we could look at life as we did in our childhood, or that of our children...so we save the little drawings, shoes, cups and toys that take us back again.

Group small assorted items on shelves: bowls, cups, spoons, rattles, together with a bib and a framed photo. Or bring toys together: a stack of blocks, a doll, tiny dishes, or books. I put the "Children's Cookbook" with the small baking utensils: sifter, rolling pin, and cutters. They fit nicely on the shelves of the miniature hutch.

The walls can hold baby quilt wall hangings, costume hats, ballet or tap shoes, scouting kerchiefs and sashes. Arrange a group of hats from Hallowe'en, plays, sports, ethnic festivals, theme parks, on wall or clipped to a line.

I still have my two crocheted dresses that I display at times from plastic hangers on a clothes rack. My mother's long-waisted dress, made in 1910, is wrapped in acid-free tissue in storage. I plan to get advice from a curator on the feasibility of cleaning crocheted work.

Antique baby clothes could be fitted on a doll of the same size, and take its place on the bed or in the cradle. I discovered that the Belgian knitted baby shawl was lacy enough to be worn as a stole.

Doll furniture and wagons are perfect ways to display the dolls and teddybears, themselves. They could read from the books, eat from the dishes, and ride in the wagon. It's only when the *visiting dolls* come that you have to worry. Then you choose a Raggedy Andy, a game or a bean bag, and close the door while the other toys *take a nap.* Our doll house now has a padlock, and we only have *open house* with supervision. At holidays we add miniature wreaths and a tree. You could just make a diorama with one room.

LINENS

Pillowcases may become pillows which aren't used daily. Sew the edging down to decorate the front. If the case is damaged, salvage the edging to sew on collars or neckline accents on a blouse. With a matching pair, they may be opened up and turned into cafe curtains.

QUILTS, COVERLETS

The Amish store their quilts in layers on the guest bed. To show them you just turn them back, one by one, rotating the top one periodically. This eliminates folding and allows the circulation of air.

I keep a quilt over the stair railing in winter, or like Carla, hanging on the back of the couch. If on a rack, it could be moved around, sometimes in front of the fireplace opening, sometimes to brighten a corner. An antique drying rack could display quilts and other linens.

Only if damaged beyond repair would I EVER cut up a quilt. Good sections could become wall hangings. I have cut smaller items from pieced squares and unfinished tops.

The child's crazy quilt my grandmother made me has a center block with my name and the date 1936 embroidered. The silks have rotted but the lining is good, so I tried to replace them by top stitching new fabric over. Fragile materials are better hung and in very low light, so it is mounted on a rod.

147

Magazines picture quilts behind headboards, as room dividers or table covers. If used as a tablecloth, have a piece of acetate plastic cut to fit the top of the table to protect the quilt from spills.

Quilts made by my friend, Judy, have won prizes, and I feel fortunate when she invites me to go to seminars. I learn a lot from my friends.

Just a thought...If children don't live with items, they won't be a part of THEIR memories. Rotate the quilts or give them a second name that includes the child's, such as "Becky's Choice" or "Heather's Hearts"...whatever. Let them enjoy the pride of future ownership, or give them now to wrap up in and take a nap.

To learn more about quilts and how they became important to the social history of the U. S., order the video, "Hearts and Hands" through the library.

SMALL COLLECTIBLES

Tiny ornaments, miniatures and related items need to be given a showcase of their own. These are sometimes called *memory boxes,* and are simply shadow boxes with sections for each item. They could house a collection of articles belonging to one person, showing unity of object, but separating them into tiny showcases. I'm thinking of my mother's stork sewing scissors, thimble, wooden darning egg and thread, bone crochet hook and tatting shuttle of her mother's. The box could be lined with calico or printed gift papers and covered with a glass front. I have seen these boxes unfinished and for sale in craft shops.

Larger ones can be built behind a picture frame with glass to house larger articles, such as the one we have containing a pitcher collection.

There are various sizes of glass domes made to display single artifacts. I have a German Christmas ornament in mine. These tend to be very expensive, so I discovered that glass candy jars minus their lids, can be turned upside down with the same result. Try a footed goblet turned over and put another item on top.

These same jars make nice containers for marbles, buttons, shells and the like. If you prefer the items be handled and admired, place them in a nice shallow bowl, or basket.

148

I find paperweights a unique way to display small significant artifacts, such as medals, a single rose, a small photo, or a brooch. We recently glued our daughter's hospital bracelet around her birth photo. The convex glass enlarges the object, so you may have to compensate. It would be a perfect place for the baby's curl from the first haircut.

Plastic photo cubes provide an inexpensive way to highlight small things. Just remove the matting and paper to create a clear box. Or stack several on top of each other, at different angles, each holding a treasure.

Some miniatures may become a pendant on a chain, or charm bracelet, or an ornament on a miniature Christmas tree. A single earring could become a tie tack or scarf pin.

Craft stores now carry clear plastic balls which open to hold treasures. It protects the antique ornaments you insert from dust and breakage.

Group small, related items together on a tray, or store them in an antique box or basket. Consider the box part of the composition; line it, and have the lid open when entertaining.

If your collection is worthy of sizeable space, purchase a glass display case mounted on legs. This could become a coffee table, perfect for protection of fragile items.

If you would like to share information with other collectors, there is an Encyclopedia of Associations at the library.

BOOKS AND ART WORK

My father passed some of his early storybooks on to me. I put most of them in the guest room, but periodically I display one on a small wooden easel in the living room. At the holidays it is "The Night Before Christmas" profusely illustrated with all of **four pictures** in it.

Nearby, we display antique Christmas cards on the table under acetate. Having a green cloth under them for a background, they are visible but protected. (See photo in Chapter 5.) More post cards are still in the albums that my father purchased at an auction years ago. They are from 1910 when he would have been six years old. In looking through "Hobbies Magazine," I discovered that certain series of these post cards are very rare. This is another item I need to research.

If you have some art work, put one piece on an artist's easel instead of hanging it on the wall. Perhaps you have some of the artist's brushes and paints, or at least a photo of the ancestor you could put with it.

We are fortunate to have an early set of Art Appreciation books graded for children and I've put them in the guest room to look at with supervision. *I realize that a lot of these suggestions are not possible if children are not guided as to their value. How do they ever learn respect if they do the same with valuable items as they do with plastic and clay? I do not believe that children can only relate to a child's world. They can learn when reminded that sometimes they may find themselves in the world of adults, and respect that time and place. I would hope we could ask our children to handle precious things in the same way they would a tiny kitten or baby chick. I only let our girls use my china doll dishes to drink their get-well tea when they were sick. Maybe we could save things until they're older, and they would consider it a privilege. I guess I'll find out now that I'm a new grandmother.*

Another book that deserves special attention is the family **Bible**. Although it is usually on the coffee table, you may find some interesting items inside the pages. I went through my grandfather's Bible, page by page, one evening, and was overjoyed to find a tiny wrinkled paper cutting of birds and flowers, which I term a *scherenschnitte*. To keep from tearing it, I very lightly applied a damp paper towel and proceeded to slowly flatten it out. I placed it on a piece of paper and covered it with a piece of glass to weight it down until it dried. Only then did I notice that the artist had reversed the painting of the design...what was pale blue on one side, was pale green on the other. It is so tiny that we framed it on a background of black in an antique frame. (See next page.)

If you find items stored in your books, why not protect them by grouping them on pages from a magnetic photo album. Additional pages can be purchased from a variety store. I found a grocery list from 1900, another strip of border art, a pressed rose, and some cards. However, Betty found a lock of red hair in hers.

Sometimes people prefer to remove the history pages from a Bible and frame them, rather than remaining folded away inside a decaying, not-to-be-handled book, where no one can see them. However, I have seen some with so many pages of history that it would ruin the Bible to remove them. You may give some thought to having the Bible re-bound, if only to bring it out for the reading of the Christmas story. The contents of these books are considered so valuable that genealogical societies are asking owners to allow them to make copies for their records. At least copy the information for others in the family or take photos of each page.

It seems that people also used **recipe books** for diaries and repositories for valuable papers. Carefully go through them for secrets they may be hiding. The recipes themselves take you

back to many hours spent in the kitchen. Display in a rack (or labeled wooden crate) in the kitchen.

Purchase an acid-free cardboard file box to store any very old documents and paper items, such as patterns, diaries, journals, cookbooks that would deteriorate if handled very often. In libraries, they would be considered Rare Books. Attend a seminar on preservation of archival materials if you want some professional advice, or speak to a museum curator at the historical society.

If you are seeking back issues of magazines, see the classified phone book under "Magazines—Back Numbers."

PHOTOGRAPHS

These usually end up in a box or, at the most, in an album. But who will visit you and ask if you have any old photos? If you arrange them in groups on the wall or a table, they draw much attention.

As we began to research our genealogy, we always asked for any photos. Seeing some inexpensive frames of the same walnut color, and of varying shapes, we set about framing our first collection. We seemed to have a sampling from both sides of the families. We needed two more frames, oval if possible. These were found at a flea market and were antique metal. It adds value to the photo of course, if the frame is also authentic to the period. We have grouped these photos around an oval mirror in the front hall over a walnut washstand. As you stand looking into the mirror you become part of the arrangement.

Two tintypes are so small that we display them with larger pictures in a section of the breakfront, with some other small related artifacts. The frames of the larger photos are crafted with fabric and pressed flowers that were part of the life of the person in the pictures.

When portraits are too large to find a place for, don't put them away without making a camera copy for your album. This also gives you a negative to make copies of your portrait for all the family.

If a valued photograph given you is already in a frame, don't feel you must leave it as you find it. Take it to a professional framer to see if she could insert an acid-free mat between the picture and the wooden frame or give you other advice concerning its preservation. Only you can judge whether or not it's worth the investment. If the frame is inappropriate for that picture, it may be perfect for another. Hopefully, each generation improves on the last, without destroying anything significant.

Photos can be mounted on the stairwell wall as though hanging on a painted tree. Or a large open picture frame could define an area for you to hang smaller ones in. Perhaps a piece of colored poster board could do the same, drawing attention to the grouping. A wallpaper border could be pasted on to finish the edge.

The basement doesn't have to be the forgotten area of the house. Just be sure the heat and humidity are in the 60°/40% range. You could create a gallery in the hall, and make a sincere effort to find one photo of everyone for three generations. Maybe you will begin to see some facial similarities that have been inherited.

My friend, Audrey, has her three daughters' yearly portraits marking the wall like pictorial growth charts.

Small photos framed alike can be fastened to a vertical hanging drapery cord with the tassel at the end.

Nice old frames, but no portraits? Have a photograph enlarged or copied by an artist, or have a mirror cut to fit the frame.

NEEDLEWORK—CROCHET

If you have inherited Grandma's doilies, they have taken on new uses today. We both had mothers who knitted and crocheted. I sewed doilies onto solid color pillows to highlight their patterns.

With some others, I created suncatchers by sewing them to metal macrame rings with nylon invisible thread. I hung them by some of the same thread in the window.

Still others I used to cover some Mason jar lids and baskets of potpourri. I starched one with sugar water and clamped it into an embroidery hoop with some colored taffeta fabric behind it.

Some filet crochet shows the design to advantage when framed against a dark background of velveteen. To heighten the impact, group with others in similar frames, keeping the fabric color the same.

Doilies of any size can be used to edge the shelves in the china cupboard and go nicely with the dishes.

But the hint I am proudest of, is to fold a large round doily almost in half, and wear it around my shoulders as a lace collar.

154

Clipped in the front with a nice pin, it is elegant! Wide antique laces can be worn wrapped around the neck and secured with a brooch. Bits may be gathered into a tiny ruffled medallion and glued to earring backs to match. More of this in Chapter 9.

Some embroideries can be framed as a sampler is, keeping the glass from touching the fabric. In fact, Lee framed mine with acetate as it could be cut with ease and was lighter to hang. In any case, they should be hung where bright light will not fade them.

My friend, Gloria, recently had her father's christening dress framed with acid-free materials. The framer was careful to allow space between glass and fabric.

Yarn—fill a hanging plant pot with balls or yarn and needles or a large basket on the floor...or do the same with rag balls.

MIRRORS

Often one beautiful mirror will send us looking for others to keep it company. They add a lot of reflected interest to a room, and you begin to see your room from a variety of angles. Near my hat collection, I have a wall of mirrors in assorted sizes and shapes, but all with a brass frame.

A mirror doubles the pleasure of a vase of flowers, lighted candles, and glittering tree lights. Try setting a centerpiece on a mirror or mirror tiles and see what happens.

REMEMBER THESE DECORATING HINTS!

1. Use plants to soften the edges of corners and angles. Place your hand over the plants in a decorating magazine to see what happens to the room!

2. Include the wall behind your furniture as part of the arrangement.

3. I think of my house as organized groupings, each a vignette by itself, with something to say. When they start running into each other, it's too much already!

4. Balance the grouping by using a variety of sizes, shapes, heights, in odd numbers, thereby eliminating a boring symmetry. It may help to use easels, stands, stacks of books.

5. There isn't a house big enough for all these things at once; rotate them with the seasons, or just when you, or they, need a change.

6. Sit in different places in a room as though you were a guest. Does the angle present a pleasing composition, or crowded, or austere?

7. Check the intensity of the sunlight and the angle at different times of the day if there is danger of heat and light damage to artifacts. Dimming the lights and using pink light bulbs is kinder to people as well.

8. Do not store or display valuable items where the humidity is lower or higher than 40-50 percent, or temperatures other than 60-70 degrees...also best for US!

9. Hang any wall art from a top line 66 inches above the floor. This is considered *eye level.*

FAMILY HISTORY is not only a chart, but all of the items the family used during their life. Each artifact we hold bears all of the scratches, dents, lines that we refer to as *character lines* in a face. I'd like to think these objects are clues to the character of our ancestors, their resourcefulness and how they chose to spend their time. I don't care how much an article is worth to a dealer when it's still in its box. I'll take the one that was chosen to be used to enrich someone's life. Only when it developed a hole or a crack or needed a new handle, was it cast aside or repaired in some creative way.

Wouldn't you love to know and hear the stories? Just like the past, we can find new uses for broken things...to hold a potted plant, or adorn a wall or hold string like my old teapot (with string coming out the spout!)

So go to family sales, comb the markets, auctions, yard sales for those items that you wish you'd saved...those that conjure up a pleasant memory, teach a child, and complete your story.

PRESERVING YOUR HEIRLOOMS

Now that you've identified all those heirlooms, and decided where you can display them as part of your decor, you should have a way to preserve the value of each of them. This can be accomplished in the following ways:

RECORD: Choose a way to record the description and value of each item, its history, location and your wishes for its disposal to the next caretaker or *keeper.*

156

INVENTORY BOX OF CARDS, or NOTEBOOK OF
CATEGORIES, or VIDEO TAPE WITH DESCRIPTION.
Include in any of these cases:
>Name of design, style, serial numbers, pottery
marks.
>Original owner, date, its use, and designated heir.
>Monetary value, including bill of sale or appraisal
papers.
>Photos good for identification and research.
>When doing video, open closets and cupboards,
making all visible, giving information
orally.

```
Category: Dishes
Item: Ironstone Dinnerware
Original price: unknown
Description: Moss Rose design - by Wood
   +Son, England - Teapot, Cream, Sugar, plates
Original Owner-James + Mary Shewbridge
Stories about item: given to my
   grandmother as a wedding present

Next caretaker: Melinda Niles
```

Send a SASE for booklet "Taking Inventory" to:
>Insurance Information Institute
>110 William Street
>New York, NY 10038

REDECORATE: Display your interest in the family by
arranging heirlooms on walls of stairwell, family room, halls, dull
corners, window sills and lintels, and under tables. Provide focus
and accents with frames, shadow boxes, racks and tables made
for your collections.

RESTORE: Wood—Without destroying the original finish and aged look that gives value to an antique, minimize scratches and restore luster with paste wax. It will also add a nice protective surface and still let the design show through. If wood is painted or antiqued, clean with sudsy warm water, but dry upright, so that both sides are exposed to prevent warping. Twig furniture should be given a coat of clear preservative every two years.

To cover scratches, you may also try coloring crayons, nutmeats, shoe polish or iodine, depending on the type of wood you are working on.

Unfinished wood can be treated with mineral oil (not vegetable) when dried out. If heavily soiled, rub oil in with a fine grade of steel wool. Change cloth when soiled and buff thoroughly. See THE WEEKEND REFINISHER by Bruce Johnson. For price, write to him at 150 Cherokee Road, Asheville, NC 28801.

Leather—Bible bindings, etc: Keep away from high heat or humidity, and water. Brush dust off and apply saddle soap with a damp cloth. Let sit for two hours and wipe off excess. Next day, buff lightly.

Frames—see "Creative Ideas" magazine, July/August 1989. Check existing wooden frames, and coat with polyurethane if unfinished where it touches the art or needlework. Raw wood emits acids which will stain and spot the work.

If paper needs regluing, use cellulose glue, which is acid-free.

Quilts—To restore quilts, fluff them in the dryer, or on the clothesline in the shade on a dry day. Only wash when you have weighed the possibilities of fading, shrinking and drying something as big and fragile as a quilt. Wet small areas and press with a blotter to test for colorfastness, and open a small seam if you think the filler is cotton and may shrink. If it has been washed several times and is in good condition, place it in the bathtub submerged in warm water and Woolite. Allow to soak for two hours and press down on the quilt to provide some gentle action. Change to rinse water using the same gentle action. When you have pressed all the water you can out of the quilt, roll it up to remove it from the tub, and unroll it onto a plastic sheet on the floor. Get as much of the water as possible out with towels and move it, plastic and all, out to the grass to dry...in the shade. It can be placed over a line when it isn't as heavy and is partially dry. Never store it until completely dry, and then never in plastic; fibers need to breathe and moisture encourages stains and mildew. An undyed sheet is the best covering for protection.

The best place to store quilts is on a bed, as they are not folded, have access to air and some light, just not direct light. It is amazing how quickly things fade when they are never moved and are exposed to bright light. I think it's neat to layer them on the guest bed, and you can show them off as you remove them from the bed to the rack, when *turning down the sheets* for your guests.

REMOVE stains:

Marble—Wet a paper towel with bleach or peroxide and place on the stain. Cover with plastic to delay evaporation. If oil stain, try acetone; if rust, use a commercial remover.

Glass—Swish dishwasher crystals around the inside with warm water.

Fabric—Try club soda, or salt and cold water. A solution of four parts water to one part white vinegar may remove yellowing. Consult the book: TEXTILES, HOME CARE AND CONSERVATION by Audie Hamilton. Never dry clean antique fabric as the chemicals may be harmful.

Store fabrics on a cardboard tube that has been covered with unbleached muslin to eliminate fold lines.

Paper—Sprinkle with talcum to remove musty odor...leave there for a month. To preserve paper, spray on solution of one milk of magnesia tablet in one quart of club soda...Let dry.

Jewelry of metal—Mix a cleaner of half ammonia and half water, and a dash of dishwashing detergent. Using a soft toothbrush, clean, rinse, and polish.

Toothpaste rubbed on some surfaces with the fingers will suffice in some cases. Add water only to rinse and dry.

Silver and Pewter—Store in cloth, not plastic. Pewter scratches can be minimized with 4/0 steel wool and a wiping with baby oil. Will melt easily, cannot be repaired. Mothballs will retard tarnish, but don't allow them to touch the silver. Wrap in waxed paper.

Copper—clean with lemon juice and a little salt.

Brass—remove stains with three parts baking soda and one part water.

Iron—Season by rubbing with vegetable oil and placing in warm oven for three hours.

Additional reading: CARING FOR YOUR CHERISHED POSSESSIONS by Levenstein and Biddle.

REPAIR: If **wooden** pieces have started to dry rot, there is little that can be done except to replace the piece. Chairs usually have to be reglued, and then kept from sources of heat. Humidity of 50-60 will keep the wood from drying out.

To tighten the seats of **cane**-bottomed chairs, sponge on a solution of very warm salt water (1 T.salt to 1 qt. water). Apply to both sides, let dry. Repeat every few months...or sit gently.

Rinse **baskets** to clean and prevent cracking.

Fabric—Mend quilts before cleaning by replacing binding, reinforcing tears or appliqueing pieces directly over the weak fabric. To help the new fabric blend in, dye it with a tea solution or bleach it in the sun before applying to the patch. It may be better to add a whole new backing to the quilt on top of the old, so as not to disturb the original stitching.

Consider mounting other forms of needlework on a foam board by stitching threads from side to side across the back. This will not require glue or fasteners which may react to the fiber. Remove starch from any needlework before storing.

Hooked **rugs** whose backing has become worn may be repaired by adding another backing of unbleached muslin over the old one, stitching where it is the weakest. Use only on floor if you have a place with low light and very little, if any, traffic.

REPLACE: Put mylar pages in place of paper pages in albums and notebooks. Mylar pages have pockets to hold individual photos or cards and allow you to see both sides, if desired.

Replace lost artifacts with a facsimile purchased at a flea market or antique shop, such as the telegrapher's key already mentioned in previous chapter.

Replace the glass in your frames with special U-V acrylic plastic to filter out harmful rays, thus protecting the subject.

RELOCATE items to better preserve them:

Letters, documents—Unfold them, remove all metal clips, staples, pins, and rubber bands. Place in acid-free folders and boxes. They will not require as much handling when well organized, and will be easier to locate when needed. Lamination requires high heat which will age paper. Learn the process of encapsulation which allows paper to breathe.

Photos, slides, and tapes—these should be stored in proper acid-free boxes or mylar pockets in three-ring notebooks, never in paper or cardboard containers or envelopes. Pack firmly or stack to prevent curling. Optimum care is where the temperature is no higher than 60-70 degrees, and remains fairly constant. They should not be exposed to bright or strong light, heat source, or dampness.

If you do not have the space and conditions to properly store your heirlooms, you may consider making a gift of them to the local historical society or museum. I'm sure they will see that your family will be able to view them at any time. The Maryland Archives is presently offering an assortment of archival materials to get you started.

Books can stand neither heat and dryness nor cold, which will crack the glue and dry out the paper until it becomes brittle. The humidity likewise will cause the pages to stain with mildew and mold, and the cover to warp. So store upright and out of direct sunlight.

REPRODUCE the most valuable of your possessions:

Make copies of the originals...photos, documents, etc., onto acid-free paper this time.

Tape record old plastic records, and reel-to-reel tapes.

Color slides should be transferred to videotape before they fade and discolor.

Large portraits that must be stored can be camera-copied to be enjoyed in albums.

So record, redecorate, restore, remove, repair, replace, relocate, and reproduce and make copies. All that's left is to...

RETIRE now, so you have time to do all these things properly!

Various issues of Americana, Yankee, Country Home, Country Living, Decorating and Crafts, Victorian Home Decorating, Antique Review, Hobbies, & AntiqueWeek.

Creative Ideas had features on preservation 1989-1990 titled "Handle With Care."

Yankee had a series titled "Forgotten Arts" c1976 that is now printed in smaller booklets.

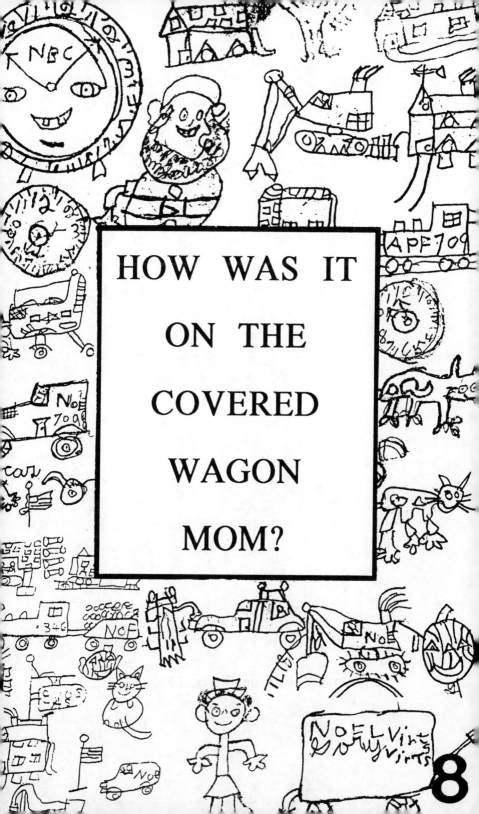

HOW WAS IT

ON THE

COVERED

WAGON

MOM?

8

Cover art by Noel Virts, 1932-1973

HOW WAS IT ON THE COVERED WAGON, MOM?

What a question to ask my mother, and at a time when all the relatives were gathered. After she recovered from the fact that I could think she was that old, she went around the house repeating it. I was enjoying the attention, but embarrassed at the reason.

Since I've started into genealogy and tuned in to history, I realized what a poor concept I had had of time periods...obviously. History had not been a continuum of events, but merely a study I had to pass to please the teacher's requirements. This I did...and got very good grades. I did what everyone does when they don't like a subject...they study the teacher and do whatever it takes to pass the test!

But I hated history! It always happened to THOSE people, never MY people...at least no teacher, even through college, had ever pointed out that MY people were somewhere being affected by the decisions made by THOSE people. I came close to getting hooked when we used a text in college titled, THE PEOPLE SHALL JUDGE, by The Staff of Social Sciences at the University of Chicago, 1947. It was a study of the letters and thoughts that led to the historic decisions, and I was drawn a little closer to the emotion of the moment.

However, I was studying to be a music teacher; what use would I ever have for history? Just become interested in genealogy, and you'll have a real need and purpose for the knowledge of history. You must know what was happening to find your ancestors. As wars were fought, boundaries changed, people migrated, disasters occurred, new states were named, records were kept in different ways and different places. It would be like looking for buried treasure without a map!

Armed with this sudden new attitude, I was so sorry that I had not realized all of this when I was a student. Since I have been a genealogist, I have been to over 70 libraries, mostly in the east where my research is located. I am there so long that they have to put me out when they close. I see the shifts change and new librarians come on duty.

I am amazed at the amount of information I have needed to learn about historical events in order to surmise where I may look for my ancestor. When I do prepare my narrative, I want to include the proper time period as a framework for my ancestor's

165

life. In this way my children will have the total picture, and will be able to identify with him.

Being a teacher myself, I wondered if there was anything I could do to influence education **today** to include genealogy in the curriculum. Thoughts don't produce, you have to communicate. It may be an idea whose time has come; at the least you will have planted a seed!

Teachers are all idea people, or they wouldn't go into the profession. They must adapt the curriculum to many different children, relate to many parents, and be able to fulfill the requirements of the administration. If you are friends with any teachers, ask their opinion on the place of genealogy in their particular school or classroom. You may find that they have already touched on its values. My fondest hope was that they would at least use it as a springboard into personalizing the unit they were about to begin.

WAYS TO SUGGEST GENEALOGY INTO THE CLASSROOM:

Volunteer to make a presentation if the teacher seems interested. Take in some family artifacts and ask if they can guess what they were used for. Ask them if they know where they got their own name, brown hair, dimples, left-handedness, quiet manner, walk, accent, abilities. That alone will bring out the composite they are.

Ask if they like detective work...looking for missing persons. Show them what you've found and charted. They will be amazed at the dates and the many surnames. This approach is more subjective for elementary school.

Probably the teacher will follow-up with giving the students an opportunity to record on a chart, **OR** make a collection of photographs, **OR** do a collage on the family qualities they are proud of. Filling out a chart is threatening to some parents who feel it will bring out experiences and information they are not ready to share with children. We, in genealogy, are careful to respect the privacy of the individual, as we want to bind the family, not cause friction. Perhaps we could look at the broader concepts and let the parents be part of the decision.

Today schools are tapping into the community for adults with special interests and skills to share them with the students. Let the school know you are willing to do this. If you would rather **provide an exhibit** than speak, specify. They will call you.

The person to write or call if you would like to affect more teachers is the **social studies supervisor** of your local system. When I did this I included an article from the "Heritage Quest" magazine to support my request, and asked to be contacted any time they would like information. He, in turn, let me know that he had sent a flier to all his teachers suggesting they contact me personally. (It helps if you represent your local society, more than just yourself. At the time, I was president of our county genealogical society.)

I also **organized a file** of suggested lesson plans and activities for local teachers. I included references that could be found in schools and libraries. This was presented to the professional library in our county staff development center, should anyone request assistance on the topic. My name and phone number is always attached as a contact person.

One of our members, Susan, has been **conducting sessions** with about 15 schools a year. Most are one-time classes, but several have been follow-ups. The skills they learn in researching, organizing and setting goals is valuable in itself. The chart is never wasted effort as it can be picked up again 20 years from now and continued. How much of our school work can we say that about?

Two middle school teachers have piloted a *hands-on* research unit for 7th and 8th grades in our county. To humanize the study of history, Jeannette Lampron Botterill and Paul Higdon, assisted by Kathy Kirkwood, have made up packets that contain laminated samples of documents. These documents, called "Tools of History," give evidence of the lifestyle of people during various time periods. Among the 30 items are the death certificate of a child, a graduation class photo, a wedding picture, county fair ribbons, a page from the census, a will, bones and fragments of pottery, audio tape, and an old map.

The students work in groups to sort the materials into categories. By scientific deduction, they try to reconstruct the

167

lives of persons in a family and decide what other *tools* may be available. Though this approach is more objective than researching your own family, it still involves "real people."

Instead of one PERSON, students could trace the migration of one ETHNIC GROUP relating to their own family.

OR choose a type of work which contributed to the origin of towns, and trace changes in the work which reflect in the community.

OR search for any clues in the community which lead to the past...cemeteries, architecture, schools, and people. Research the origin of the names of streets, hills, and areas of the community. In all of the planning for the new city of Columbia, Maryland, I've always been glad that they named the villages for the original land grants, thus blending the old with the new. This reminds us all that we may build new houses, but the land was claimed first by others who will be remembered for their contributions.

I also had some requests by G/T (Gifted/Talented) teachers to **be a mentor** to students who had chosen genealogy as their personal project. Now we're getting down to *one to one;* a real chance to follow a student's enthusiasm, and be responsible for passing on your own. It then is intergenerational and you're creating mutual respect. For a retired teacher, it's a chance to be active again, and use those skills you identify with.

You're working away with the individual, and then comes the time for these students to be part of the **FAIR at the end of the year.** Now the whole school will see the results, and the pride of the students who did such fine work...teachers, parents and other students. I was so proud to be invited, and to receive a certificate of thanks!

In some states there are **displays and prizes** awarded for excellent exhibits. More and more genealogical and historical research is being presented. Students choose topics that rival some college research papers I've read.

These awards could be publicized in the paper and on local stations, thereby involving the **whole community.**

Well, the day I had hoped for finally arrived...a request from Jeannette and Paul to work with other teachers who were writing a **new social studies curriculum** and planning to include genealogy. I prepared an outline with 14 educational objectives, hoping to influence these history teachers on the overall importance of the topic. I took books, I took charts, I took personal projects I had created with children...all to first motivate the teachers who would then motivate the student.

Was I surprised to find that they had **also** brought books, charts, and questions about attending my genealogy workshops and joining the society! We all shared resources that are new in the field, and we will keep in touch as partners. What more could you ask?

Following are the educational goals and objectives that justify the inclusion of genealogy into the curriculum:

GENEALOGY: A PERSONAL VIEW OF HISTORY

Goal—To better understand the periods of history when viewed through the lives and decisions of our ancestors.

Objectives and **Activities** to implement them:

1. History can be learned in many ways, and genealogy allows each student to see it through the eyes of his ancestors, as well as the author of the text. He identifies personally, in that it didn't happen to **those** people, it happened to **his** people.

2. Students learn to identify certain time periods in a personal way, by getting to know what was happening socially, economically, geographically, politically to his ancestors. (Time lines, role playing, printing a newspaper of the period.)

3. Genealogy creates an environment that values individual personality differences and contributions. Each ancestor is a contributor in a chain leading to you, and no story is like the other. Genetically we are unique and full of capability. (Encourages self-esteem and self-expression. Students can feel they have great potential.)

4. Students learn valuable skills as they use the processes involved in research: documentation, organization, recording,

interviewing, deductive reasoning, use of maps, courthouse records, gazetteers, and other references and indexes. (Completing a documented study of an ancestor or a portion of their heritage, and presenting it.)

5. Learning is enhanced by the element of *discovery,* and the amount a student learns is directly proportionate to his motivation, persistence and amount of time spent. In this way the student participates in his own learning and is self-directed.

(Each step a genealogist takes is like detective work: Where was he last seen? Who were his friends? What was his work? Which was his church? Where did he live and pay taxes? Whom did he marry? Was he in the military? Each clue leads us closer to our goal and we must know the history of the area and times to be successful.)

6. Basic concepts in the reasons for migration, and the places they chose to settle are reinforced by the tracing of ancestry. The census helps us pinpoint those places.

(People migrated because of bad economic, political, or social conditions just as they do today. They generally chose areas and conditions where they could pursue their former work, or where they could afford to travel, etc.)

7 In order to do some of our research, genealogists learn to better communicate with a purpose...to extract information with respect to the person or institution that has it. We write letters, interview with tape or video recorder, visit archives, courthouses, and libraries. The cooperation we receive is often relative to our approach, so we learn to meet people on their terms if we need their help.

(We are asked to be specific, brief, patient and know which type of document or book we need. Librarians will not help you with your research *per se.* If writing a relative, be considerate of his time, but assure him he is an important part of your story.)

8. Creative writing projects have ready-made subjects in genealogy. The topic is personal, original, anecdotal. It can take many forms: letters, diary, news article, typical day in the life of Grandpa Jones. Many adult genealogies have been written, and each is unique, because each has different things to tell. Some are

embellished with art work, some have charts done in calligraphy— all showing a pride in their roots.

(Accounts in other's histories of hardships of immigration, clearing the land, etc., give background to students whose stories lack details.)

9. The product of our research can take many forms, thus allowing a less academic, non-verbal student to prepare a project. Preparing a bulletin board, photo album, computer chart, group project on the history of the town, oral histories, photocopies of various types of documents are examples they may pursue.

10. Genealogical research is often original and much appreciated by the family, which puts the student in the position of family historian. He knows he is making a contribution because nothing about his family has ever been collected and organized before.

(It provides a positive, meaningful link to a student's parents, and involves them in his learning.)

11. Genealogy traces us all back to many of the ethnic groups who were once minorities, thereby helping the minority students to feel more valued. Everyone is in a minority from time to time...even left-handed people. It's a time to teach respect for our differences and be proud of them.

(Perhaps the teacher could diagram the ethnic makeup of the class as though they were migrating together. What would their choices be when they arrived? Discuss.)

12. Genealogy constantly challenges the student. To find a new ancestor gives two parents to start looking for. Each person decides how far he wants to go with his research. He may pick it up again years from now, and it will still be valid, if proven originally.

(This encourages the setting of goals and the incentive to achieve them, if time permits.)

13. Knowledge is not acquired for its own sake, doled out from the teacher, but it takes on a problem-solving focus with the motivation from the student.

14. We **must** know our history, or we cannot find these

ancestors. The country evolved according to the needs of the people, at different rates, in different areas, for different reasons. Names of people and towns were changed or disappeared. Wars took their toll, as well as disease and natural disasters. Some ancestors were famous and well-documented; but most dug the roads, cleared the forests, built the railroads and lived simple lives. They aren't mentioned in the books, so we have to write them up. But we have to find them first...like digging for treasure.

FURTHER STUDY PROJECTS:
Time capsule
Video/Radio—"You Are There"
History of Surnames
History of your artifacts—display
Styles of Architecture—models, drawings
Oral history—One topic, many people/One person, many topics
Senior citizens memories—local nursing/retirement home
Genetics- nature vs. nurture—discussion
Photography collection, interpretation
History of costume and dress
Clues in the town cemetery—Glenwood project
Vocational history of a family or town through the years
Video/story "Reunion Of The Barger Bunch"
The Town Between The Tracks—written by a class w/interviews
Grandma's Attic—volunteering at the Historical Society
Henry Hall Grows Up In Clarksville—black schools
An exhibit in the Social Studies Fair—prizes
Recreate a one-room school—invite retired teachers to share
Visit a Mormon Family History Center, receive help & name of
       pen pal
Contact the Genealogical Society and get help from a member

LEARNING BEGINS AT HOME...
where the family began.

Remember the old Chinese adage "We hear, we forget; We see, we remember; We do, we understand."
We learn what we live, so we try to make past memories a part of the present, and build on it. Others have argued that *the past is over and done; no one can change it, so let's move on.* We do move on to improve and learn from the past, holding on to

meaningful traditions.

Create opportunities for your children to become involved with your memories of the past. Take them with you as you review your ancestry, and these times will become the memories of tomorrow...the things you did together. It then becomes **THEIR** ancestry as well! I'd like to suggest many activities that will allow you and your child, or grandchild, choices. I will put them into age groupings as a beginning activity; but many of them may be continued into adulthood.

VERY YOUNG—PRESCHOOL

* BOOKS—Baby books usually have a double page for the family tree, so right away you realize you have added another little limb to the tree. Anything you can't fill in reminds you to get working on it. Use full names if at all possible, or initials if known.

Keep a journal about the baby, or the whole family if you have other children. Have it handy for quick entries, and date it at the time you enter something. Just use a blank book, as diaries are confining and every day is not unique! Include all kinds of funny, poignant, and even distressing things as they occur. You will be surprised how many times you will forget which day something happened, and be glad you can look it up.

A child can paste pictures from magazines to fill a large calendar and mark special days...the day they got new shoes, a bicycle, another tooth, a letter, and a candle for a birthday. It's a way to chronicle each day and talk about what was good. These can be purchased at book and stationery stores.

Choose photos of family members to put into a small album, one the child can carry around and keep with her toys. After looking at it together, a one-year old may be able to find the right photo when you ask, "Where is Ashley?"

As they grow older you may want to prepare a larger album so you can add names under the photo. Include pets and photos to go with *house, dog, car, ball, swing,* etc. It then becomes a reading book.

It would be especially appropriate if photos can be taken

when relatives and friends present a gift. You would always remember to associate the right person with the gift when talking about it in the future.

For several years, we photographed each of our daughters sitting with all the gifts they received at Christmas, so we would remember the year. It helps recall the toy before it became lost or broken.

* Rock and sing some of the lullabies and folk songs from your childhood. Think of those with motions or funny words. Or you may leave the rhyming word out and let the child supply it...such as in "Hush Little Baby, don't say a **word**."

This is the way folk songs are passed along, as *hand-me-downs* from the past, changing as they go. Teach them to the children and tell them when you first heard them.

We used to sit in the swing on the porch after we had our baths and clean clothes on. Mom used to sing songs and we played that we were riding on the train. The train would stop when she called the station, and one would get off and another get on.

* Play and share some games from your past, such as marbles, checkers, hopscotch, Hangman, Uncle Wiggily, or jump rope to the rhymes...(talk about aerobic exercise!) The book KIDS' AMERICA can give you more ideas.

We once had a family get together in the summer when we set up all the old games around stations in the yard. We made up score cards that explained how to win a prize. Two 70-year old cousins tied for first place! (See Chapter 3 for details).

* Show and tell about the artifacts you still have from the past. Tell how you got it, to whom it first belonged, and how and when it was used. There are bound to be a lot of questions. If you treat these items as though they are the only ones in the whole wide world, the children will know why they cannot play with them often.

You may have an old mechanical bank which they can operate to save some coins. I have an ice shaver which I made snowballs with, as did my Grandma. While we had the block of ice, I was able to relate stories of the ice truck and the little pieces we grabbed as the ice pick did its job.

* Some modern toys are copies of antique ones...such as a stereoptican and Viewmaster. It is interesting to compare how things have changed.

* Bake something with the children, using the old toys if you have them. Sift the flour, stir the soup, break the bread crumbs, shape the ball cookies, and knead the bread dough. Sometime you can bake potatoes wrapped in foil in the fireplace embers, toast hot dogs or cook a kettle of stew for a winter picnic. Relate it to cowboys on the open range.

* When you tell stories, let them be about you when you were a child. If you want them to be more mysterious, give yourself a fictitious name like Daney (which was really what the neighbors called me when I was little). "Once upon a time there was a little girl named _____." Tell about the times you were afraid, or embarrassed, or got into trouble, or had an exciting trip. Mine would be about my first ride on a train, when I had to spend the night before at Grandma's and sleep in her feather bed. It was so soft, it sort of smothered me, and I could hardly get out of it in the morning.
   You might consider writing these down in a book for grandchildren far away...or better still, tape them. There is something warm and personal in hearing your voice instead of imagining it coming from print. Small children can turn the recorder on when their mother is too busy to read. Recently there was a contest sponsored by a national magazine inviting children to pass these stories on. Prizes were awarded for the most unique. In **our** schools, stories are used to celebrate Grandparent's Day.
   Doris wrote about her school days in 1914—describing in detail a typical day, the clothes she wore, the rules, subjects, teachers, games, seasonal activities and unusual happenings.

   There are also story-telling festivals held in some areas of the country to celebrate the art and folklore of the past. People all over are beginning to celebrate the past in many ways, and genealogists are enjoying every minute of it. We have a responsibility to our ancestors or the past will be lost. I watch and sympathize with the Indians who have so little left of the proud people they used to be.

* You may want to write a letter to your grandchild at any time, to be opened when he is 16 or 21, with some of your hopes for him in his lifetime, should you not be here to tell him. He will realize how very much you meant to him.

* When you put up a growth chart for your little one, choose one of wood or cloth so it can be taken with you when you move. Our pencil marks are on the door frame in the house where I grew up, probably painted over three or four times by now. If you do the measuring at birthday time, you will be able to write the year as well. A really neat idea would be to add a photo in a small needlepoint frame. The design could take on the appearance of a tree or beanstalk, easy to do freehand.

* When my father first fell in love with a tape recorder, we couldn't have a private conversation in the house. Little did I realize that I would be grateful for those *baby rhymes and expressions* that he picked up. One special one was when I was saying "This little piggy said,"...instead of "Wee, wee, all the way home," our daughter, Teri, said, "Ouch!" Try to get some of the recitations, spontaneous songs, and imitations on tape as the little ones think them up. Let them *read* you a book, or should you say, *the pictures.* Be sure to label it later by saying on the tape who it is, and when and where. You will not always remember or be able to distinguish the voices.

* To decorate their son's room, Steve and Debbie made enlargements of illustrations from their favorite children's story books, such as Curious George, Pippi Longstocking, Alice in Wonderland, Bartholomew Cubbins, and Winnie the Pooh. Matted and framed they make a colorful and classic addition to enrich Eric's life.

* Grow something...if it's only grass seed to sit the antique bunny figurine in. (By the way, did you know that there is a tiny bunny sitting in each bloom of old-fashioned common larkspur? Not the double species, but the mixed pink, blue and lavender that reseeds itself.) Put some paper-white narcissus in that special

176

green bowl and watch them come to flower in the spring.

Plant a tree for each child on his first birthday in a spot that you can watch from year to year. It will be a symbol of your thoughts of him as he grows with the tree. Sounds like photo time again! There are so many nice stories of sheltering trees...perhaps the gift of a book would be nice as well.

Continue the customs of your parents who did special holiday things. It's not **what** you do, but **why** you're doing it. Talk about them each time, keep them alive. If you didn't come from a family filled with tradition, then start some of your own. But think hard...what did you look forward to at each holiday that seemed to be necessary for your happiness?

* Children can turn out some pretty meaningful art work if given the materials and the inspiration. After an exciting day at the zoo or a walk down the block, ask them to draw what they saw, or their favorite part of the day. While they tell you about it, print the story to go with it, or just give it a title.

Ask them to paint a seasonal picture, and guide them in their choice of colors by talking about it first. None of these things is a new idea; it's just a reminder that these experiences create shared memories and time you spent together. When they think of you, they will think of special times, not just a photo in the album.

I want my children to hear me singing with them and playing the piano, feel the prick of the pins when I was sewing and fitting clothes on them, see me sitting in the audience when they were in a program, wading in the creek, feeding the ducks, watching a sunset and trying to catch it on film.

* Treasure boxes can be started whenever a child finds something that is truly his...to admire, to own, to later replace if he wants. If this shows there is beauty in little things, then it is worth every bit of it. The myriad of shells, bugs, butterflies, odd-shaped sticks, shiny sparkly rocks, part of a broken toy dug from the ground, all spark conversation, and an opportunity to share thoughts between you. There is beauty in little people too, and we need to seek it out.

One of my best gifts was a wood shaving with two knot-holes that seven-year-old Mindy had found on the ground. She presented it to me for my collection of owls.

* Try drawing a silhouette of the child on white paper. Tape the paper to the wall and seat the child, turned profile, in front of it. Direct a bright light on the child so it casts a distinct shadow on the paper. Trace the profile with chalk, pencil or pen. Cut out and mount on black board, and frame. Trim the frame with buttons, braid or lace. This makes a good keepsake, and may be managed by an older child. Tell them this was the way they made a portrait before there were cameras. Look for some the next time you go to a museum.

* Children who can manage scissors may enjoy creating a collage of their favorite things: colors, foods, TV and music stars, play activities, trip souvenirs, toys, names or photos of friends, movie ads, clothing. Using old catalogs and magazines, ribbons, feathers, or whatever, let them paste everything helter-skelter over a large piece of poster board...call it "WHEN I WAS FIVE." It's a way to say who they were at five years old or whatever age.

* Two of our grandchildren have given us huge cookies with their handprint in the middle...not hardly anything you can save. But a salt and flour play dough could be treated the same way, glued to a plaque and sealed with acrylic spray. Be sure to label the name and age of child.

* Keep some unbreakable artifacts in a treasure box so that children may choose some for you to talk about—an old photo, an award, a report card, an old book, an army emblem, etc.

* This is the best time to take walks and discover...because everything is new to them, and it's exciting to see them marvel in what we take for granted. After you've discovered all you can see, take time to cover your eyes and just listen. You don't have your sight to help you, so you listen more closely.

Take time in summer to put your ear to the ground and listen...sounds like a busy world down there. Who is walking in the grass? Time to talk about Indians and how they could tell about weather, danger, time, where to find animals. I love the poem "Indian Children" by Annette Wynne and have

178

memorized it so I could quote it at the most appropriate times. Look for it in the collection titled STORY AND VERSE FOR CHILDREN by Miriam Blanton Huber.

The town leader, Mr. Gross, believed that everyone should have at his command a wealth of literature, quotations and poetry, to be able to make a point in an eloquent fashion. He was a wonderful friend, and in his honor I used one of his quotes as a drill for our re-created one-room school. He visited that day with other retired teachers, and his eyes twinkled in appreciation when he heard the lines. "Life's Mirror" by Madeline Bridges teaches us to share our best with others.

ELEMENTARY AGE ACTIVITIES

Now a child is being tested as to how he can keep up with the rest of his peers, and still find someone who cares about him as an individual. Genealogy reminds him that he is an important part of a long line of proud ancestry. That will never change, no matter what doesn't work out at school. So we can be a partner with the school, and provide him with experiences and material that will enrich his studies.

* Help him make a list of all the qualities that he is proud of...that he feels makes him unique. Include physical, emotional, and mental aptitude. Is there someone in his family line who may have passed this on? Put their name beside the quality. Point them out on the family tree.

Sometimes these qualities may include shyness, dimples, longer toes, crooked fingers, poor at reading, good at singing, chosen for soccer team, hates broccoli. If we can find role models for the good things and someone to blame the bad on, it makes us feel we're not alone. And best of all, it isn't life-threatening! We try to accentuate the positive.

* Try to recruit your child as a partner in learning about his ancestors. Compare it to jumping in a Time Machine, or taking a Quantum Leap. If he saw **Back To The Future** he may understand how we transfer our thinking to another day and age.

* Buy him his own copy of MY BACKYARD HISTORY BOOK by David Weitzman, for parents and children together; it involves looking at your family, home and community for clues to the past. I wish every family had one as it contains so many interesting ideas for all ages.

* If your child would like a workbook to fill in with his personal family facts, then MY FAMILY TREE WORKBOOK by Rosemary Chorzempa, Dover Publishing, is great. It provides a framework for a young person to make an effort to complete. Don't ever push him to finish, because you never really finish ALL you can do. You can be proud of whatever he records, knowing that it means more for the child to do it himself. He may pick it up again...years from now. The history will still be out there waiting for him to find it.

* A book containing lots of projects from the past to make and re-create is KIDS' AMERICA by Steven Caney. It begins with a chapter on Genealogy, including meaning of your name, how to make a coat-of-arms, even words to the song "I'm My Own Grandpa." Just about everything kids used and enjoyed in the past is explained and directions given for reproducing. This book may be in your school library.

* Fifth grade students of my sister-in-law, Nancy, completed a history of their town by interviewing townspeople and writing and illustrating articles. I contributed some historical materials they could quote for background. It was published by the Parent-Teacher Organization with the title "Brunswick, Maryland—The Town Between The Tracks."

* Other projects initiated by the schools include linking up students with nursing and retirement home residents. This was very successful in Frederick, Maryland where I read that the residents signed up if they were willing to be interviewed. Lasting friendships were formed and visits and cards were exchanged long after the initial meeting. This is a great way for students to learn about the past, and how to communicate with older people.

* Another way you may encourage communication is to ask a young person to label your old photos. In the process they will begin to notice similarities, and ask questions about where the

180

photo was taken, and what was going on. Just be sure to give them a hard, smooth surface to work on, and to use a soft pencil, not a felt pen, as it may bleed through. If the pictures are already in an album, write the names in a small notebook by page numbers so it becomes a key...fasten it to the inside back cover so it stays with the album.

* There are many interesting artifacts in the homes of the grandparents, but they may be hidden away in a trunk or box. So I have prepared a "Treasure Hunt" to provide a reason for the articles to be shared...if only for a moment. Use it for your young people and offer some sort of reward if they find everything.

```
      TREASURE HUNT FOR FAMILY HISTORY.........1988
                      BY_____
_____OLD PHOTO OF GRANDMA
_____OLD PHOTO OF GRANDPA
_____OLD BIBLE
_____QUILT
_____OLD JEWELRY
_____OLD WATCH
_____ANTIQUE SHOP TOOL
_____ANTIQUE KITCHEN TOOL
_____OLD CHAIR
_____HANDMADE FURNITURE
_____OLDEST BED
_____OLD STORY BOOK OR SCHOOL BOOK
_____OLD BUTTONS, FROM A UNIFORM OR EVEN SHOES
_____BABY CUP OR SPOON
_____OLD KEY
_____ANTIQUE CLOCK
_____LANTERN OR OIL LAMP
_____OLD TICKETS OR PROGRAMS
_____OLD SCHOOL REPORT CARDS OR PAPERS
_____OLD LETTER
_____RECIPE BOOK AT LEAST 30 YEARS OLD
_____A WEDDING PICTURE
_____A SCHOOL CLASS PICTURE
_____A MEDAL OR AWARD
_____A DEGREE OR DIPLOMA
_____A FAMILY TREE
_____OLD GAME OR TOY
_____OLD DOLL
_____OLD HAT
_____OLD GLASS DISH
_____OLD PITCHER
_____PHOTO OF MOTHER OR DAD AS A BABY
_____PHOTO OF YOU AS A BABY
_____PHOTO OF AN OLD CAR, NAME OF MAKE_____
_____A TREE OR BUSH AT LEAST 20 YEARS OLD
_____AN OLD POSTCARD
_____A LOCK OF HAIR
_____ANYTHING ELSE THAT IS VERY, VERY OLD
```

* You can give children a keener sense of the geography of the world if you keep a world globe visible, perhaps in the center of the table. That way you can refer to it in ordinary conversation, especially when speaking of your ancestry. If you live with these things you absorb them as you would fine art and good music. You can't sit down with children and announce, "Tonight we're going to listen to some good music, or talk about Van Gogh." Boring! But if you live with it, they will absorb it as part of the atmosphere...a sort of "subliminal learning."

As a genealogist you can point out the country of origin, and the route your ancestors took to arrive in America. They didn't all come from the same country, so you have an excuse to talk about Grandmother's people as different from Grandpa's line.

* There are genealogy badges to work for in both Boy and Girl Scouts. Encourage your child to pursue this goal with your help. If you don't feel qualified, ask if the local genealogical society would act as mentors to the troop. Advanced scouts must do a community service project, and many in our area have chosen the beautification of neglected graveyards. They lay paths, build footbridges and reset tombstones, clearing away brush and brambles.

* Pretend the TV has broken down some weekend night. Role play that you are pioneers and have to make up your games with whatever you can find. Simulate immigration on a crowded boat. What would YOU bring with you? And play *What would you do if...* and set it back in the old days. Make sure the whole family participates as a unit trying to stay alive and well. It was dangerous to set out alone.

* Take children with you to help diagram the cemetery and mark the location of the family stones. If they help you transcribe, discreetly check their information before you leave each stone. Help them choose and make a rubbing as a memento. Buy or gather some flowers for them to place at each site. (See Chapter 13 for more details.)

Invite a child to go fishing with you and get better acquainted while you wait for a bite. My husband values the time he had hunting and fishing with his dad or granddad. The quiet misty mornings were good, and I suppose he felt accepted by the adults...even after he hooked his granddad in the lip with a wild cast.

* Suggest to your son or grandson that you could help him make something for his mother for a gift. Suggest a craft and pass on your skill. If he has an idea of what it should be, so much the better. The important thing is the time you will spend together.

Any craft can be enjoyed more when preparing a secret gift for someone. Not only is the skill passed on, but stories of how long it took you to become good at it. Young people have so many choices these days that they may choose not to complete any similar items, but they will have an appreciation of what it takes when others do.

Genealogy doesn't demand that we live like our ancestors, but that we gain an appreciation for what they went through in their days and times to live and be happy. If they could do it in those times, how much easier it should be for us in these!

* Have your child make his own greeting cards. They are much more appreciated, and make wonderful keepsakes. We leave each other notes which, if kept, are funny years later.

* Let her start a collection of autographs. Instead of just a lot of signatures, have each person finish the sentence, "I remember the day you..." so it will be the memory of a particular event as well. It's always interesting to know what people CHOOSE to remember. They see you from different angles and through different eyes. This would be interesting for graduating seniors, or even for adults when they retire.

* Have your child draw a picture of the family, with a description of each to accompany it. An older sibling could help print the story.

* Collages could now be more wordy, filled with adjectives, more personal souvenirs gathered from real life events. This project is more popular with those who don't want to fill diaries.

* Diaries or journals give opportunities to tell whole stories, including all those who were involved. Since it is to be filled with secret feelings, it is a good source later of emotional development

and working things out. Again, journals allow more space, more freedom. Make a gift of one with the title "THAT WAS THE YEAR THAT WAS...199_."

* Find excuses to write letters to your child or grandchild. Choose a special birthday, or create an award for something special and write a letter to go with it. I still have some special letters and I treasure them. Include some puzzles, poems, cartoons, and surprises that make getting a letter from you a celebration. I read of one grandpa who deliberately misspelled words so his grandchild could correct him. You might head your letter with ANOTHER LETTER FROM MR. BOTCHIGALLUPI...(a name that was abused in our family).

* If you have girls you may be interested in buying or having a dollhouse built in the style of the house you grew up in. They could help you furnish it, and it would provide a setting for you to re-create stories of your childhood. Or perhaps you had to move or sell a cabin or summer house where you had happy memories. Having a model of it would give the whole family a hobby furnishing it with souvenirs and mementoes.

* A model train layout does the same for boys and fathers, who put all their energy and time into re-creating a railroad town they once knew, or wish they had known. My husband's father retired from working on the railroad to fixing up his own *town* and spent part of every day repairing and running his trains.

He could have given any person a complete story of his work, the names of the locomotives, cars, stories of accidents and a typical day's work, and names of people he worked with. We forget to interview those who are closest to us. Everyone is an authority on something. What would you really like to know about Grandpa? Then you have to ask him! He doesn't know you're interested.

* Whenever your child needs to write a story, encourage him to choose an ancestor or relative. Perhaps he can interview the relative about his life, or the way he completes his work, or whatever he feels knowledgeable about. An older person will respond to a child as someone to whom he is leaving a legacy, where an adult would be perceived as prying. Sometimes it's better to send a child.

184

Work with the school in a partnership, accepting the fact that we are all teaching, just from a different perspective. To bring family and community together, Jackie Reed has developed a "Name a person" chart to assist the student in gathering information on his history. With her permission, a sample is included on this page. Together we get a total picture of the child...but know it is constantly changing as we all grow in understanding and appreciation.

FAMILY AND COMMUNITY HISTORY

Name a person who:

Has a famous or notorious ancestor	Knows when his ancestors came to America	Has a grandparent who attended the same school (or a school in this community)
Has a relative who is over 90 years old	Learned a special skill from a grandparent	Knows how this town or city got its name
Can name the oldest building in the community	Has attended a family reunion	Has talked to someone who has lived more than 50 years in the community

HIGH SCHOOL—YOUNG ADULT

By now the treasure box has graduated to a trunk full of pressed flowers, photos, letters, or sports awards, scout badges, and baseball caps. The social life is recorded in scrapbooks and diaries, or sandwiched in between rehearsals for the play or part-time jobs. Who has time for genealogy?

* Many class assignments are completed when students use ancestral facts as background. It is personal, unique, and given documentary proof. So as previously suggested, let your knowledge of genealogy provide you with subjects.

* In science class, mention the deductive reasoning that goes into the research of an ancestor. There is no place for assumption; things must be proven step-by-step. Just as the theory of evolution had to evolve in stages, so does the evolution of your family line. Each generation is related to the last, but has its own identity, as do the members of that generation.

Genetics has a direct link with genealogy in trying to understand the predisposition of certain medical problems. More and more, people are consulting their family tree to assist them in making decisions, and setting their lifestyle.

* History classes require study of the events and decisions that shaped the lives of people during a particular period. The people mentioned in the textbooks are rarely our people, but the ones who were chosen to represent us at the moment. Your ancestors were somewhere at that same moment...so ask yourself...IT'S 1865...DO YOU KNOW WHERE YOUR ANCESTORS ARE? Where were they living? How did this affect them?

A good chart to invest in is a "historiograph." It has a line for every year from 1620 to 1900 for you to write in the ancestor who was born then. Crossing this line in seven different categories are other statistics of that particular year; current president, inventions, disasters, wars, etc. When you have trouble finding your ancestors, you have all these possibilities. The chart has space for adding any that relate to your particular area. Developed by Carlton Smith (no relation!), they are available by mail.

Write for information:
The Genealogist's Historiograph
c/o Carlton M. Smith
3219 Cobblestone Drive
Santa Rosa, CA 95404

SCHOLARSHIPS—A knowledge of your family genealogy could lead to a college scholarship. If you can research back to prove your ties with colonial war heroes, you may be eligible for a grant of money. There are only a few given, so you are in competition with other high school seniors and undergraduate students; but they are offered every year. For more information, write to Colonial Dames of America, 421 East 61st Street, New York, NY 10021.

* English and creative writing classes are times when you can look to your ancestry for character sketches, short stories, essays or almost any form of writing. For fiction, you just elaborate on the plot and give details that you wish were true. I get discouraged sometimes when I can't find out more about my great-grandfather, and I'm tempted to add a lot of fiction...but I know that's a *no-no* and I stick to the truth, be it ever so humble!

When I was 13, I decided to add my name to a pen pal column, and over the next two years I found myself corresponding with more than 40 teenagers. I enjoyed getting their pictures, and hearing about their activities and opinions. We wrote using different inks, in circles, slang, a poem now and then...but little did I realize that one of my letters would be read to the class. I had handed it in when the assignment was to write a good letter. Heaven knows, I had had enough practice! Genealogy links you to a large circle of new *cousins,* and your mailbox can be constantly filled if this is what you like.

You could be adding a nice dimension to both your writing and your genealogy if you interview your living relative, do an oral history, type a transcript, and take some photos. If that is above the call of duty, save it for sociology.

* Sociology—Could it be possible for you to do a study on the past in your particular school area? I hope that the teachers realize that the *process* of researching is more important to a student than

having the whole class study the same thing from a book. To personalize education is to make it come alive and be valuable long after the school years are over. **Education goes on all of our lives**, so the more we can relate it to the student's daily life, the larger purpose it will serve.

Coincidentally, I visited the public library in Charlestown, WV at just the right time. An unusual display on a turntable was filled with photographs and neatly lettered labels that spelled "Bakerton—A Company Town." It had antique photos of classmates in front of the school, men at the store and the railroad station, folks enjoying the Sunday School picnic, an area named Frog Hollow, and the annual fair of the Stock and Agricultural Society.

The student included maps, a time line and a genealogy chart. How I wished my family name was Baker of Bakerton! Then I noticed the student's name...Heather Moler. She **IS** a cousin whose parents I had gotten information from seven years before. When I wrote to congratulate her, she related that this was the fifth project for which she has won a Grand Prize at the county social studies fair and was entered again at the state level each year. She has chosen subjects on which there is little recorded, so she knows she is making a unique contribution. She has had to interview local people and do original research. This area includes information on her own family as they have lived here for many generations. To give you some ideas, I'll list her topics:

"The Washington Homes of Jefferson County"
"Friend's Orebank"—early industry
"Julia Davis: A Living Legacy"—90-year old author
"Storer College"—first black college in WV.

She credits her father with helping her build the display, but that was probably easier for him than the research.

* Special Projects are pursued in our schools under the Gifted/Talented teacher's guidance. Students with the time and motivation may choose topics which enrich their regular classes. One of these is GENEALOGY. Many of us in the genealogical society have been asked to be mentors and give students help whenever they need it.

If you would like to have a guidebook written just for young people, I recommend ROOTS FOR KIDS, by Susan Provost Beller, Betterway Publishers.

* Math is my worst subject...I think because there is no room to be creative...the answer better be right! I guess this is why I find early land plats hard to read...so many perches, rods, between two red maples and a large white stone. You have to learn the language of measurement as you do much of the old vocabulary, before you can start to do the configuration. But all of this is very important to the surveyor, the geographer, the archaeologist...each of whom is very much a part of genealogy.

* Geography—If you have traced any of your family line, you probably represent many parts of the U.S. and several countries of the world. Learning to understand *where they're coming from* will give you a personal interest in the area as it relates to their work, access to water, path of migration and quality of living. Maps are very important to our research as they help us visualize relationships of counties and countries to one another. Geography becomes less abstract, as it is the scene where our story takes place; so we feel a personal need to know.

* Economics reminds us we must budget our money for college, hoping to have some left for spending, and a date now and then. Save the budget records you tried to manage on, and they will make some interesting reading later on. You can only go as far as your income will let you, so it will be a good indication of your lifestyle at the time.

   I put myself through college, dividing each paycheck six different ways. I still have the metal bank I used, and I remember I only had $12 left each month to spend on the *extras.*

* In studying government and civics, genealogy provides a genuine need to use the courthouse and legal records housed therein. Not many citizens find themselves using these records from the past until they have a problem. A routine field trip does not educate as well as a personal search for clues about your ancestors. Perhaps students could choose a person from the indexes to follow through as an exercise, if their ancestry is from another county or state.

* Language—If the student has a choice, he may profit more from the language of his ancestry. Correspondence to the old country reminds us of the barriers this would remove. Answers often

have to be translated, names are hard to decipher, and grammatical differences are encountered. When study overseas is a possibility, students could stay with cousins who are still in their country of origin.

* What about all those odd jobs...did they prepare you in any way for your real career? Why not write your feelings about each job you had, what you learned about yourself, and your choices for work in the future. Include the dates, salary and hours. After making many mistakes on the job, I convinced myself that working with food was not my calling. One job as a waitress only lasted a day. Fifteen years later, I received a check from a co-worker who confessed she had stolen my tips, and wanted to be relieved of the guilt. If I cashed the check, she would know I had accepted her apology.

Another job was running a Humpty Dumpty Ice Cream truck with my boyfriend (now husband). It was at this time that I found I had an inclination for putting things on top of cars and trucks, temporarily out of my way. The trouble is...I would forget, and go driving off with these items flying in all directions. When it was whole boxes of popsicles, a lot of our profit was lost in a mass of twisted sticks and frozen *glop*, which of course had to be eaten right away. Funny thing...it was always my favorite...banana!

* And those dates...though details are forever secret, do a little personality analysis. Project into the future and try to predict where they'll be. It'll come in handy at the twentieth reunion when everyone's fortune is made, as they say. I tried to visualize myself married to these fellows when I was in high school. Now we see each other as just friends trying to enjoy life while we stay out of debt and the doctor's office!

* Describe a typical day and your feelings about each of your subjects in school and the teachers. Usually your feelings for both were about the same.

* Psychology—Though you're trying so hard to blend with your peers and be accepted socially, try to keep in the back of your mind that you are a unique individual who will graduate into a world apart from these same friends. Will the activities and

190

education allow you to function wherever you go? Do you feel you excel in **something**? Then develop that **something** until you're the best at it.

We are a unique combination of qualities which will sustain us, if we let them, but first we have to identify them...and find someone who will respect them at home and in our work. They call it **nature vs. nurture**.

* Journal—Find some way to record the way you were at a certain time, a certain age. It will show you how much you've changed, matured...all the stages you go through to improve your thinking. Girls tend to reveal their feelings more than boys, so they will do more evaluating. Neither has to share it with anyone but the journal.

At least keep a chronology of your life. This need only be a list of any important events in your life...a capsule version of the news, according to you. Include awards, milestones of any kind, activities, plays, trips, parties, new friends, accidents, moving dates, new car, apartment, community disasters, illness and changes in the family. Doesn't take long...and believe me...you will forget unless you do.

* Grandparents are special and although they can't hold you on their laps any more, they're hoping you'll drop in and share the events of your life. Ask them what they were doing at your age. Perhaps there's some way you can be an apprentice to them as they go about their day. You could talk and learn at the same time. Hunt them up in their garden, workshop, or kitchen and find out what they enjoy about life. Some have told me that they don't tell you things because "You never asked!"

The photos may still need labeling, the artifacts are waiting to tell their stories, and most of all, you can learn more about your parents from them. You can discuss things about your parents that you do not understand, and they will take a calmer attitude because they are not directly involved.

This is the age when you begin to visit on your own and not as part of the whole family, sharing your time and being compared with brothers and sisters. The fact that YOU chose to come is a big compliment to your grandparents.

* Community projects may add clout to your resume someday. Volunteering at the hospital, at the library to read to children, at the historical society as a docent, to do oral histories, to record cemetery inscriptions, take photographs of historical significance, to clip and file old newspapers, to write short articles for the newspaper, or to organize teens to beautify a portion of the town or do a service project.

* Understanding problems of a minority becomes apparent when we take the part of the ancestor arriving into this new nation. The voyage itself was a big decision and considered worth the hardship. But only the Indians were not immigrants to this country, and each group had to assimilate with those already here.

Sign out a film, such as THE IMMIGRANT EXPERIENCE: THE LONG, LONG JOURNEY—a 30-minute film which tells the story of the American dream and the American reality, as it was lived by a Polish family who came to America in 1907. Distributed by Learning Corporation of America, it is suitable for upper elementary to adult—and follows the story of one Polish boy as he was pushed around. Then look at your own background, which probably represents several ethnic groups, and see if you aren't a little more tolerant.

This is the decade of ecology, called a "reverence for beginnings—streams to oceans—going back to salvage the good we threw out with the bad." We preserve or lose. (See the parallel with genealogy?)

In summary, genealogy allows you to develop skills in every area you've been interested in. Best of all, you are able to present your findings in many forms...a story, an album, a bulletin board, a computer chart, a group project, exhibit, and audio and video taped interviews. While doing your class work, you're making a contribution to the family...and that's a great combination!

If you want to drop your research now, take good care of it. It will be a good beginning when you pick it up in your retirement years...if you can wait that long!

Lewis, Sunie, YOU AND YOUR GRANDCHILDREN, Special ways to keep in touch. Price Stern Sloan, 1990

Caney, Steven, KIDS' AMERICA. New York: Workman Publishing, 1978

Chorapenza, Rosemary, MY FAMILY TREE WORKBOOK. New York: Dover Publications, 1982

Chorapenza, Rosemary, DESIGN YOUR OWN COAT OF ARMS. New York: Dover Publications, 1987

Weitzman, David, MY BACKYARD HISTORY BOOK. Boston: Little, Brown, and Co., 1975

Beller, Susan Provost, ROOTS FOR KIDS. White Hall, VA: Betterway Publications, Inc., 1989

Wigginton, Eliot, FOXFIRE BOOKS, VOLS. 1-9. New York: Anchor Books, 1972

Reader's Digest Association, Inc, BACK TO BASICS. New York: 1981

Wolfman, Ira, DO PEOPLE GROW ON FAMILY TREES? New York: Workman Publishing. 1991

Perl, Lila, THE GREAT ANCESTOR HUNT. New York: Clarion Books, 1989

CREATE

A
MEMORY

9

CREATE A MEMORY

When my mother passed away unexpectedly, I could hardly believe that the house wouldn't be filled with all her activity...and the sound of her humming as she worked on her various projects. I walked through the silent rooms, picking up her hairbrush with the strands of gray still there, throwing out plant cuttings that had never rooted, closing music on the organ she would never play again, and then I came to her sewing. The quilt she was always going to make, the dried flowers she was going to use, the antique photograph she was going to find a frame for.

Suddenly, there was something I could do for her...we had often said there will never be enough time to do all the things we want. So I worked feverishly for the next three months, completing many of her projects. I can't believe the amount of work I turned out because I was so motivated! I was so pleased I could do it, that when I finished each one it was as though I held it up for her to see...a sort of memorial gift in her honor.

Now I read in the *grief manuals* that it is good to keep the memory of a loved one alive by completing some unfinished business. To me, it was the natural thing to do.

Many of our memories of family are connected to articles they once owned. To only record the dates and stories from the past is to miss the clues that lie in the bits and pieces we find hidden away in trunks, boxes, and scrapbooks. These storehouses may be in the attic, basement, toolshed, sewing box, recipe books, Bibles, or even behind frames. I hasten to remind you to ask cousins to look in their grandparent's effects for similar items, and allow you to touch, photograph and record their existence, as you share a common heritage. Some of our most valued possessions were in the homes of daughters who now had a different surname. If you show a sincere desire to revere the memory of their family, you may receive the item for safekeeping.

As I have stated before, I have tried every conceivable way to encourage my family and friends to pursue genealogy. I have found that people think of it as long, involved charts, endless research, which only old *musty-dusty* people pursue. We genealogists are on a scale from those who have a box of old photos, to those who belong to the DAR.

Why even Confucius in 479 B.C. said, "We should keep the dead before our eyes, and honor them as though still living." So, I would like to give you some ways that you can bring these bits and pieces of memory out of the boxes and trunks, out where others may enjoy them. These are ideas for highlighting your artifacts by crafting, sewing, framing, and adapting and combining them in new ways. It makes them visible, preserves them, and reminds guests and family where your heart is. Hopefully, they will comment on them, which will then provide an opportunity for you to extol all the virtues of genealogy.

PHOTOS

These are the most available remnants of the past, and some of the most interesting. In addition to the hints in another chapter, I found a way to use several things together to create a bigger picture of my mother. I had a small oval portrait of her with soft sepia tones. In addition, I had a box of pressed flowers...pansies, roses and fern...that she intended to do something with. So I purchased a shadow box frame with an oval inset and went about gluing the flowers around the corners with silicone adhesive. I also included some money plant *coins* that she always grew and took to the fair. There was even a tiny blue beetle that she saved. It has a special place in the corner. This portrait is the cover of Chapter 2.

If you have some special fabric from the past you may want to fashion a padded frame to add meaning and interest to a photo. In my case, I had some rose brocade from the drapes my mother made for the living room. I foolishly sold the rest, but saved about one yard, which makes it even more valuable to me because of its scarcity. Allowing about two inches extra width, I cut the sections for the frame. I put a thin layer of batting on the frame and covered it with the fabric, gluing it down on the back. I allowed it to dry overnight to be sure it was secure. Then I stapled a fabric-covered cardboard backing the exact size of the frame to finish the edges and back.

Craft and fabric stores sell other patterns for fabric frames, padded, shirred, or embroidered. Choose a muted shade or a small print that won't overpower the photo. Perhaps you can add tiny ribbon roses, stiffened ribbon bows, or small buttons. A miniature bow tie or buckle could be added for a man's portrait, and the frame covered with tie silk. You will be creating an heirloom by giving it your special touch.

I created a calendar by choosing photos of our daughter when she was very young. Using a small commercial calendar, I was able to glue an appropriate photo in place of the printed picture. I related each to the season.

Photos can now be transferred to fabric to create unique sweatshirts, aprons, team teeshirts, reunion mementoes, and quilt squares. A medium solution is brushed onto a photo-copied picture, **never** the original. By following directions, this photo is then pressed onto the cloth item and your project is complete. Ask for the product at your craft store.

DOCUMENTS

Consider framing those old unusual documents, marriage certificates, awards, family charts. Children learn their values by seeing and living with these possessions. Adults are reminded that they may have similar documents hidden away in drawers. My friend, Audrey, had the family pages from her Bible photo-copied in color, and framed. My German family tree has a hand-drawn border and two doves sketched in the center over the lettering. It's lovely and personal because someone cared to do it. Having German background of Frey, Boger, and Wertz, I now know why I enjoy drawing and the decorative arts.

Frakturs, or painted German certificates, are starting to be documented, as are quilts and family Bibles. These rare personal items are privately owned and valued, but you may see an inventory that includes some of your ancestors. Just this week I found one of the Axline family in Loudoun County, Virginia...a birth certificate for a brother of my ancestor...and the artwork was beautiful. I want to try to copy it for his brother. Certainly his parents made one, but it probably was lost. To make your own fraktur, see Calligraphy in this chapter.

If you would like to have a keepsake of a modern wedding ceremony on an antique Victorian replica, including a photo, write Victorian Certificates, 2035 St. Andrews Circle, Carmel, ID 46032; (317)844-5648.

Though some preservationists do not support laminating, it seems a good way to me to protect the surface of the document. It is the application of heat that may dry out the paper. The two documents I laminated were of heavy document paper, and are in good condition. Newsprint obituaries have turned brown although completely sealed. If you decide to frame them under glass you should have acid free matting to slow down any browning of the paper. Better to frame a copy, as the ink of the original will fade in bright light.

Other ways of preserving documents include mylar pockets which fit into notebooks, or in acid-free folders in a box or cabinet. I have chosen the folders until I have time to prepare my notebooks.

If you have many obituaries, and newspaper clippings, photocopy them for permanence, keeping the originals in an acid-free box or file. It is a good idea to copy all important papers, so you do not handle the original as often.

We made a set of place mats by laminating colorful souvenir menus from a variety of restaurants.

There is also an interesting birthday or anniversary gift produced by Hallmark called "The Birthday Times." If you provide the card shop with the full name and birthdate, they have a computer print a page of the news of that day. It includes inventions, songs, headlines, other famous people who share that day, etc. They will do a similar page for anniversaries. Though they come with an envelope, Teri framed ours for a gift.

GRAVESTONE RUBBINGS

Hopefully, you have discovered a beautiful folk art stone of your ancestor's. You applied the paper, created the rubbing and now you're ready to display it. I mounted mine on a piece of foam board cut to fit a plain black documentary frame. For hints on how to make a rubbing, see Chapter 13.

Remember you can do a rubbing of someone else's ancestor to evoke interest and conversation. Just be sure to own up to the truth!

Wythe County, VA has a wealth of unusual folk art gravestones which are featured in the book FOLK ART IN STONE by Klaus Wust. It is out of print but may be found in your library. I have several rubbings that I plan to use as designs for embroidered, stenciled and appliqued pillows. The weeping willow and tree of life are my favorites. Each symbol has a meaning.

A monument maker uses rubbings as patterns to create new stones for a family plot. You may think of other patterns you would like rubbings of, such as stained glass, jewelry and silverware patterns, wooden trims, and the brass symbols used in heraldry and the church. It comes in handy if you need to match, repair or duplicate the pattern in another art form.

As a matter of fact, I should make a rubbing of the carving on the headboard of the bed my great-great-grandfather Hood built. We were given the bed for a youth bed for our first daughter. After removing five layers of paint, we discovered a large rose with stems of leaves flowing from it. I should stencil a pillow and curtains with the same design. The same idea could be used on note cards and gift paper as well. For a brochure on making rubbings, write to:

Oldstone Enterprises
Publication Department
77 Summer Street
Boston, MA 02110

ETHNIC TIES

Display your ethnic background by using touches of the native language around your house. Purchase or create a plaque to put over the door that says "Welcome to our home!" or "Willkommen!"

Other sayings or mottoes on the wall of the guest room such as "Have a good sleep" in French or Swedish. A wood burning tool or power router would handle the heavy jobs, but the same greeting could be painted, embroidered or cross-stitched. Craft stores carry plaques of all sizes just waiting for your design.

If you can't get to the Old Country, attend some of the ethnic festivals held in the states. Some of the larger cities celebrate their ethnic neighborhoods on special summer weekends. Maybe this would be the time to make a collection of hats, scarves, dolls or baskets, items from the area. They would make a nice wall grouping.

This would be the time to listen to the music, watch the dancing or learn the steps, observe the crafts and try the food. (Ask for recipes.)

When you serve a company meal, write the menu using ethnic names for the dishes and display it on the buffet. And of course when you sit down to eat, play Julia Child with a cheerful "Bon appetit!", "Esse gute!" or whatever.

When we were first learning vocabulary in French class we used to change our slang to French. Perhaps we could choose some phrases to use at appropriate times, such as time to clean your room, come home on time, pardon, good luck and congratulations. Maybe **this** would get some attention; somehow my English was always ignored!

While we're still at the table, what about having the globe as a centerpiece instead of gathering dust back in the study? Or you could make a set of place mats, laminating maps of the countries your ancestry is from. Of course you highlight the area or village they lived in. You can create these with clear Contact paper. Perhaps you'd like to use an opaque design for the back to make them reversible when you don't want to be intellectual. I figure if they expect you to read the backs of the cereal boxes, we can do the same with place mats. **There is no way people are going to get out of my house without knowing I'm a genealogist!**

When our Australian friends, the Harrises, were living here, they brought gifts of paintings and records done by Australian artists; travel posters, books, and slide talks to educate us...but what we needed most was a dictionary to understand their quaint little vocabulary. It was easy to see how proud they were of their country!

COATS-OF-ARMS

These can be purchased if you realize that there is no ONE coat-of-arms for each family name. Each new family with the same name incorporated something different in their version. They felt related, but with individual qualities, which I'm sure we do in our families. So when you display the commercial ones, explain that this is the one which Sir _____ had commissioned for **his** family.

Again, if you are artistic, you can buy the wooden shield plaque and re-create your version. The main parts surrounding the shield are: the crest, helmet, wreath, mantle, supporter, motto, and compartment. For a good book on this topic, look for DESIGNING YOUR OWN COAT-OF-ARMS, by Rosemary A. Chorzempa, published by Dover. It is a simple introduction to heraldry for all ages.

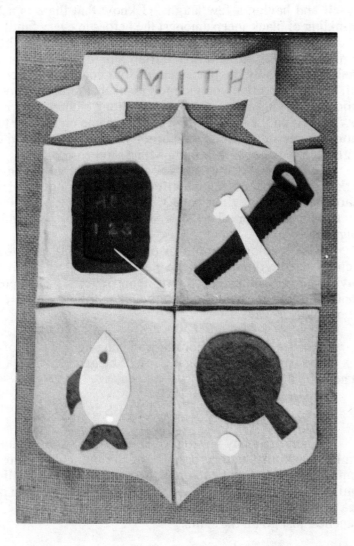

Because I want to appeal to a larger number of people, I like the idea of creating a more informal type of coat-of-arms. This gets the idea across, and once you have their interest, you explain the historical background. Many persons go into genealogy to become respected for their vast knowledge and productive use of their time. I also am doing the same, but am not concerned that my image will suffer if I appear to be enjoying myself and having a few laughs. I know that there is a liberal sprinkling of black sheep amongst the heroes in every family.

This informal version is not the coat with eight arms coming from it; but a larger burlap shield, divided into four smaller sections by the placement of four contrasting sections of felt. Into each section you glue felt items that represent your four major identifying interests. You cut a long ribbon, fold it into a bow, glue it on the top and print your surname on it. The top and bottom edges are trimmed with bright colors of fringe and tassels to give it a regal look. It is hung with a satin cord.

Example: My husband's SMITH coat-of-arms is made of dark green burlap, the smaller sections of turquoise and chartreuse. (See previous page.) These designs tell you that Lee is a teacher educator who fishes, does wood-working, and plays pingpong.

Use a coloring book for other motifs and 3-D touches, such as needle/thread, college patch, flower pot, knife/fork, playing cards, boat, palette, sports item. But creative people don't want to be told everything; just give them the idea, right? Then get out of their way!

I have seen a latch hooked wall hanging of a coat-of-arms. Ask at the craft store...but again, it will be generic. Check books on heraldry at the library.

FAMILY TREES

There are many versions of family trees. There is no better symbol of family history because of the branching, and a tree shape is the easiest shape to draw. So paint one on the wall of the family room, hang framed photos on it. The stairwell is a perfect area as you can add branches as you need them. To see the higher branches, just go up the stairs.

The holidays have always been a time for families to rejoice in shared memories. Every trim from mantle to door is an opportunity to display those treasures we have gathered over the years. However, the tree seems to command our attention, towering over our heads and glittering with old and new ornaments. Why not add some other personal items not usually thought of at Christmas? In fact these items are so important to me that I've trimmed a smaller tree with them so they could be noticed.

Besides some very old antique ornaments you'd see an Indian clothespin doll I made 50 years ago for a school assignment, a pair of felt doll shoes I made when I dressed dolls for the poor, a blue ribbon award for a plaster sculpture of Mindy's, an Indian corn necklace bought for Teri, a sand dollar found on a Georgia beach in November, clip clothespin angels—gifts to my youth choir, yarn Santas made for lapel pins, a bracelet, a baby spoon, a tiny God's Eye, tiny framed cross-stitch tributes from dear friends, reindeer finger puppets, charms from summer trips, cardboard napkin rings made by children, crocheted snowflakes from Mom, baby booties or socks, baby shower favors, silk flowers from the wedding, bookmarks, pin cushion tomatoes and strawberry sachets, cookie cutters, needle & thread, yarn & tiny needles, fishing flies or floats, gift ties, party blow-outs and other favors, or dollhouse miniatures...to remember a particular person or event.

The smaller tree I put these articles on is the same one I bought at the local department store for our first Christmas. My husband had been drafted shortly after we were married, and I was not about to spend our first holiday without a tree. So before I left to go to the army camp, I took my suitcase to the store and asked if they had a tree that would fit in it. This is the 38th year we've enjoyed it.

On another occasion, let the children use styrofoam eggs as heads and trim them with various yarns, beads, wire, etc. to represent members of the family, or themselves. These can then be hung on a limb to illustrate a branch of the family tree. Simply stick the limb into a vase of sand. You could photocopy ancestor photos and put them in miniature frames. These would make nice gifts to those who share our heritage.

Children may also fashion humorous trees of natural materials, sticks of different sizes and lengths nailed together side by side. Another *family* may be depicted with corn cobs, sticks, nuts, pine cones, gum tree balls glued on a six-inch diameter slice of wood. In both cases, glue on the tiny movable eyes and attach a flat stick on which you print *Family Tree*. It just illustrates the fact that no two relatives are alike!

Norman Rockwell painted his version to show all the personality types, from pirate to general to colonial dame. I have a print mounted for framing.

We used an original design of a family tree for the cover of a family calendar. This turned out to be a good activity for the Burgee reunion, as we had everyone present write their names on a blank calendar. They noted birthdays and anniversaries, and signed their address on another sheet. We promised to mail them out if they would leave postage. See Chapter 3 for details.

Treat your documented family tree chart like a work of art, framed and in a place of honor. The first 12-generation chart I had I used as a working tool...a giant crossword puzzle. Eight years later, I now have another complete chart on the wall in the basement to add to as I find new surnames. I make sure every house tour ends up there, so everyone can see what it can amount to, without hearing a long story.

Our daughter, Mindy, made us a counted cross-stitch tree with blocks to be embroidered as babies are born. It also has appropriate verses of scripture until the blocks are needed. (See Chapter cover.) She's already creating heirlooms. Anything that is created by heart and hands leaves its mark that you were here, and you cared enough to show it.

CALLIGRAPHY

There are lovely family charts that can be purchased, which, when filled in, make nice gifts for appreciative members of the family. Besides the standard tree form, they also come in circles and rainbow shapes. Perhaps you have taken a calligraphy course, and now you can show off your skill.

If you haven't thought of it, just let me hasten to say that you don't need the course if you are willing to practice with the

206

instructions that come with the pens. Do buy the proper nibs or pens and the rest will come with practice. There are always new alphabet styles to learn, and new ideas for working with different layouts and projects. But your main concern is that it is in a flowing style that is legible.

This skill in calligraphy can also turn out some very nice German fraktur replicas for birth and marriage announcements. You may even copy old designs from folk art books, and create the whole certificate freehand. Perhaps the art stores have some appropriate stencils you could do in soft watercolors on parchment. I have had good results using a sponge brush. You control the amount of color by your pressure on the sponge. It is always good to experiment on scrap paper first. When your design is finished and dry, lightly pencil in lines and your lettering. Spacing is very important, and the more relaxed you are, the more graceful the flow of the lettering. I'm very impatient myself, and hate to practice because it takes so much time with no result. But I try to tell myself that a few days practice is worth it if you are creating something for a lifetime.

The nice thing about folk art is that its charm comes from its simplicity. It is better to create an heirloom than to buy something that is mass-produced. Remember, handwork never looks perfect; in fact, the Indians deliberately put a mistake in the design of their baskets and rugs, because only God is perfect! Think of all the gifts you have received that showed more thought and time was spent than money.

As we learn a craft, we keep a sample of our early attempts, which will improve later on. You'll have a measure of your progress and an appreciation.

Calligraphy adds a nice touch to note paper and reunion invitations featuring photos of the ancestral home or marriage portrait of the honored couple. The photo can be copied and the writing added last. Add your initials somewhere to document. Though the original is black and white, multiple copies can be run on colored paper, and folded.

A favorite recipe can be written in script on a ceramic tile and trimmed with related fruit or vegetable motif on the corner. Be sure to sign the name of the cook and the date. This tile could hang on the wall or be used as a trivet.

FABRIC

The sight of certain fabrics brings back memories, and most women will comment on the color and design of outfits they are wearing in old photos. In families such as ours, someone was always sewing for a new baby, a costume for a play, a special gown for the prom or wedding, an Easter outfit, a blouse for a gift, curtains for the kitchen, bonnets to sell at the fair, a collar to turn for a few more wearings; tighter here, looser there when the figure had blossomed too little or too much. I have been hanging onto so many scraps of fabric that I feel my life is one big patchwork.

Several years ago, I decided to cut a four and a half-inch square from every fabric I'd ever used and sew them together into a quilt top. Since I am still sewing, I am still adding...so my quilt top is hanging over the stair railing as a conversation piece. Every now and then when I do a program, I take it with me to use as a tablecloth under my projects.

You may want to create a fabric still life. A basket or bowl shape can be glued to a felt-covered board. As each project is finished, cut a flower out and paste it into the basket. I think I'd be on my tenth still life by now, or some Monet creation that continued into the next room!

My kind of quilt has finally come into vogue...they call it a *charm quilt*. Each piece is of a different material, and every piece is often cut the same shape. It isn't that I don't like the organized look of two or three colors; but when am I ever going to use all these other colors?

If you own an heirloom quilt of any quality, please call a local quilting group and have it documented. This simply means letting them know its pattern, the year it was made and by whom. Quilters represent our heritage as a nation, and our respect for individual contributions. Did you know that quilts helped women achieve the right to vote? Check it out! Order the video, "Hearts and Hands," mentioned in Chapter 7. This 64-minute video shows the beauty and use of quilts between 1820 and 1917.

If you have antique baby clothes, consider finding a doll who can wear them...hopefully one in the family. Or make a simple rag doll the size of the dress and/or bonnet. There's always a teddy bear. Ours is wearing my brother Noel's eyeglasses and a band aid that our granddaughter, Heather, placed there.

A Girl Scout sash with all the badges makes a great wall hanging. Other pins and ribbons could be added. My mother even made my uniform so I have a few pieces of fabric and buttons.

Fabric makes nice padded album covers, and if some starch solution is added, you can cover paperback recipe books and journals...

> Fabric Stiffener Recipe: Mix 4 T. flour in 1 c. cold water. Slowly add 1 c. boiling water...bring to a boil; take off heat and stir in 1 1/2 T. sugar. When cool, store in refrigerator.

Coat fabric on back while damp, cut to fit phone book, recipe box, books, albums. Make gift cards, napkin rings and ribbon by letting dry first, then cut with shears into shapes.

Small pieces of fabric make up into pillows to be autographed. Dresden Plate quilt pattern is good for this; our friend, Eva, made one for an anniversary party gift. This and other circle designs look nice in a hoop on the wall.

A memory quilt could be made by handing out six-inch squares to be trimmed with embroidery, cross-stitch, tube-paints, stencils, designs with iron-on tape, crayons or markers. When returned, a quilter could assemble them with a plain colored lattice between. Both those who give and receive would share a memory! If you want to copy a design, place quilt on a copy machine.

Small items are more quickly accomplished, and still become heirlooms. Try making a doll quilt, perhaps in the Tumbling Block pattern which has straight seams, and use some miniature prints. My Bow-Tie doll quilt goes well in the cradle with my old doll.

Some antique dealers even sell the rag balls that were prepared for making rag rugs...just rolled up strips of old fabric. I think anyone can duplicate that look! They'd look colorful in a basket! The strips could be wound around clothesline or macrame cord for a basket...they cost a lot at the shops. But we're not buying; we're using **our own** heirlooms and saving pieces of **our** past.

Do you have some of those old Indian blankets or jacquard spreads from the 1930's that eventually ended up in the car, in case you needed to get out and get under? Well, maybe there are some portions that can be made into pillows. Call it recycling...get in style!

I found some pieced patchwork strips my mother said she was learning on. The uneven stitches were of the nine-patch design done in red and white. She would laugh to see the squares now cut into folk animal shapes that prance along the back of our couch. Little did she dream that she would end up sewing a wedding dress someday!

Table runners provide a way to record who attended a get-together. A design providing sections with the date could be autographed with tube paints. I made one for the holidays of green burlap and painted on two bare tree shapes with roots at either end. Using felt of many colors, I cut three-inch leaves and glued them on both trees. Each tree represented relatives from mine and my husband's families. We asked them to write their names on one of the leaves. This is how we were able to depict the fact that we both have the same Uncle Charlie. His leaf is at the center, where both trees meet. We just found out by doing our family histories that Charlie married twice; first Lee's great aunt Emma Nelson, then my great aunt Mollie Coates. It's a small world!

Since my father was a bee-keeper, and my mother made beeswax candles, I fashioned two pillows whose designs were in keeping: the Honeybee and the hexagons of Grandmother's Flower Garden in shades of gold to represent honeycomb. I embroidered a bee near the center.

Wall hangings can be created to highlight a special time of your life. Since we are both teachers, I have always been intrigued by the Schoolhouse quilt pattern. So I made a small hanging with the pattern in the middle. Above the design, I embroidered the names of the four schools I had taught in, and below I added my husband's three. Beside the hanging on each side, I placed a small slate stenciled with the alphabet.

Wedding albums can be covered with an appropriate fabric, and presented to family members. Satin from the bridal dresses could be used, as well as laces and ribbons from the bouquets. Roses can also be made from fabric for trim.

When I made maternity clothes for our daughter, Teri, I made a baby comforter from the scraps. It's fun making something from nothing...and giving it meaning as well!

An easy way to create patchwork in a hit and miss design is to choose three colors and cut each in strips about 3-1/2 inches wide. Cut these strips in varying lengths from 4 to 7 inches. Alternating colors, sew these strips together until you have a proper length. Sew this to other strips prepared the same way, and you will be delighted with the graphic design. I made a pad for the piano bench of red, gold and black. It turned out so well that I added a pad to the black rocker as well.

LACE

Old lace handkerchiefs can become sachets by filling with potpourri and tying with ribbon. Other lengths of antique lace may be added to trim blouses, guest towels or pillowcases. Recently, I saw small drawstring bags created from lace over white or pastel cotton.

Laces may be taken from damaged linens and used on doll clothes, frames, ornaments, framed collages, albums, or combined with dried flowers. You will want to limit the need to wash the lace.

If you have several yards of wide lace, it can be fashioned into a jabot or neck scarf. Another easy idea that worked well was a large lace heart for the table or door. Just fold 1 yard of wide lace in half length-wise and sew a half-inch casing along the fold. Shape a coat hanger into a heart, separating the wire at the top. Thread the lace onto the wire heart, and trim with ribbons and flowers. It makes a great door decoration, and two of them sticking into a block of styrofoam acts as a centerpiece for a wedding shower or reception. Of course, you cover the foam with more lace or flowers.

Lace that is starched and filled with dried flowers gives a Victorian look to a home or holiday tree.

Create notepaper by photocopying lace onto pastel paper.

211

ETHNIC CRAFTS

When I found the small scherenschnitte paper-cutting in the Wertz Bible and restored it, I became very curious as to whether I could try to make one of my own. I really wanted to test out this genetic predisposition theory. I purchased a book which gave a few designs and some background information, used my nail scissors and turned out two or three. They are much too large and some are more like Valentines, but I learned to appreciate the skill and time it would take to develop a work of art. Maybe when I'm confined to a wheelchair...but then will I be able to see...oh well. I can say I tried it **once**.

Decide what crafts represent your heritage, and purchase or create some samples: Swedish weaving on guest towels, Carolina seagrass baskets, Indian clay pots, English crewel work, Italian glass and marble, Irish woolen coverlet or crystal.

Attend ethnic festivals and purchase items to wear or display, such as a clan tartan. Buy a doll dressed in native costume, or a hat and scarf to wear. In the summer, some cities celebrate their neighborhoods by holding festivals of food, dancing, and crafts. I'll have to suggest they have a heritage booth where we can sign up under our family name. We may find some new cousins this way...it's worth a try.

NEEDLEWORK, SAMPLERS, CROCHET, KNITTING

Embroidered scarves and doilies may be used as shelf liners with your heirloom dishes. The edges of the mantel or cupboard shelf will have a softer look if scarves extend over them.

Samplers and other needlework may be framed under glass. (Don't let work touch glass.) If handles are attached to the narrow ends of a rectangular frame, it becomes a tray. When not in use, it reverts to a framed artifact. Always use acid-free matting to keep the wood and fabric separated, or seal the wood with polyurethane.

Samplers may be created in cross-stitch today by working the child's name and date in center and surrounding it with symbols of their interests. Possibilities include pets, bicycle, sports items, ballet slippers, musical instruments, dolls, etc.

Scout badges, awards, souvenir pins, slogan buttons could be added later. Craft stores carry an assortment of patterns.

Mottoes worked on perforated papers make nice Victorian touches when framed. Perhaps you remember a saying that was a hallmark in your family...sort of words to live by. Or perhaps there was the line of a poem or song. The same motto or motif may be cross-stitched and inserted in a plastic cup made to hold designs. A child could design a paper insert instead, to be changed anytime.

Knitted articles may become pillows if a row of machine stitching precedes any cutting. This holds the stitches in place and prevents unraveling. Cut pillow shape outside the row of machine stitching. Let this row of stitching act as a guide when you attach the back section. If desired, additional designs may be added to a plain color pillow in duplicate stitch with needle and yarn. Do this before adding the back.

I have purchased sweaters, robes, sweatshirts and added monograms and motifs that I thought appropriate. This saves time, but still has a personal handmade touch.

For children and teens, you may want to turn their old tee-shirts into pillows. Simply sew the neckline together and abbreviate the sleeves, sewing them shut. After stuffing, sew the bottom shut as well. Some of those slogans and colorful designs would brighten up a room, and make one more appearance before the rag bag.

I found some of Mom's crocheted window blind pulls make nice napkin rings, but I only have three. That's something else I can look for at the flea market.

I wanted to do something different for the table at a baby shower, so I put a pink sheet under the crocheted cloth. I was reminded of the crocheted dress Mom made me when I was five, that I wore with different colored slips.

A crocheted table runner could become a valance or curtain for a narrow window.

While traveling in New England, I noticed that doilies had been used to accent each of the panes that framed the door. Each was different..perhaps hanging with nylon thread from a small nail, or pressed to the glass with water-soluble glue.

Consider sewing a doily to the cover of an album to give it the look of an heirloom. I've even seen them glued to a lampshade.

I remember my Grandma crocheting baskets and stiffening them with sugar water. They held a glass tumbler and cut flowers. I would love to have one of hers. Today the stores are showing doilies starched into baskets, bonnets, and folded into fans trimmed with flowers and lace. I never learned to crochet, but now we have classes at the local craft shops, and I guess soon there will be a video. (Check at the library.)

Small pieces cut from damaged needlework can be filled with potpourri and made into sachets. Larger sections can be incorporated into wall hangings or table runners.

Pieces from an anti-macassar set (crocheted chair set) can be framed on contrasting velvet or satin background. This is a good idea for any type of filet crochet to bring out the motif.

Needlepoint designs can be incorporated into many objects...clear plastic lined cups, lids of boxes, jars, plaques. I have several pieces that were never finished. These could be abbreviated and sections used for eyeglass cases, covers for a sewing kit, bookmark, pincushion, or a design on a plain tote bag. If large enough to cover a small stool, try finishing it as a two generation project.

BUTTONS, JEWELRY

I used to look through my mother's button box, and there were as many stories about that collection as there were about the photos. I recently went through it again, and took out the most unusual to display. There are Girl Scout uniform buttons, two from the U.S. Post Office uniform my father wore when carrying mail, some shoe buttons, some from a W.W.II pea jacket, overall fasteners my brothers wore, metallic ones that sparkled, some made of mother-of-pearl, leather, small white ones from the long underwear, and there was even one from the *teddy-bear* coat that I begged for. In the days of the *depression* and before, buttons were removed from old clothes to be used on the next project. Clothes were cut down to fit the next child in line, and buttons would reappear.

You may want to put the collection in a special jar with a cross-stitch button design on the top...the Mason type with the open screw-on lid is just perfect for needlework. Mine are still in the original rusty old candy box. But I guess there is something to be said for humble origins.

I have seen some mosaic designs made by gluing buttons onto a board covered with fabric and framed. But I think I'll try attaching mine to a styrofoam cone, with tacky glue, pins, or pressure on the shank type to create a *button tree*. When beginning, balance your collection over the whole tree. Then some broken necklaces can be festooned around in the spaces. Scatter the glitter around to perk up the dark metal. Add a base that is simply a dowel wrapped with braid and placed in half a styrofoam ball. A real neat idea would be to stand the tree on a carousel with a music button that plays "These Are A Few Of My Favorite Things."

Some very plain wooden frames gain the shine of mother-of-pearl by gluing on many sizes of white pearl buttons. By forming neat rows or clustering them at the corners, you could form a sort of mosaic. Wooden and leather with a few shiny military buttons would give a masculine look to a portrait.

An attractive bracelet can be created by stringing buttons on a length of round elastic. Two matching ones can be glued to earring backs, either clip or pierced. And a matching pin can be created from another used as the center of a silk flower. Usually we don't have that many of one kind to make a set. Large buttons can trim shoes when glued to a clip made for this purpose. Look for jewelry findings at your craft store.

If you find this a fascinating hobby, there is a National Button Society where you can learn more about it. The address is 2773 Juno Place, Akron, Ohio 44313. Founded in 1938, it has 2350 members in 43 state groups; also has Junior and Shut-in sections.

Consider starting a charm bracelet for a granddaughter. Present charms whenever she has an achievement. Suggest that she add her baby ring, diary key, Girl Scout pin, heart locket, photo charm. The bracelet can be pinned to a small banner when not being worn. A wide ribbon could be fashioned into a bell pull hanging for this purpose.

My neighbor, Anna, created some very attractive gold shadowbox frames that hold pins when they're not being worn. In place of a photo, she fashioned a green velveteen cushion in the oval center.

WOODWORKING

If you can frame your own pictures, you are adding even more value to them. You may have barn siding or driftwood you can use that represents the people in the picture. Frames do not always need to be mitered; the sides can be butted together.

My father fashioned a small grandfather clock case to hold **his** grandfather's pocket watch. The interesting thing is that he carved it from a piece of barn beam from his childhood farm in Loudoun County, Virginia.

If you have pieces of the old tobacco barn, you could cut out shore birds or folk animals as Lee did.

We have a beautiful lamp made from a burned-out chunk of a redwood tree. We bought it as a souvenir in California. Another lamp is made from a bannister post of the altar railing at church. When they remodeled they were throwing them away.

Many heirlooms can be turned into lamps, but if you do not want to damage them by making a hole for the electrical fixture, simply prepare a base big enough for the artifact to sit on and place the conduit rod behind it. We have some toys that we plan to use now that our children are having children. It's a neat way to keep them and still use them. One in particular is a Jack-in-the-box.

Everyone should be blessed with a woodworker who will make shelves and racks to order for your collections. Someone who will add framing to a room, and boards with shelves and pegs to hang things on, would be a godsend. Perhaps he can make a hinged screen for photos and art work, or turn an autographed door into a table.

216

Speaking of tables, my cousin Eliza has a unique one made from a square metal register cover. It sits on wrought iron legs near her fireplace. That's one thing that won't dry out from the heat!

Shadowboxes and memory boxes need special sized nooks for each object to be highlighted. Maybe just a horizontal strip of molding along the wall will provide a shallow tray where you can display a variety of objects, making quick changes from time to time.

Be sure to document your originals with a date and signature. Rubber stamps can be purchased to give it a professional look, but be sure to sign your own name and date in permanent ink.

Our children have been blessed to have many things hand-crafted by their dad...from tables and chairs to step stools, swingsets and playhouses. The best heirloom is the dollhouse which we can add to over the years. It was formerly our camping chuckbox. We got the idea as a present for our middle daughter, Robin. The library has several books on dollhouses. (745.59)

We got lots of ideas, and while Lee tiled the floors and papered the walls, I sewed linens and gathered up tiny items all over the house. Here was a place for my piano jewelry box, tiny ceramic dolls, and wooden furniture I had used in **my** orange crate dollhouse. We hardly bought anything. Lee turned small cereal boxes into chests of drawers, a toy watch into a mantel clock, and four red buttons became burners on the stove.

There is as much joy in the making as in the playing, so we have kept it at our house until this mobile society stops whirling around. I'm afraid the movers wouldn't recognize the gem that it is. Anyway some things you go to Grandmother's house to see, and only when you're old enough to take care, does the lock come off.

We don't buy anything we can make or recycle...we call it being creative! Can you believe that the stairs torn out when my in laws remodeled their kitchen in 1956 are now holding shoes in my closet as shelves? They've served five different reincarnations and still live on. How dull to live with everything new...with no stories to tell and warranties so short you have to buy insurance to cover them! My German ancestors would be proud of me.

WALLPAPER

It brought back thoughts of the kitchen back home when I saw that apple wallpaper! I had used scraps of it to cover a box for paper clips, pencils and such on my desk...and there it was, under some papers. Yes, my mother also wallpapered and we would cover books and notebooks with the leftover paper.

When we moved (for the last time!) to this house, we almost got a divorce trying to wallpaper together. But something good DID come out of it. Again, it was the kitchen, and we chose a small red and blue check paper. I began to imagine it in a quilt design, and marking the squares and triangles of the Ohio Star pattern, I cut out the sections and glued them on the center of each of the twin pantry doors. To outline the edges I traced them with a fine black marker. It was just what we needed to coordinate the woodwork with the walls, and took almost no time at all. I love it!

Come to think of it, you should be able to do the same with notepaper, or a box, or on gift paper...I think I'll cut out a whole batch of them with my new rotary wheel.

218

STENCILING, PAINTING

This will add sparkle to some of the artifacts that you want to use as decor. You can buy items at craft fairs, but they have no personal sentimental value to you. You're reviving the old and blending it with the new!

My friend, Gloria, stenciled a neat border of ivy and flowers to frame the wall above the fireplace, and repeated it on the wooden cornice her husband, Ray, built over the window nearby. Gloria and I have too many things that would get lost on wallpaper, so this is a way to soften the arrangement.

Make yourself an old sign to hang outside the door, identifying the "Inn" and year it was "established." Stencil a slate for phone messages. I have had good luck with a sponge; the problem can come from too thick or thin paint...so do plenty of experimenting. Stencil a design on a child's rocker, around a mirror, on gift paper. You can purchase some stencils for gift paper or cards that say "Celebrate," "For You," "It's A Boy," etc.

Drawings of the family home, place of business or pet can become a special picture or note paper. It's an opportunity for the artist in the family to get involved. Years ago, I painted our family cat's portrait from a photo Mindy took, and when Tigger passed away at the age of 20, Mindy returned the original to me in a beautiful frame.

SCRAPBOOKS

Create collections having to do with one particular subject. If you plan to add more items later, obtain a scrapbook with posts that expand. The following are the types of collections it may hold:

1. Story of your town...history, diagram of Main St., naming all the storekeepers and homes you can remember, old newspaper articles and photos, and tragic disasters that changed the town in some way. I gave my father clippings to read and enter to help him feel useful.

2. In memory of a special person...to remember a life that has ended; or to tell someone "these foolish things remind me of you."

3. The story of your life in mementoes, awards, tickets, publicity, to pass on to your children. A framed collage can grow from a valentine, travel post card, a letter, military induction notice, wedding or graduation invitation, and have all related items glued around it.

4. A new scrapbook as a gift for a child to save his own memories in. Put a family tree in the front.

5. Give to an elderly person to clip the daily paper as a contribution to the library.

6. To keep a collection of graduation pictures and articles concerning the alumni as distinguished citizens.

7. For a history of a particular organization or lodge, including members roster, activities and awards.

8. After the wedding of Tim and Jane, she wanted a way to remember each of the gifts they had received. So on each page of an album she created designs using the gift paper, coordinating flat ribbon, and card enclosed. On the card she noted the gift. This is one time that the care taken in wrapping the gift will be appreciated for as long as the gift itself.

9. To share foods and culinary traditions, try assembling a recipe book. By telling of family favorites and including some stories behind them, we get to know each other and see how each makes a special contribution. (More details in Chapter 4.)

10. An autograph book is another collection that will take on meaning as years go by. Though usually thought of as childhood scribbling, choose a guest book, give it a colorful cover and ask all to sign before they leave. You may want to add what you served or how you spent your time on that occasion.

Now that you have chosen a goal, choose a cover that highlights it. Recently, I saw three-ring binders with clear plastic covers which would hold a special design. Consider making it attractive with colorful collage, title, photos, to show what's inside. If you cannot find these binders do the same with clear contact paper.

Make some of the padded fabric covers with a framed photo of the owner attached to the outside. Eva made one of these for each of her children. Somewhere add your name and date.

Preserving scrapbooks is very hard to do when they are of

the thin rough paper simply glued together. The items were usually just pasted in, or worse, taped and falling apart. I have tried to save some of mine, page by page, in mylar pockets to keep items with their original pages. My two post card albums have beautiful covers, but the heavy paper pages are crumbling more each time I try to take them out to read the backs. So I am reassembling the cards in mylar pages made especially for cards. This way both sides may be read, and enjoyed without handling. I can also re-group them in sets for identification. Take a look and get advice from antique and flea market dealers. You can bet they know the way to preserve the market value of an item.

If you are motivated to try any of the crafts in this chapter, the world is waiting to help you. There are so many magazines on the market, craft stores with materials and also classes, craft videos in the library to sign out, semester classes at the community college. Craft fairs are being held year round where you may get advice and referral for instruction.

If you are planning to work with an heirloom that cannot be replaced, get some professional advice from a preservation source...usually the local historical society or museum director. I have a brief section on some of the methods I am aware of toward the end of Chapter 7 on Heirlooms.

Whatever you do to create a memory, imagine someone 50 years from now coming across the things you have so lovingly preserved. Will they know who did the work, who the first owner was, the date and your desires concerning its care?

No matter what you create, find a way to sign and date it. Name labels can be ordered and sewn in, but a personal and inexpensive way would be to use a laundry marking pen and cloth tape. A piece of iron-on tape works well also. If something is presented to you as a handmade gift, have the person autograph it. This will show how much respect you have for their work; and you want them to be remembered.

Your lack of organization may cause items to be thrown out by family members who do not have the time to organize them. So label, sign, and date them. Put them into notebooks, acid-free boxes, albums, and keep an inventory of the most valuable in your safe deposit box. The sentimental and historical value of most of these things is inestimable. All of us in genealogy can tell you countless stories beginning with, "If only..." and "I waited too long to..." "too soon old, too late smart!" You know...

So craft it, frame it, sew it, mount it, paint it to redesign your bits and pieces into heirlooms. Help them speak to new generations and give them a second life where they will become symbols of the past and yourselves. You've inherited the talent and the memories; all you have to do is pass it on!

PRESCRIPTION:
Try genealogy!
...Dr. D. Smith

10

Rx GENEALOGY

In this day and age there seems to be a prescription for everything, and there are more ailments than ever. A lot of the maladies can be traced to depression from lack of self-worth, a feeling of uselessness when we are no longer working our jobs or raising our children. I'd like to prescribe a dose of **genealogy**. Of course, that means to many, putting TIME in a bottle...or so goes the song. But let me reiterate that you can spend a little or a lot of time tracing your family history, or encouraging others to revere the past.

When you find your office force is getting along very well without you, and you no longer have a *position*, create your own position. Find other ways to make a contribution that will be more lasting than helping the company make money. Your experience has given you many skills that can now be used to create something just for you and your family. Organizing data, using computers, communicating your needs to others, setting daily goals and feeling the challenge to meet them are all part of the field of genealogy. You'll love the hours, the boss, and the challenges...because you set them yourself! You are independently wealthy with time and the choice of what you'll do with it.

Try Genealogy! It will challenge you every step of the way, and the goals will be self-satisfying! You'll become so absorbed with your detective work that it is only the growling of your stomach and the dizziness that makes you look at the clock. Every blank on that chart is like a mountain to climb just because it's there! Every generation opens new doors, poses new problems to solve, and gives new insight and direction.

And you have the freedom of choice to put it down and take a vacation anytime you want...no stressful deadlines! You'll probably opt for a trip near the ancestral home...just in case you want to drop in.

GENEALOGY IS...MOVING FORWARD INTO THE PAST

Instead of "Back To The Future," we can solve many problems by moving "Forward Into The Past." Our behaviors and beliefs sometimes create **patterns** that have been repeated for

225

generations. Our options on how to raise our children, spend our money, choose a career or religion are rarely our own, but those that we grew up with. Then there are the strains that mobility, job security, alcoholism, and abuse may bring to a marriage of our parents.

If these are causing us problems, we need to examine why and how they came to be. Knowing this, we may be able to improve on them and not keep repeating them. This, then, is known as the **nurturing** part of our character.

But the other side of us is totally set by our genetic makeup, our **nature**...those 100,000 genes on 23 chromosomes, some of which carry on the same qualities as our ancestors. So we should be extremely interested in who they were and what they were able to do.

Now multiply that by two separate individuals getting married and trying to agree, and accept each other's personality enough to raise children, and it's amazing when it works! We can't predict every situation that is going to need a decision, so we pray that love will find a way.

As you consider your parents, grandparents, and siblings, why not make a family diagram, sometimes called a "genogram." Beside each first name write occupation, birth order, education level, cause of death, marital history, and any labels which describe their character (workaholic, worrier, hypochondriac, etc). It will help you to study and analyze objectively some of the qualities that you have inherited over many generations. Though you will want to blame them, you'll become much more tolerant and understanding. You see, they can also go back two generations to look at their heritage.

I'm sure by now that you have had to examine your medical family history for any predisposition to diseases and weaknesses. You can then start to know yourself and take care before something flares up. Because you are unique, you start to learn which medicines **you** can't take, which foods give **you** a reaction, and you try to ward off those hereditary ills. We adopted a four-year old little girl, and we had very little of her history to give to the doctors. What we thought to be *baby fat* later turned out to be a thyroid condition.

Because I am a genealogist, the family has asked me to check our ancestry for anyone with an eye problem. It is very important to trace the RP that one member has. I have been told of

226

a cousin who was blind for most all of his life. Since he is deceased, I must write to his son and check it out. Family historians are starting to give doctors the information they need to trace what they feel is a *defective gene* leading to some of the major illnesses.

Studies are being done for cancer of the colon, breast, and ovaries, manic-depression, and Alzheimer's Disease. This will single out those *at risk* even before tests are run.

Scientists are even studying the proliferation of surnames to trace migration patterns. It seems that certain genetic diseases predominate in one ethnic group more than another, and by studying their migration they can see the spread of the disease. As long as there is active migration there is more diversity and less concentration of the gene through intermarriage. Studying by surnames provides a simpler way to pinpoint the genetic strain.

This reminds me of identifying the ethnic groups of people who settled the west by studying the foods they were eating, and the way they were prepared. Though you may know just when certain groups were motivated to migrate, the quicker evidence was found by looking at the surnames of the families.

It's exciting to me that there is a need in the technical world for knowledge of the past. It proves it is part of the present, a part we would do well to know and use to make the present better. Forward into the Past!

True, genealogy is our link to the past, but if we're going to progress, we should do a little family housecleaning and throw out the "junk" that isn't worth saving. I think they call it "maturity."

Try to be the one who puts an end to these family feuds. We need to cement relationships, heal emotional wounds, and renew contacts. Lack of communication is what makes any problem become worse. As you visit all the family, you truly need their information, but listen for anything that has caused friction, and do your best to say all the good you can. In other words, accentuate the positive; eliminate the negative. If you really are puzzled by some of the reactions, better avoid the issue and go to something else. Try getting the lady's age; that should do it!

Keep in mind that more important than charts is bringing the family together to support each other. Often you just need an excuse to get reacquainted, and your charts and questions will do it. If you can't get in a visit, ask a trusted friend if they will help you, so you can complete your research accurately; or send your grandchild!

Let me share a series of problems to which I feel genealogy has an answer:

IF you don't feel you have a purpose in life, consider preparing your family history. You can work alone, just writing stories of your past, and what you remember that was pleasant and funny. You may choose just one special person who influenced your life.

IF you feel lonely a lot of the time, you need to have a reason to get out with people. Go to a meeting of the local genealogical society, as a visitor. Enjoy the speaker, mention the surnames of your grandparents and where they lived, and you will be introduced to others researching that area and maybe that name. They may be carpooling to one of the research libraries, and you can ride together.

IF you have recently suffered the death of a spouse or close friend, prepare an album in memory of him/her. Or just write all your memories in a letter as though you are talking with him again. I recall, in "Hello Dolly," how Dolly would look up at the heavens and talk to Ephraim and ask him his advice. Keep writing as long as you want and need to.

IF you have some deep *concerns* but no quick answers, you need to concentrate on something else. Genealogy is so absorbing as you search for clues to your ancestry, that the time will fly. It moves you into the thinking of another age and time, when the problems weren't yours. Many of us go without lunch if we have the right book! Yes, we're addicted!

IF you have low self-esteem, what you need is an illustrious ancestor you can talk about! You need to research in those big heavy leather ledgers from the 1700's, and read those wills in their colonial vocabulary and ornate handwriting. After all, you are an important link and they are depending on you to keep their memory alive!

IF none of your choices has worked out, and you feel you're a complete failure, you have not fully explored the other sides of yourself. We are unique, even complex, machines capable of many other skills than the ones we've tried. The army says, "Be all that you can be," and it's a known fact that most of us only scratch the surface of what our brain is capable of doing. So try research...genealogy...and while you're filling out your chart, you may find a part of history that nothing has been written about. I could easily be an archaeologist...just imagine being the one who sees a treasure for the first time! But if I did that, then I wouldn't have time for this...maybe next year!

IF you didn't get to go to college, now's your chance! Community colleges offer courses in genealogy. And if you're over 60 you may register for Elderhostel courses and stay right on campus—one of 1600 in 40 countries. Just write for free catalog to: Elderhostel, Inc.
75 Federal Street
Boston, MA 02110

IF you think the only time you use the courthouse is when you have jury duty, or are in trouble, you will find that genealogists and any taxpayer may examine the records...with respect to those who work there. Wills, land records, marriage, and many other records reveal how your ancestor lived when he was in that county.

IF you enjoy using computers, genealogy will give you many hours of pleasure...entering new material as you find it, and printing it out in four or five types of charts and lists. Many genealogists need help getting started because computer stores are not knowledgeable about our needs. We lean very heavily on one member who has been generous with his experience, and helps us make choices.

IF you don't feel needed, volunteer at the local historical society or library. There you will meet others who clip old newspapers, sort memorabilia, file books and papers, and meet some people doing research for myriad reasons—authors, students, new residents, historians, sociologists, and those genealogists again!

Historical and genealogical societies share the same focus, to record the history of an area; so we complement each other. One features the structures, and the other, the people who built them. One is incomplete without the other. So that's another quest of mine...to bring historical and genealogical societies closer together, at least in understanding.

IF you enjoy sharing information with visitors, train to be a docent and lead tours around the museum displays. You will always be learning as the people ask questions and add information to your talk.

IF you like to work with young people, you could meet them at their schools and the library as a mentor. More and more people from the community are sharing their skills to inspire young people to pursue genealogy as a personal look at history. Let the schools know you are willing and able! The Roman orator Cicero, writing in 44 B. C., noted that older adults "as they become less capable of physical exertion, should redouble their intellectual activity; and their principal occupation should be to assist the young, their friends and, above all, their country with their wisdom and sagacity."

IF you don't get any but "junk mail," become a genealogist who has entered the Family Registry of the Mormon library and you will hear from genealogists all over the country who share your surname. They welcome non-Mormons. Of course you are expected to answer at least once. If you expect a reply, you should always enclose a SASE. I had 45 penpals when I was only 13. Two of them became lifelong friends, and we visited years later, which you may want to do with newly found cousins.

IF you find it hard to visit the retirement home again and again, work on your genealogy and interview while there; or take your friend/parent on a drive where he used to live. As he talks about happier times, record on tape or paper.

IF you need activities for all generations at get-togethers, ask for stories from everyone's childhood; that way, everyone can relate and be involved. Of course, you tape record.

IF the community is changing and you miss the *good old days*, collect memorabilia, photos, write articles, ask the local paper to run some material from the past. Form an historical society or commission, or just meet at the round table as "Knights of the Good Old Days."

IF I had more time, I'd go to lots of auctions. Besides completing some of my sets of antique glassware, I would try to buy some items I remember from childhood. Anyway, I'm always looking for the portrait of my great-grandfather, Jacob Boger. I foolishly left it in a storage room when we rented the house, and it was gone when the renters moved out. It was so large I didn't have a place for it. We should have at least taken a picture of it. The frame was beautiful, and I'm sure it was quickly removed and sold. But I'm hoping poor Jacob is waiting to be sold in someone's flea market and I can buy him back. I'm told people buy them to have *instant ancestors*!

I would also bid on books and family Bibles. You could go early and at least copy the family information from those offered for sale. I know a friend who has bought so many, that her husband is threatening divorce. We keep files of Bible copies at the library. Twice a year some of our members hold a Bible Copying Day, and offer a prize to the person who brings in the oldest Bible. These books once took the place of safe deposit boxes, in that they not only held the family records, but lists, deeds, photos, pressed flowers, and maybe, a lock of hair.

IF you are victimized by a grumpy fault-finding relative, this may indicate boredom and lack of purpose in life. Try to help the person set new goals, such as labeling old photos, cataloging the artifacts...where they came from, telling stories on a tape, describing items in a vintage catalog or the photos in an album. You truly need this information, and they should feel important to your cause.

IF you hate cloudy, dreary days, spend them in a library researching your ancestors. The time goes fast and you may come home with a lot of pictures and material copied for your files.

IF you're going through a midlife crisis, attend some workshops to meet people and become a student again. If you concentrate your research, you could become an authority on that particular topic. You would be in demand as a speaker.

231

IF you fear you're losing your memory, you need some mental stimulation. If you don't use it, you lose it! They know now that memory is a complex, changing process that depends on your emotional and general health, which can improve with practice or deteriorate through disuse. I find that I have the names on my six-generation family chart pretty well memorized. When I need a name, I can picture my chart and it flashes into my mind. But then I've been using my charts for ten years. Just digesting the new facts we find, and drawing clues from it gives us a lot of practice.

Any time you recount and assess, the memory is strengthened and valued. Two or more persons who share backgrounds will motivate each other...sort of group therapy!

IF you're concerned with all the clutter in your house, take a good look at its value as artifacts from the past. After preparing a card about its name, origin and background, find a decorative way to display it in your house, donate it to the local museum, or make a gift of it to a relative who will care for it. Be certain you know the market value before you sell it. Consult a price guide.

IF you don't understand your parents' attitudes, study their lives as they were growing up, and walk a while in their shoes. Patterns are hard to break, and parenting is a learning experience all your life. None of us is perfect, and we're always trying to become...

IF you are a single parent, I think a child could maintain his security from a chart that represents ALL that he is; a record for him to look at and study, where all the broken parts are there together. He could complete portions of his chart on visits with each parent. Parents may want to tell stories or make tapes about their own childhood, and how much they see in their child that takes them back. This would be truly quality time and gets beyond any contemporary problem; seems better than material rewards and whirlwind activities.

IF you have problems relating to your siblings, genealogy is an opportunity to gain a new respect. As an adult, you no longer need to compete for your parent's attention, and can try to get to know them as friends. As your parents pass away, you will probably share more of your childhood. Then you'll realize that you saw it through different eyes and angles. Your perception was affected by your age and place in the family, your ability to cope and your emotional maturity, among other things. Talk it out and see...did they see and hear the same things as you?

IF you've been taken ill and need an activity that you can do at home, subscribe to a rental library. After an initial membership fee, they will send you books for the cost of postage, and you may work on your genealogy at home.

Some of the volumes you need may be available on inter-library loan at your public library. Make certain they can be circulated or loaned. If the doctor recently told you or your relative to slow down, be inactive physically for a while, buy that person a nicely bound Family Tree book ($10) with all the names, dates and information waiting to be filled in. All you need is a memory and the time to complete some of it and your satisfaction will speed your recovery.

IF a child is recuperating from an illness, have him fill out a Family Tree Workbook by Rosemary Chorzempa, adding photos. In addition, he can write letters to distant relatives asking for information he needs to know. He will be receiving surprises in the mail. People seldom let a child down. (See Chapter 8 for bibliography.)

IF you or your parent are fluent in a foreign language, you would be in great demand to translate letters from the old country. Genealogists correspond overseas to learn about their ancestry, but often need help in reading the records. Volunteer at the nearest Mormon library or genealogical society. It motivates some of us to learn the language ourselves, especially if we plan a trip in the future.

IF you are searching for a missing contemporary, you follow some of the same routes as a genealogist. Trace to the area that you feel they lived most of their early life, what kind of work they were doing, or possibly in the service, and check the phone directories, or city directories, old and new. Also take a look at a book titled SEARCH, A Handbook For Adoptees by Jayne Askin, if this is your concern.

Recently, there was information made available that you could write a personal letter asking your relative to contact you and address the envelope to him. Place this into another envelope with a request that the letter be forwarded to his current address, and mail it to the Social Security Administration at the following address:

Office of Central Records Operations
300 North Greene Street, Room 1312
Tower Metro West
Baltimore, Maryland 21201

IF you don't have the time, but would like your family history to be researched, there are professional genealogists who submit their rates on request. Ask at the local historical society or public library for their names.

IF I desire, how may I locate a genealogical society? Look in your phone book, ask at the library or historical society. Consult Meyer's Directory of Genealogical Societies in the U. S. A. and Canada.

Genealogical groups are organized like any self-help group...for the purpose of sharing ideas and improving your skills to further growth in your area of interest. One person can put a request in the paper for all those interested in studying family history to meet. Those who come together decide when and where they will meet again. An experienced researcher can be invited from the nearest town, and you're on your way.

IF you work on genealogy, there will be painful parts of the past you will want to forget. We always have to work on it, but I have found that in recording genealogy, we organize our good thoughts as a tribute, a celebration of life. Crowd out the bad by filling your story with happy, positive memories. Those are the ones we can choose to surround ourselves with...just like supportive friends! We are as happy as we make up our minds to be.

IF you feel genealogy is too big a job for you, you need to know that research is always done a step at a time. You set short-term goals, and you are only limited by your time and motivation. Don't think of a whole chart; record all you can find about one family. There is no ONE way to record your family's history; it depends on YOUR goals. Those who try to fill up a chart often don't know much about their own grandfather. So it's the choice of a lot about a few persons, or a little about a lot of persons. Whatever you do will be more than anyone else in your family has done, so it will be appreciated.

IF you are the caregiver of an elderly parent, try to strike a balance between *give and take*. My husband and I have been in this role for many years, but we have not had to *live in*. However, I feel much better about *giving* when I know I am going to receive *something* in return, if it's only a smile.

The rewards I strive for are simple: to find out about this feeble person's younger days, any memories that are there, any comments I may attach importance to...anything I may add to the family history. Time to be with these people is running out...maybe I should ask about some of the artifacts, label photos with their help, talk about aunts and uncles whom I haven't gotten to know. Just an impression would be helpful; otherwise they'll just be a names on the chart. I know it's hard, practically impossible with some, but I try singing hymns, taking dolls, mementoes, anything that may take them "home again." I don't give up easily; genealogy will strengthen that!

IF you want to publish a book, leave something in print that will be a legacy for years to come, then write the story of your family, or yourself. Do it for your own satisfaction. If others join in, you will be doubly rewarded. The information is out there waiting for you to find it...accept the challenge and learn something new every day. You'll find it hard to stop! Dr. Wayne Dyer says, "Take charge of your life!"

IF you want to stay young while you're researching, keep moving! You'll get a workout as good as the spa as you lift those heavy courthouse ledgers, walk the stairs instead of using the elevators, improve your circulation and upper arm muscles as you manually wind that microfilm. Do those deep knee bends when the oversized book you need is on the bottom shelf. Be glad when the metered parking spaces close by are full and you are forced to park two blocks away. And why else would I be eating my bag lunch in the sunshine on the marble steps of the Library of

Congress? Genealogy can pep you up and get you out...you've got to run if you want to catch up with those ancestors. They're migrating all over the place!

IF the time comes when I'm alone and have to settle down a little, it won't be to a retirement home. I'm going to suggest to three of my female genealogist friends that we share a LARGE apartment house across the street from the library in Fort Wayne, Indiana or the Mormon Library in Salt Lake City, Utah. I want my demise to catch me by surprise!

I guess you could say that I'm hooked on genealogy, a sort of *born again* feeling. It's the first time I've found a vehicle to communicate a lot of feelings it takes to get along in this world. **So Rx Genealogy and pass it around!**

PASSPORT

TO A

PLEASANT

RESEARCH

EXPERIENCE

Duane Smith

Travel Agent

11

INTERVIEW YOUR FAMILY

All of the things mentioned in this book are part of your genealogy, or family history: artifacts, recipes, tapes, holiday memories, tombstones, autograph books, letters, trips, reunions, obituaries, awards, documents...the list is endless. Many of the stories behind these items exist only in the memory of family members. When they are gone, all their memories will go as well...unless. Deuteronomy 32:7 "Cast thy mind back to the old days; nay, trace the record of each succeeding generation; ask thy father what news he has to tell, thy forefathers, what word they have for thee."

Here is where we come in; the ones who decide to save those memories for future family to appreciate. Each generation tried to help the next; to make the most of things and improve on them.

It is amazing how many people do not know the maiden name of their own grandmother. Of course, it will not bring a curse on them...but it's like cutting down a 100-year-old tree, as though another will appear in its place tomorrow. Most of what we have today is because of yesterday.

We who enjoy this study are drawn to it because we can decide, in our individual ways, how we will record it. When we get together we enjoy the many ways to go about it, and learn of new projects we may try. These I have tried to share in this book so you have choices. You may spend a lot of time, or a little. You may record your stories of one person who changed your life, or the way the whole family brought qualities to help you on your journey. By that time, you may want to find out just where this whole clan originated, and how they became what you know today as YOUR FAMILY.

The one process you must employ is to write things down, NOW! If it's only one sheet of paper and a hand drawn chart, start with yourself as number 1, and write down as many **full** names of parents and grandparents as you know. When recording the women use their maiden names, as that is their blood line.

Also, add the date (day, month, and year in 4 digits) and place of their births and deaths...the city and state. Interview the family, especially the eldest. Get a genealogist's chart and fill it out with more detail. Get the children to help, or take it on as an extra credit project for school. It is part of history and social studies in our county. Below is a sample of mine.

These charts may be purchased at the local Mormon library, the genealogical society, or by ordering a catalog from the Everton Publishers, Inc., P.O. Box 368, Logan UT 84321.

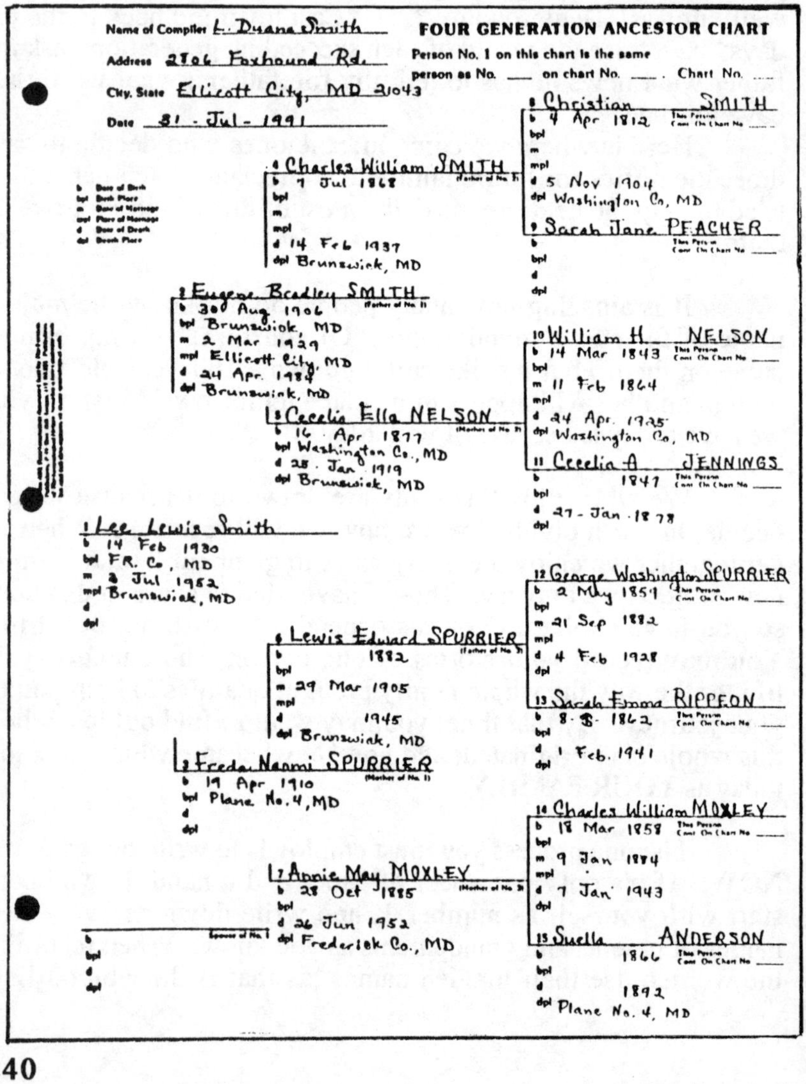

Name of Compiler *L. Duana Smith*   **FOUR GENERATION ANCESTOR CHART**

Address *2706 Foxhound Rd.*   Person No. 1 on this chart is the same

City, State *Ellicott City, MD 21043*   person as No. ____ on chart No. ____ . Chart No. ____

Date *31 - Jul - 1991*

Chart entries (handwritten):

- 1 Lee Lewis Smith — b 14 Feb 1930, bpl FR. Co., MD, m 3 Jul 1952, mpl Brunswick, MD
- 2 Charles William SMITH — b 7 Jul 1868, m, d 14 Feb 1937, dpl Brunswick, MD
- 3 Freda Naomi SPURRIER — b 19 Apr 1910, bpl Plane No. 4, MD
- 4 Eugene Bradley SMITH — b 30 Aug 1906, bpl Brunswick, MD, m 2 Mar 1929, mpl Ellicott City, MD, d 24 Apr 1989, dpl Brunswick, MD
- 5 Cecelia Ella NELSON — b 16 Apr 1877, bpl Washington Co., MD, d 25 Jan 1919, dpl Brunswick, MD
- 6 Lewis Edward SPURRIER — b 1882, m 29 Mar 1905, d 1945, dpl Brunswick, MD
- 7 Annie May MOXLEY — b 25 Oct 1885, d 26 Jun 1952, dpl Frederick Co., MD
- 8 Christian SMITH — b 4 Apr 1812
- 9 Sarah Jane PEACHER
- 10 William H NELSON — b 14 Mar 1843, m 11 Feb 1864, d 24 Apr 1925, dpl Washington Co., MD
- 11 Cecelia A JENNINGS — b 1847, d 27 Jan 1878
- 12 George Washington SPURRIER — b 2 May 1851, m 21 Sep 1882, d 4 Feb 1928
- 13 Sarah Emma RIPPEON — b 8 - 8 - 1862, d 1 Feb 1941
- 14 Charles William MOXLEY — b 18 Mar 1858, m 9 Jan 1884, d 7 Jan 1943
- 15 Suella ANDERSON — b 1866, d 1892, dpl Plane No. 4, MD

These charts serve a very practical purpose: when dates are needed for obituaries, for remembering special birthdays, and anniversaries, the names and ages of visiting cousins or to settle many arguments.

A **generational chart** is the easiest for all to understand and preserve. It shows **relationships** and **dates** and **places**, so everyone may see at a glance.

Next, for every couple on **that** chart, you should create a **ONE FAMILY CHART** like this one:

FAMILY GROUP No. 6		Husband's Full Name Lewis Edward SPURRIER				
This Information Obtained From		Day Month Year	City, Town or Place	County or Province, etc.	State or Country	Add. Info. on Husban
	Birth	1882	Plane No. 4	Frederick	MD	
Church records	Chr'nd	at Marvin Chapel Methodist, Mt. Airy, MD				
	Mar.	29.3.1905				
Cemetery Gravestones	Death	1945	Brunswick	Frederick	MD	
	Burial		Marvin Chapel Cem.			
Family records	Places of Residence					
	Occupation R. R. Engineer	Church Affiliation Meth.		Military Rec. —		
	His Father George W. Spurrier		Mother's Maiden Name Rippeon, Sarah			
		Wife's Full Maiden Name Annie May MOXLEY				
		Day Month Year	City, Town or Place	County or Province, etc.	State or Country	Add. Info. on Wife
	Birth	28 Oct 1885	Plane No. 4	Frederick	MD	
	Chr'nd					
	Death	26 Jun 1952	Brunswick	Frederick	MD	
	Burial		Marvin Chapel Cem. Mt. Airy MD			
Compiler L. Duane Smith	Places of Residence					
Address 2806 Foxhound	Occupation if other than Housewife		Church Affiliation			
City, State Ellicott City, MD						
Date 31 Jul 1991	Her Father Charles W. Moxley		Mother's Maiden Name Sue Anderson			
Sex	Children's Names in Full (arrange in order of birth)	Children's Data	Day Month Year	City, Town or Place	County or Province, etc.	State or Country	Add. Info. on Children
1 Earl Lewis	Birth	6 Apr 1906	Plane No. 4	Frederick Co., MD	
Full Name of Spouse Clara E Gordon	Mar.				
	Death	7 Aug 1980	Brunswick		
	Burial	9 Aug 1980	Mt. Airy		
2 Freda Naomi	Birth	14 Apr 1910	Plane No. 4		
Full Name of Spouse Eugene Bradley Smith	Mar.	2 Mar 1929	Ellicott City, Howard Co., MD		
	Death				
	Burial				
3	Birth				
Full Name of Spouse	Mar.				
	Death				
	Burial				
4	Birth				
Full Name of Spouse	Mar.				
	Death				
	Burial				
5	Birth				
Full Name of Spouse	Mar.				
	Death				
	Burial				
6	Birth				
Full Name of Spouse	Mar.				
	Death				
	Burial				
7	Birth				
Full Name of Spouse	Mar.				
	Death				
	Burial				
8	Birth				
Full Name of Spouse	Mar.				
	Death				
	Burial				
9	Birth				
Full Name of Spouse	Mar.				
	Death				
	Burial				
10	Birth				
Full Name of Spouse	Mar.				
	Death				
	Burial				

Now that's a good start! So you still have some blanks? **Visit** any relatives who live nearby; those who have lived the longest. If they know any stories, ask permission to **tape record**. Perhaps when you have more time, you'll **write** Great Aunt Mary, and ask her to fill in what she can. Maybe you'll want to put your charts in an album to show now and then, and ask for additions and corrections.

And wouldn't it be nice if you had some photos to go with these names? They would look nice in the album as well. When you write, you could also ask Great Aunt Mary if she has any **photos**.

There are a lot of names on the chart you never knew because those ancestors died before you were born. The next time you go by the **graveyard**, you can try to find the tombstones. There may be interesting verses, and you may get clues as to how they died. If not, the old newspapers may have the **obituaries** written up. They're on microfilm now in most of the **libraries** in the county seats. And when they died, they usually left a **will** telling the family how their estate was to be divided. Just having a reason to go to the probate office in the **court house** may provide a meaningful experience. You'll be in the middle of a lot of activity, but the records are open to you.

Now I have really made it as easy as I can to get started...at any age. It gets to be a search for a missing person in much the same way as a detective.

Where was he last seen?
Who were his friends?
Where did he live and work?
Did he go by any other name?
Was he ever in trouble?
Did he own any land or business?
Whom did he marry? Where was she from? Who were
    her parents?
Which church did he attend?
Did he ever hold office, attend a lodge?
Was he ever in the military; fight a war?
Where did he die? Where buried?

You start wondering if you really can find this person; you'll give it a try. After all, there must have been more your grandfather did than sit in the rocker, smoke his pipe and ask when dinner would be ready. What was he like as a boy and how

242

did he meet Grandma? After you trace his life, reading the wills, diaries, letters, seeing the signatures, or maybe a lock of hair in the Bible, you'll know some of the answers you didn't have time to ask.

VISIT THE LIBRARY

Although searching for your family history may begin with interviews of relatives, you soon find that you must go to printed materials to supplement and verify the clues you have been given. These records are kept in repositories and public libraries, each of which is unique in many ways.

I heard a story once of a very unusual visitor to a library that was next to the zoo. When the keeper came around to check the monkey cage, he found one of them named Joe was missing. "Does anyone know where Joe is?," the keeper asked. "I think he went over to the library to check out some books," replied one of the others. This was highly unlikely, but the keeper had to find him. When he arrived at the library, there was Joe standing at the check-out counter with two books, "ORIGIN OF THE SPECIES" by Darwin, and the "BIBLE." "I won't punish you, Joe," said the keeper, "if you have a good reason for signing out those books." Joe answered, "I'm sorry, but I just had to find out if I'm my brother's keeper or my keeper's brother!"

We just have to find out who our ancestors are, and knowing that collections vary from one to another, I began my search. Ten years and 70 libraries later, I can tell you what I discovered as I made my survey throughout three states.

I'm still looking for the "perfect library;" you know, the one in an historic setting, free parking close by, open 9:00 A.M. to midnight, open stacks (shelves), indexed by surname, copiers five cents, special collections, self-threading microfilm readers with push-button controls. One with soft couches for brief naps, lamps for better atmosphere, staffed with cheerful librarians who are also genealogists, convenient rest rooms, and drink machines and lunch area inside the building.

Would you believe each of these conditions exists in a library right now...but not all in the SAME one. (I'm still working on a patent for the self-threading microfilm reader!)

LIBRARIES ARE ALL DIFFERENT. They reflect the community in which they are located, and are influenced by the clientele, temperament and management style of the director, philosophy of their board, supervisory style of the department heads, and the attitudes of the staff toward one another and the user. The political, social, economic, ethnic, and educational area in which a library exists has a great effect. Some form a liaison with genealogical societies.

LIBRARIANS ARE ALL DIFFERENT. They are human beings who obviously have a love of books, but hopefully, not at the expense of their patrons. We genealogists are not always made to feel welcome. On one of my research visits the librarian told me he only tolerates genealogists, because he is a history professor at heart. I said to him, "History without genealogy is only geography." He quietly tolerated me the rest of the day.

Emerson expressed these same ideas in his Essay on History, " *There is no history, only biography...what it [soul] does not see, what it does not live, it will not know. Every law which the state enacts indicates a fact in human nature; that is all. Civil history, natural history, the history of art and literature—all must be explained from individual history, or must remain words. The trivial experience of everyday is always verifying some old prediction to us, and converting into things for us, the words and signs which we had heard and seen without heed.* " So I feel we are well supported that history and genealogy go hand in hand.

As I went from library to library, I asked each librarian how we could present ourselves in order to receive the best assistance. I related my experiences and explained that, as library chairman for my society, I was preparing a survey . Most of them asked that we:

1. Be specific and not tell long stories, as they have many other patrons to serve.

2. Be knowledgeable...have clear-cut goals. Know what area, time period, and type of information we desire.

3. Be patient. Not all librarians are genealogists, so take that into consideration. Read a "how-to-book" instead of expecting hints from the staff.

244

We really need each other...the genealogist depends on the libraries to connect them with the materials of research. The librarian needs to provide such a climate that they support the taxpayer. I read several library service books, such as SNOW-BALLS IN THE BOOK DROP by Will Manley, PATRONS ARE PEOPLE by Sarah Wallace, and DOING RESEARCH by R. Baker; watched a videotape on research interviews, and read chapters in the book, LIBRARY SERVICE FOR THE GEN-EALOGIST by J. Carlyle Parker (929.1) to see what they had to say in our behalf. In summary, they agree that genealogists need and deserve service, and libraries should try to have at least one person qualified to assist them.

Let us not forget that anyone who works with the public puts up with a lot of intolerance, and lack of respect. Also, have you noticed that the library is probably the only place in town where a vagrant can use the rest room and sit on the sofas to take a nap. I have seen many bedrolls under chairs, and a book in the hand of a dozing *patron*. There is a lot of responsibility here that complicates their day. When I, as a teacher, was called a *public servant*, I felt there was no respect for my position nor my years of education. So it is with librarians.

But how about the PERFECT PATRON? Some of us are known as people who make ridiculous demands, and tell long stories. I have a few communication skills that I think will help:

1. Take time to establish rapport with the staff. They are the keepers of the *gold* you hope to discover. Ask if there is a genealogical specialist. Use the librarian's name whenever possible.
2. If they like you, they may bend the rules a little.
3. If the first librarian gives you a cold reception, ask if there is someone on the staff who CAN help you.
4. Expect to be referred to a book, instead of a short course in genealogy. "Could you refer me to a book on...?"
5. Wait until the shift changes; you may find the next person more helpful.
6. Do respect others' time and quiet for research.
7. Above all, put yourself in the librarian's place. She may have just dealt with a vagrant, silenced a teenage gathering, has a migraine, or had a $100 book stolen; and, it picked *today* to

happen! We are ALL responsible for giving genealogists a better name.

PASSPORT TO A PLEASANT LIBRARY EXPERIENCE

Let's take a field trip to a library, any library. I'll be your travel agent and prepare you for the trip.

SURVIVAL BAG—filled with items you may need to fit any emergency if the bus drops you off for all day. In this bag goes your **notebook**, a mechanical lead **pencil** (no sharpening), full-page **magnifier** sheet (to figure out old handwriting), an **address book** with your surnames (use at card catalog), **name labels** (for signing in or to give to a new friend), **post-it notes** (mark pages for copier), **coin holder** for dimes and quarters for copier, driver's license for **identification** (don't leave home without it), **eye drops, cough drops**, special **glasses** for reading microfilm (no bifocals!), **tissues**, and **lunch** bag (or buy).

Be ready for this bag to either be inspected, or put into a locker before you enter some libraries. So much has been stolen that we are all under scrutiny. As you develop a system of organization, you may only need to bring the family charts of a few families, and some paper to note clues. A lot of background material you will photocopy from its original source.

PREPARATION FOR TRIP—As the librarian suggests, be specific with clear-cut goals. You can only do this by doing some homework. Consult the DIRECTORY OF GENEALOGICAL LIBRARIES IN U.S. AND CANADA by P. W. Filby to obtain the hours, address, head librarian, and holdings you may expect to find. It is helpful to photocopy the pages in the Filby volume which pertain to the area libraries you plan to visit. Also, I have made copies of the bibliography for certain states from his book, AMERICAN AND BRITISH GENEALOGY AND HERALDRY. He has chosen basic references to each state's research. Find it in R929.016F.

Take along your four-generational chart with names, county, state locations included. This gives everyone a visual

246

framework of your research needs. Verbal stories and poorly pronounced surnames make it hard for communication to take place. Be sure to note the various spellings the name may come under. I feel this is a standard way to introduce ourselves to anyone we want to interest in helping us.

To properly evaluate material and ask specific questions of the library staff, compile information from your family charts and include:

Estimate time frame he lived in; 30 yrs=1 generation
His last known residence: city, county, state
State and county name at <u>that time</u>
Census area was called then; numbered
Ethnic group represented; migration pattern
Church affiliation
Wars which occurred in that area
Family-owned land
Name and location of wife's family—check for records
Occupation; government-related?

If you have never done any genealogical research before, visit your local library and sign out a "how-to" book in the 929's and a history of your area from the 975's. Many librarians say that we expect them to teach us, but they can only direct us to the books we need. Others are listed at the end of the chapter.

TRAVEL ARRANGEMENTS—If any of your research is reasonably close, you should consider car-pooling. Societies usually plan field trips, and many choose this over going alone for many reasons. If you are a beginner, you will learn a lot just by discussing your needs as you ride along. You will have an introduction to the libraries from experienced people who will orient you to the facility and how it operates.

We help each other with directions, reading street signs in heavy traffic, parking and gasoline costs, research methods, and help with microfilm readers (I think there are 25 different types). In addition, we have someone along with whom we can rejoice, commiserate, and eat lunch. Also, remember, there's safety in numbers.

Most of us find ourselves researching so much, we have to combine it with our social life. After all, where else can you find a listening ear to those wonderful stories of serendipity?

I must recommend motorhomes; they are a wonderful way to bring comfort to research trips. It is the perfect answer to the reluctant spouse who doesn't know what to do while you're doing *that stuff* again!

SPEAKING THE LANGUAGE—When you're taking a trip to a new area, you don't want to appear to be an outsider, so you try to read maps and learn the language. So it is with terms used in reference to libraries.

I've prepared a glossary of terms that I learned little by little. You can take a class and get a list of these, but you really learn them by using them, just as you do a foreign language.

HOW TO SPEAK LIBRARIANESE

ABSTRACT - a brief statement of essential thoughts; a summary
ARCHIVES - DOCUMENTS which are non-current records of organizations preserved for their continuing value
ATLAS - collection of maps
AUDIO-RECORDINGS - department housing oral histories
CARD CATALOG - organized under AUTHOR-TITLE or SUBJECT; may be on MICRO-FISCHE or COMPUTER
CIRCULATION DESK - main desk, for sign out & information
CLASSIFICATION OF PRINTED MATTER - either DEWEY DECIMAL (#) or LIBRARY OF CONGRESS (letter)
CLOSED STACKS - material to be retrieved by librarian; call slips?
COMPENDIUM - a SUMMARY or ABSTRACT containing essential information in a brief form
CURATOR - arranges a collection into an order based on archival principles, manuscript techniques and research needs
DOCUMENT IDENTIFICATION - correspondence, diaries, minutes, proceedings, printed material, financial documents, photographs, literary productions, legal, scrapbooks, maps, charts, diagrams
EXTANT - existing
GAZETTEER - an alphabetical index of geographical names
GENEALOGICAL SPECIALIST - one trained in the holdings & procedure dealing with genealogy
INTER-LIBRARY LOAN - to obtain a book from another library
LIBRARIAN - one who is trained & responsible for the care of materials & area; who will assist you if approached with respect
MANUMISSIONS - records dealing with the freedom of slaves
MANUSCRIPTS - bodies of personal papers with significant unity; often unpub
MAPS - designate land forms; CHARTS refer to land & sea
MICROFORMS - microfilm, microfische, microcards, microprints-separate index
MORTALITY SCHEDULES - lists of persons who died within the past year
MUSEUM - a collection for conservation, research & interpretation
OPEN STACKS - shelves open to public
PROVENANCE - the office that created or received records
PUBLISHED - printed material w/call #, found on appropriate shelf
RARE BOOKS - used under close supervision; xeroxing may be denied
REFERENCE SECTION - non-circulating
RESERVE - to obtain a book not on the shelf
SERIALS-PERIODICALS - area housing magazines, journals, & newspapers
SPECIAL COLLECTIONS - materials unique to this library, different hours?
STILL PICTURES - drawings, paintings & photos in their various forms
UNPUBLISHED MATERIAL - refers to personal papers, often incomplete & unorganized; not in print; usually in vertical files or boxes
VIDEO-CASSETTE AREA - visuals with separate index
VERTICAL FILES - cabinets of clippings, pamphlets, or unpublished materials; separate index?
VITAL RECORDS - birth, marriage, divorce & death

ITINERARY OF TOUR—POINTS OF INTEREST

INFORMATION OR REFERENCE DESK: Introduce yourself as a genealogist, and request any handouts or guides they may have.

TAKE TIME TO READ the handout so you will know the layout and policies of this facility; locate microfilm readers, copiers.

SURNAME REGISTRY FOR VISITORS: You may indicate which surnames you are researching, and ask for others to correspond.

BOOKS MAY HAVE TO BE REQUESTED ON CALL SLIPS, rather than be on open stacks...use address labels.

BOOKS YOU FINISH WITH have special collection places; do not reshelve.

SPECIAL COLLECTIONS OR AREAS: Some libraries cater to researchers in genealogy and history. These may have separate indexes. Ex. Rare books, Manuscripts, Photos.

CARD CATALOGS (or on microfische) will provide call numbers under Surname (all spellings), County, City, State, Ethnic group, Religious denominations, and Genealogy.

FOREIGN LANGUAGE DICTIONARIES help with ethnic research, old letters, wills, tombstones. R400

CITY & TELEPHONE DIRECTORIES go back many years, and prove residence and occupation of ancestor. R929

NEWSPAPERS on microfilm give credence and drama to some of the family stories you've heard. Special Area?

BEGINNERS will want to consult the **how-to** books. 929.1

INDEXES, BIBLIOGRAPHIES will show what family histories have already been published. R016

COUNTY HISTORIES include the names of many families and background on the vocational development of the area. 974-5

ETHNIC MIGRATION AND PASSENGER LISTS R929.72

STATE HISTORY will follow the colonists as they migrate and open up new regions. 973-978

U. S. HISTORY and its various regions include military accounts. 973

CENSUS SCHEDULES pinpoint the area of residence for the head of family only from 1790 on; will name entire family from 1850 on. R 015.73—consult index book for page on microfilm.

TOMBSTONE INSCRIPTIONS reveal birth and death dates and clues to church membership. Volumes 929.3, some in periodicals indexed in 929.105.

MARRIAGE RECORDS published by counties give wife's maiden name and establish residence. R 929.3

CHURCH HISTORIES often include baptisms and marriages. 200

SCRAPBOOKS may contain clippings, obituaries and unique memorabilia. (Vertical file)

MAPS & ATLASES help establish the exact location of a piece of land. Early maps include mills and plat names. 912

GAZETTEERS give meaning to unfamiliar place names. R910.3

HERALDRY & PEERAGE volumes will show pedigree and coats-of-arms for the oldest families. 929.6

PASSENGER LISTS tell the immigrant's name, age, ship, and embarkation port. R973

COURT RECORDS include books of will abstracts and indexes and lists of land holdings. R929.3 or 975.2

VITAL STATISTICS may be documented by ordering by mail. See 312.5 and R929.1U for addresses for birth, marriage, and death certificates.

TAX LISTS, ASSESSMENT RECORDS, RENT ROLLS 929.3

OATHS OF ALLEGIANCE, NATURALIZATIONS R929.3

ORAL HISTORIES, VIDEOS, FILM, and SLIDES may give first hand accounts. (Special areas)

PERIODICALS and INDEX will locate short documented articles on genealogy and history. R929.105. Back issues may be signed out.

NEWSLETTERS from genealogical societies provide link to related regions. (Special areas)

TECHNOLOGY, APPLIED SCIENCES will help you investigate the development of the career in which your ancestor was involved. 600

ARTS will promote study of the value of your antiques and artifacts. 700

EUROPEAN HISTORY volumes will put together the turmoil that caused your ancestor to migrate. 940

BONDED PASSENGERS—If your ancestor was an indentured servant or slave, he may be considered property and named with the land holdings in the will of his owner. R929.3

PATRIOTIC & HEREDITARY SOCIETIES keep very complete records in order to maintain strict membership. See FOUNDERS AND PATRIOTS R929.2 or MAYFLOWER INDEX 369.1

ADOPTION brings unique problems to tracing lineage, so consult R362.734A, if needed.

GENETICS is playing a larger part in medical research. See newly published books in 610.

LIBRARY SERVICES:
> Location of microfilm and readers...is use limited?
> Location of copier, the cost, staff or patron operated?
> Rest rooms, lunch room, drink machines, cafeteria?

Record the hours, holdings, address and phone number for future reference.

Other services that the library offers are networking, interlibrary loan, or putting books on reserve. You may inquire about other libraries and genealogical societies in the area.

If you plan a research trip out of town, call ahead to be sure the library will be open, ask if a specialist will be there at that time, and if certain materials can be made available for you.

A SURVEY OF LIBRARIES

I've been to libraries as intimidating as the Library of Congress, and as small as the renovated butcher shop in Loudoun County, Virginia, where, in the only notebook they had, I found three of my families. So I'm firmly convinced that the best library is the one where you find what you're looking for, and feel welcome while you do it.

Each library impresses me in a different way. Though one has a wonderful collection, it lacks service and books are not reshelved. Another locks up everything, including you, and will only get you one book at a time. One has the papers of a noted genealogist, another, a magnificent photo collection. Still another has the most complete newspaper inventory, and the one in the next county has a wonderful set of church records. Some are noisy teenage gathering places; others treat local history to a room of its own, which the local genealogical society maintains and contributes to. Each library is a testimony to the community's support and appreciation, and a boon to the visitor who feels welcomed.

Some of the best genealogical libraries are maintained by the Church of Jesus Christ of the Latter Day Saints (Mormon). There are branches called Family History Centers all over the country; they welcome non-Mormons doing research. Their records include all ethnic and church groups of the countries of the world. Call one of their churches to find the location of one near you.

The library has much to help you, and you could probably browse around for hours in a random approach to research. But I like to meet the reference librarian as though I were Alice in Wonderland needing all the direction she can give me. I like to give them the opportunity to show me that this is a great facility, and I'm going to come back home feeling like I was treated like a respected researcher.

It is encouraging to note that there is even a library for the deaf, blind, and those who have motor difficulties. Supported by a non-profit corporation, the address is:

Genealogical Library for the Blind
and Physically Handicapped
4176 English Oak Drive
Doraville, GA 30340

LEARN TO COMMUNICATE

One of the biggest lessons we've learned in interviewing relatives, is that you have to ask the right questions. When we've stumbled on to some juicy fact that we wished we'd known before, a relative says, "You never asked; I didn't know you were interested in that!" Another quote that comes to mind is, "Seek and ye shall find, knock and the door will be opened, ask and it shall be given." Oh, how I wish it were that simple. Our family histories would fall into place so much easier, if we learn to communicate.

Communication is defined as follows: "to impart, share, make known; to exchange information by talk, gestures, writing, sympathetic relationship." We genealogists employ all these means in an attempt to find out all we can about our ancestors. We have such a sincere need to know and learn that we will develop whatever skills we need to accomplish our purpose.

253

This then points out how important motivation is to any project. People involved in communication, such as teachers and preachers, learn early on that if YOU are motivated, you will find a way to get your idea across. As a young choir director, I felt I could never do an adequate job of getting singers to follow my lead. Then I realized that if I showed my love for a piece of music, I transferred the attention from myself to the product we were going to produce together. And in the singing we would have worshipped the moment. Moments are like that, you know...never the same...and gone so quickly.

In today's world we study people's motives. We are suspicious that money is all they want at our expense. I try to establish that my motives are simply to record all that is important about my family so they will never be forgotten. There is so much about them that I need to know, and I would appreciate their help.

When approaching a possible *new cousin* I try to put myself in his place. You don't communicate with anyone until you identify where *they're coming from*...their background of experience, the value of their time, their attitude and their age level. The funny thing is that they're going to be doing the same thing to you. It's called gaining their respect, and there isn't enough of it today. After all, these new-found cousins were doing very well living out their lives without benefit of genealogy. Why should they get involved in someone else's project?

Now comes your opportunity to make a testimonial on how your life has been enriched by this quest. Show your enthusiasm for all the new things you've learned, telling a few anonymous stories that have made your ancestors interesting people. Then remind them that some of these ancestors are also theirs. If they become **partners** in this research by giving you information, you will end up with something you've produced together.

I like to express the far-reaching value of leaving something for posterity that will only become more important as the years go by. And if we record now what we know to be true, the record will be as complete as we desire it to be...not just fragments in someone's faded memory. I constantly remind people that this is one project that you can pursue a little or a lot. **Whatever you do is more than has been done before.**

The only thing you should remember is that you have a responsibility to make an **accurate** record that has some sort of proof, or state that this is just an assumption, or a family story. These stories are necessary, and interesting and just plain facts alone make for a boring history. But you want to be a **responsible** writer who is leaving something of real value, so you do all you can to check out the validity of your records. Any reader of any literature should consider the source, before forming an opinion. We aren't all professionals, but we can give the source of our information, even if it was Grandmother Sally, as she sat on her porch stringing beans.

But wait, we've forgotten to show our badge, our credentials! I never ask for anything without giving as well. It's just a neighborly thing to do....aren't we talking *family* here? I would, first of all, introduce myself by mentioning a family person we may have in common. I state that I am a teacher by profession who just became interested in finding all the cousins in my family.

I would not mention writing a book at this time for several reasons. It puts the product ahead of the importance of the person; and the cousin suddenly suspects he is just going to become another consumer. I want to be appreciated for the unique contribution I can make to a project before I enter into it. Is the purpose of this pursuit to make money or to bring the family together? First things first. As I said earlier, each time you present yourself, you are also being scrutinized, and they don't **have** to participate.

Another item I take with me is my four-generation chart which shows how I relate to the family line. This acts as a quick **visual aid** which does not get bogged down in a lot of genealogical jargon. This could separate you from your potential disciple. This chart serves a lot of purposes as an introduction. It spells out that you have a plan, and that it can be looked upon as a new form of crossword puzzle.

In scanning it they will see all the **allied families** that come into the heritage through the wives, (which at that time you remind them, is 50% of their lineage). You can usually use some of the **alternate spellings** so they can see that the name was often changed. You can point out the early deaths, the tragic stories you've heard that altered their lives, the importance of recurring middle names, mentioning the other family members who have contributed some of that very information. This has never failed to evoke questions and comments of interest. It may even get you some new immediate leads on surnames they see. You will be showing them visually how many people they are descended from. The blanks on the chart point out that there are missing links that still hold secrets. All this to whet their appetites for more that brings the family together.

At this point, you bring out a **one-family chart** and begin to fill it in to get them started. If you feel they want to, by all means ask them to fill it in for you. Point out that this chart shows siblings who may have photos and information, and you need their married names.

Depending on the time element and availability of your new acquaintance, it may be wise to call again as a **follow-up**. By this time, you will have had time to digest this new information, and perhaps make copies of your charts to mail back. If the new friend has shared photos, you may want to make camera copies and give them a negative in appreciation. Then they can have multiple copies to share with their children as a result of your visit. This is one of the many ways my husband gets involved. We keep our camera and an adjustable copy stand in the trunk of the car. **You must capture the moment.**

I cannot say enough times that *you may never pass this way again, and find the same people available to share with you.* Events in both our lives change our plans, and genealogy has you going in many directions, trying to capture these valuable stories before they get away.

To us as genealogists, **communication** is everything, and we do well to cultivate all its forms to aid us. Unless we learn to communicate our needs, we make it difficult to retrieve information from the librarians, record-holding agencies, and even fellow researchers. We have to realize that these persons serve many others, and their time is valuable.

Try to set up a sympathetic relationship by joining a society of researchers, or visit a relative, or make an appointment with a librarian, any one of whom becomes a **partner** in your research. All the letter writing in the world does not reap the rewards of real live conversation with someone who can help us.

But sometimes you cannot make a long trip until summer, and you want to make an initial contact. Here are some hints to make **letter writing** easier:

• Introduce yourself in a warm personal way, giving some of your background and experience. Discuss your goals briefly, including publishing of a book if this is true. (People value their privacy today...there's so little of it left.)
• State the common ancestry you are seeking.
• Be specific. Enclose a portion of your chart with a brief explanation.
• Keep it simple. This is not a genealogist, and you want to appeal to everyone, no matter what his background.
• You may prefer to just list up to five questions that can be quickly answered, instead of a chart to be filled out.
• **Always enclose** a SASE for a prompt reply. (Self Addressed Stamped Envelope)

Sometimes you find someone else researching the same surname as you...people you haven't met in other states who are descended from the brothers and sisters of your ancestor. You can get their names from the Latter Day Saints library, societies and periodicals. This makes you feel supported as you share your information. You can never have too many cousins, *as long as they don't all visit at the same time.*

GET YOUR SPOUSE INVOLVED

Though it's important to feel our families appreciate our research, we become especially anxious when our spouses are not involved. Most of us are completing information for our children's legacy, so we want to include our spouse's ancestors as well.

The *don't bother me with that stuff* syndrome is the same one that takes over when our spouse is reluctant to go to church. It does no good to agonize over it. Anyway, I well remember that until ten years ago I felt no urgency to get into genealogy either. I found out my parents had been interviewed by my cousin, Audrey, who was already convinced of the merits of genealogy. That's fine for her, I thought, and maybe someday I'll talk to her about it. I had not yet confronted the fragility of life in a personal way. So I try to be patient with all those who have not yet had a *conversion.*

In all these cases, if you show an excitement, an enthusiasm for what you are doing, others may become curious about it. If you try to show how rewarding it has been for you, they may want some of those rewards. Though you feel, as I do, that you are learning so much, and becoming adept at research, you must not flaunt that attitude. It may be misunderstood as conceit.

Instead, communicate the fact that you simply care about your heritage, and don't want your family to be forgotten. Relate some of the unusual facts you've found, and assure your spouse that there's a whole set out there waiting for him/her as well. I automatically wrote in as much of my spouse's history as I could find, and asked him to come in the library with me a few times. He could bring his own work from the office. We worked at the same table, and everytime I found an interesting fact, I showed it to him. I got him to fill out some call slips on his family areas. He agreed to do one stack of books, if I would get them. He neatly wrote them out, and searched the indexes, and then said he was going out for coffee. I didn't see him until lunchtime.

That was his attitude, until one day I persuaded him to read his great-grandfather's will from the large leather-bound ledger. In the ornate writing he read, "And I leave to my wife, Drucie, my house..." Well he was hooked! "Look at that...he called Drucilla, Drucie; how about that!" It seems that this dry research suddenly took on a real human aspect, and this William Spurrier was someone he may want to know.

He still is too active to sit there and read very long; says he's *too busy living life to read or write about it.* But I want to tell you the long list of things he DOES do. Because we live with people, we do not own them. We can only hope they will support us when we need it, and understand our goals, especially when they are not **their** goals.

1. To begin with, we communicate well because we had a lot in common when we married years ago. Our relatives and ancestors lived very near each other, so we are at home in the territory.

2. He is always happy to take me along on business trips; and while he goes to meetings, I go to the library. He searches them out and checks the hours, drops me off with a "Good luck!" and picks me up with "Did you find anyone?" I have no parking problems.

258

3. He keeps his ears open at the office, and suggests co-workers call me if interested in genealogy, and I will help them.

4. He has asked others if their family history has been written; could he borrow a copy for me to preview?

5. He saves me all his dimes and quarters for photocopying.

6. He likes to learn new skills, so experimented with copying our antique photos. He now takes the camera and copy stand on all our trips. While I take down notes and tape interviews, he copies their photos. He recently bought us a camcorder. Now we'll really turn out some productions!

7. He has heard so many different personal stories from my research, that by now he knows each new cousin represents a new outlook and perspective on life.

8. He can always think of other things to do while I'm in a library...grease the car, get a haircut, look up an old friend, take his desk work to the city park where he won't be interrupted with phone calls. If he were miserable, I would be, and I'd go with other researchers. I don't want to feel so indebted.

9. He studied the genealogy software to be knowledgeable about printing out charts and various lists for me. I enter all the research which I personally have done in the library, and he extracts it in whatever form I need.

10. If I go to present a program, he often accompanies me and sets up the audio-visual equipment I need. I am not oriented to machines so I appreciate the assistance. I think women make a mistake when they show men they do not need them. People step aside when not needed, and made to feel that way. We are so busy that we split up the skills to complement one another. Whoever is better at it, does it!

11. He has business contacts who give me lots of ideas for publishing my book, getting publicity, securing speakers for

programs, workshops in leadership, media techniques. He calls it
being my agent.

12. He approaches every Monday with, "Where are you
going this week?" instead of "Are you still doing that?" I guess
it's called respect. If we were all alike we wouldn't need respect
and tolerance.

13. He took the time to help me design a brochure and
certificates of appreciation for our society, and suggested borders
and layout. He proofreads and gives me new ideas. He makes all
my projects *happen.*

14. He will do research if my goals are clear and
objectives specific. I guess it's similar to me helping him in HIS
office.

15. He bought an RV...no, not out of desperation so we
could camp in the library parking lot, and he could watch the ball
game. But that is partly right! We had the RV before I got into
genealogy, but found it gave us more choices. When we go to a
library, he can be comfortable, and I can grab a sandwich and rest
a while. If parking is a problem he moves on to the city park.
More about RVs in Chapter 14.

16. He saw that my papers were going to be
overwhelming, and it would be hard to get into bed at night. So
he helped me fix up a room in the basement with a desk made of a
door resting on two file cabinets.

17. He has made frames and assisted with mounting
heirlooms on the wall as decor.

18. He has helped me with transcribing tombstones by
holding back the brambles, and lifting fallen stones, while I did
the recording.

19. He really got hooked when I found an article and
portrait of his great-grandfather, Christian Smith, in a 1901 issue
of the B&O Magazine. It described the old gentleman's entire
career on the railroad from a teamster to an engineer. His blind

wife died a tragic death when she caught her clothes on fire at the fireplace. The newspaper obituary, the stories of a haunted house, all turned a genealogy in a drama to be told. He recently volunteered to speak to our society. He's come a long way.

I realize that some of these things may not apply for **women spouses.** But I always think it foolish for women to stay completely away from their husband's interests. Even if you don't enjoy research, you meet some of the people your husband works and shares with. Genealogists are interested in anyone with a surname and a family history. We all qualify on those terms. Attend the society meetings and hear some of the interesting speakers. Many speak on artifacts, trips to other lands, local historical areas, photographs, and much of the time they are illustrated by slides or visuals. A family history includes a husband AND wife, so let us get to know the OTHER side of the family...at least **once!**

I think it all boils down to the fact that we have something to be enthusiastic about, and the opportunity to share it. Before I get too philosophical here, I might mention that my spouse knows that I have something I can do for the two months he will be watching sports on TV. Things have a way of justifying themselves.

ORGANIZE YOUR NOTES

As I implied, I'm one of the lucky persons whose husband says I'll put up another shelf, build on a room, or buy another file cabinet when I complain about all the paper I have strewn around the house. He patiently steps over the piles on the floor, waits while I clear off the bed so he can go to sleep, and foolishly hands me the genealogy mail when I should be starting dinner.

I have been through just about every stage of organization that you could possibly try; and I DO believe that they should change with your needs. Diversity is our strength as societies, and as we observe what works for others, we can choose what is best for us. I want to share some of the methods for your consideration.

In the beginning, about nine years ago, I could suffice with a small address book. In it I had written all the names, about

20, with approximate birth and death dates, maybe spouses. In each library, I took it to the card catalog and copied lists of references. I had also included my husband's line to keep him involved. He is my support system and I wanted him to have something personal to rejoice about as well. I was taking notes in a notebook which I tried to alphabetize to add to surname files when I got home. With most all my research in the same counties I found it hard to stick to one or two surnames.

My friend, Audrey, uses index cards for vital statistics. These she organizes into the file box when she returns home. Each card holds the info on one household with dates and children's names. She cross-indexes with the spouse's name. Dividers could have the name of the family line or be sorted alphabetically. See samples below:

```
Bauer, William Ernest        Ba 3
b.  5/23/1878   d. 2/12/1957   see
Baltimore, Md.   USA           Ba4
m.  4/30/1902  Myers, Agnes
Occ. strawhat mfg. M.S. Levy Co.
Father Bauer George
Mother Bauer, Bonnett, Elizabeth
Children William Frederick
Ethel Agnes      Mary Elizabeth
```

```
Bauer, Myers, Agnes           Ba4
b.  12/16/1880   d. 11/23/1940 see
Baltimore, Md.   USA           Ba 3
m.  4/30/1902 Bauer, Wm. E.
occ.  housewife
Father  Myers, Frederick
Mother Myers, Miller, Elizabeth
Children  William Frederick
Ethel Agnes,   Mary Elizabeth
```

We're starting to find more information now, and we need more space, so we notice the person with a whole **notebook of family charts**. These are divided by family and can be quickly filled in with new information, having spaces for each type. There is always lots of paper for other notes. Keep these rules in mind: libraries only allow **pencils**; write only on **one side of your paper**. Reserve a page for Future Research to record references or clues to pursue on your next visit.

Let me suggest, at this stage, that it is a good idea to keep a **bibliography page** in the front of your notebook. Number each reference and include the complete title, author, call number, library housing it. When you need to give it as a reference, just write the #. All logging is good, but if you find yourself re-copying, it takes too much time.

To remember when I answered letters and what I sent, I either make a copy of my answer, or note right on the letter the date and what I sent and keep it in my **correspondence file**. It gets pretty embarrassing if you send the same thing twice; and you do forget because it may be months before you find new items to exchange.

Some persons, like Jim, take a whole **file box** to the library, or files in a nice neat briefcase. Now they look so business-like and professional. They are the same ones that take time to go to a nice restaurant for a lunch break, I suppose. Often, I am dropped off for the whole day and have to have my survival bag for any emergency that may occur.

But people with **file folders** obviously maintain a cabinet at home with a drawer of family files. Into these go all manner of paper...maps, narrative from published histories, charts, and primary source material. A file can just be a cardboard box of legal sized width. When I asked one friend about her files, she assured me she only brings worksheets from the files to the library, leaving the source materials at home for safe keeping. One member relates that she has two copies of her collection and keeps one in the freezer in case of fire. Another has a copy with another relative.

My research became so fruitful for a time, that I needed visual representation. So I invested in a **12-generation chart** . I had learned some calligraphy, so I spent a weekend proudly entering names on it. I would only put in ink the ones that had been verified, the rest would be in pencil. I found myself getting out that chart so many times to show relatives and get them interested, that it became dog-eared. So my resourceful husband suggested he photocopy the chart in sections and mount it on large legal folders. This also enabled me to take it to libraries as a reference tool, and not knock out a whole table when I opened it up. There is only SO much space you are allowed.

The basement is where I have what is now MY room. Here you can see evidence of most all these methods of organization. I believe most of us who are addicted and spending years at this will use a combination of methods. My area consists of shelves holding books and boxes for periodicals. A four-drawer **file cabinet** holds handouts and articles on general and specific topics, state files hold library and local aids for trips. Another drawer holds **surname files** of research notes, charts and related information. The notebook I take to libraries directly relates to these files. I leave the documents here for safe keeping. One of the drawers is reserved this year for the Howard County Genealogical Society and a file for each of 12 committees.

Prominently taking over a desk along the wall is an Apple Macintosh **computer, printer, and typewriter.** A clock, calendar, phone and a clamp-on lamp completes all I need to feel organized. The computer was a big decision and you must learn how to speak to it, or it will not work for you. But work for you it will, and will print out your charts in so many ways. You will feel as though you've published your book when you see it so neatly displayed. It can be understood by everyone, and stands less chance of being thrown away. The charts it prints are more concise, and can be used as worksheets in the libraries. Printed for only one family at a time, you can file them into your notebook and divide your larger chart. Printed as an ahnentafel (German for ancestor table), it will give friends a list of surnames and dates.

If you choose software which will print out lists in certain order, you may want to list all the ancestors by areas of research. It will make up a listing of a particular county and state when you plan a visit. I have print-outs for every county and state I am currently researching in. When you live in a high-tech world, use it to help you, if you can.

I have not discussed collecting photos. Often relegated to boxes and albums, I would like to recommend using 3-ring pages and mounting them together as families with charts nearby. I plan to insert these photo pages between the narrative stories, maps, and charts to complete my family story. Eventually, I will fill several notebooks divided into family groups. Let me also bring to your attention one suggestion on using maps to enhance your story. Don't forget the value of enlarging or reducing maps to pinpoint certain areas. Reducing often allows you to show relationships without having to cut or fold-out something of unwieldy size. This idea is from Peter, a retired geographer, who also showed me how he photocopies group photos, leaving space around them. This becomes a key on which he labels the individuals in the group, or adds information about the occasion.

Overall, I find that a loose-leaf notebook is my answer to the best method. It can be reorganized or supplemented without much trouble. It is inexpensive but the contents are invaluable. Being organized just means having respect for the materials and the time you have spent gathering them. Keep them in such a way that they will serve you and allow even a stranger to understand and retrieve them. I assume no responsibility for the success of these methods, as it is inversely proportional to your years of accumulation, the size of your office, and the patience of your spouse or housemate.

Stryker-Rodda, Harriet, HOW TO CLIMB YOUR FAMILY TREE. Baltimore, MD: Genealogical Publishing Co. 1983

Ichholz, Alice, THE RED BOOK. UT: Ancestry Publishing Co., 1989. American state, county and town sources

Eakle, Arlene & Johni Cerny, THE SOURCE. UT: Ancestry Publishing Co. 1984. Ackermann and Towle, GENEALOGICAL AND PERIODICAL ANNUAL INDEX

Ackermann and Towle, GENEALOGICAL And PERIODICAL INDEX. MD: Heritage Books, Inc. 1987

EVERY

MEETING

OF PERSONS

IS AN

EXCHANGE

OF GIFTS

12

PERSONS ARE GIFTS

Persons are gifts which God sends to me...wrapped!

Some are wrapped very beautifully; they are attractive when I first see them. Some come in very ordinary wrapping paper. Others have been mishandled in the mail. Once in a while there is a "Special Delivery!"

Some persons are gifts which come loosely wrapped; others, very tightly...but the wrapping is not the gift. Sometimes the gift is very easy to open up, but often I need others to help. Maybe they have been opened up before and thrown away.

I am a person, therefore, I am a gift, too. A gift to myself, first of all. God gave myself to me! Perhaps I've never accepted the gift that I am.

I love the gift which those who love me give me; why not the gift from God?

And I am a gift to other persons. Do others have to be content with the wrapping, never permitted to enjoy the gifts?

EVERY MEETING OF PERSONS
IS AN EXCHANGE OF GIFTS

Let us celebrate the gifts who come to us...some regularly, some sporadically. Let us unwrap with reverence and rejoice to discover the many gifts of God.

(Excerpts used with permission of
Sister Anne Marie Gardiner, SSND)

EVERY MEETING OF PERSONS
IS AN EXCHANGE OF GIFTS

So look into the rewards of your local genealogical society. After finding out that your family thinks you've got to be crazy to spend all that time in research, you long for a group that understands you. Maybe here you'll get some group therapy! When you tell them the symptoms you're having, perhaps they will suggest a cure.

Check the phone book and call for information about the group; go to at least one meeting. Maybe they will help make it simpler, and certainly more pleasurable, having people who share your frustrations and celebrate your discoveries.

Let me tell you of my first experience. My phone call put me in touch with an enthusiastic person who gave me the address of a school, and mentioned that they meet once a month in the media center. This is to encourage sharing and display of materials that are brought by the members. After a business meeting of 12 committee activity reports, the program speaker brought everyone insight into research techniques. Refreshments were available later, and the sales and browsing tables continued.

After attending, signing in the guest book, receiving a name badge, I was asked to introduce myself along with other visitors during the business meeting. I felt like one of the group already when I gave the four surnames I was researching. Several members spoke to me afterward. They also directed me to their computerized surname indexes, which have all the names the members are researching, and the locality. I found a member that very night who shares the same ancestor with me. Needless to say, I joined...and four years later found I was president.

Not being up on Robert's Rules of Order, I wasn't sure I could handle it. Then I remembered some of my teaching background, and realized that *participatory management* would involve everyone. Anyhow that makes us all responsible for the success or failure of a project.

Remembering Sister Anne Marie's meditation that the sharing of our gifts enriches us all, I prepared a Gift List of types of committees and activities we (the board) would like to RECEIVE volunteers for. In exchange the members were to prepare a list of programs they would like to have GIVEN. But it wasn't that simple. A lot of lists were not handed in, but still the short-term goals were set. Big projects were divided into small portions, so we always had a measure of success.

We still had no program chairman, and that is the main focus of our meetings. We decided to ask a different member for each month to be the program leader, contact the speaker, see to his/her needs, introduce and thank him afterward. That turned out to be a wonderful idea because:

    a. It got more members responsibly involved.
    b. It provided visual interest and recognition.
    c. It gave me support, as president, for the total
       success of the meeting.
    d. It allowed each leader the freedom to present in
       a way comfortable to him/her.

I prepared a list of program topics from various sources, and especially asked the membership for ideas. I deliberately avoided ethnic subjects, as only a portion of the membership would come. I chose more basic topics, such as: use of MAPS, NEWSPAPERS, PASSENGER LISTS, MIGRATION, holdings of local LIBRARIES, PERIODICALS, PATRIOTIC ORGANI-ZATIONS, MILITARY RECORDS. I found that some of the members who suggested topics became the best program leaders. They were acquainted with the speakers, who sometimes were their neighbors.

Since we had so many different program leaders, I thought it a good idea to prepare a guide sheet outlining all of the appropriate procedures in setting up programs. If you should want to use this, write me for a copy.

If you haven't much money to pay a renowned speaker, you may want to each contribute a portion of the fee, as though you were attending a regional conference. Some speakers may come to represent their COMPANIES and set up DISPLAYS to sell. In this case, there should be no fee. I'm thinking of genealogical BOOKSTORES, and PUBLISHING HOUSES who guide you as you write your book. We found the latter an extremely good talk with slide illustrations.

The local COMMUNITY COLLEGE may have some medical professors to speak on genetics, HISTORY professors who specialize in European countries, PSYCHOLOGY teachers who give insight into the importance of self-esteem as related to genealogy. The English department offers a course in creative WRITING. They may even offer a speaker on GENEALOGY as ours does.

The public SCHOOL TEACHERS may have conducted projects involving genealogy with their students. Working with video and theater, they have presented local history through a child's eyes. One middle school conducts a study by visiting a nearby cemetery and spending the day.

Watch the newspapers for articles on new AUTHORS, local history SEMINARS and TOURS, ARCHAEOLOGY, MILITARY REENACTMENTS, CIVIL WAR buffs. They may never have thought of themselves as genealogists, but they have a story to tell.

I cannot remind you enough to look to the expertise in the MEMBERSHIP. Unless you have known each other all your lives, you have no idea what unique experiences they have had that may help you with your research. Some that come to mind are: BOOK REVIEWS representing a wide variety, membership in PATRIOTIC SOCIETIES, OVERSEAS RESEARCH trips and how to prepare for them, and little known library collections we've discovered. I share ideas with many other societies, and one had a forum consisting of members who each chose a different chapter of THE SOURCE. This huge, wonderful book we use like a dictionary, with never enough time to read the whole thing.

Another source to look into are RETIRED PERSONS who can give you the benefit of their experience. I'm thinking of a retired doctor who researches CIVIL WAR MEDICINE and speaks in costume, and an ANTIQUE dealer who teaches you to evaluate your artifacts.

Some local elderly TEACHERS who like to reminisce may give you a first hand look at the early days of your county. In fact, someone could interview them, and show some of those ORAL HISTORY techniques. Often the HISTORICAL SOCIETY sponsors these projects.

And don't forget the BLACK HISTORY of the area. It is studied through looking at the white history as well. Perhaps there is a resident who could relive the *not-so-good old days.* Every new member is a new set of experiences. The diversity of our group gives us all more resources to choose from. **Every meeting of persons is an exchange of gifts.**

Some societies turn at least one annual meeting into a workshop. We learn some skills with hands-on experience. Ideas for these include bringing in photos to be camera-copied, doing research from member's volumes (varying the topics from ethnic, church records, geographic collections). Learning to use preservation techniques and use of the computer for genealogy are two more. Other workshop topics are listed below:

• Challenge the group to *come to terms with terms* by defining a list of 100 most encountered by the genealogist. Use a reference titled CONCISE GENEALOGICAL DICTIONARY by Maureen and Glen Harris—Ancestry, Inc. Reward the winner with a free membership.

• Encourage communication with at least one meeting to get better acquainted.

• Bring in ethnic FOODS and a folk DANCE teacher.

• Have a SHOW AND TELL, leaving the item or story up to the inspired. Better find out how many in advance to allow enough time. Set a timer.

• ROLE PLAY your favorite ancestor, wear his name tag, apparel, or carry an artifact that he used. Answer all questions as though you were he.

• Show a film, possibly on immigration, discuss.

• Schedule the meeting in another location and build your program around it. "A Walk Through the Courthouse" or "Genealogy in the Public Library" helps us become familiar with local resources. Encourage car-pooling for those resistant to change, and provide good maps.

It is especially beneficial to invite speakers from your own community. It shows we are in liaison with one another, and we recognize their contributions. We may even meet on another occasion as neighbors, and if we need additional information at a later date, they are close by. On a practical note, neighbors don't have to allow travel time and expense.

I definitely believe all visiting speakers should be offered an honorarium, no matter how small, in appreciation of their expertise and the time they spent preparing their talk. If they represent a government facility, they will probably not accept it, as it is part of their job. Other speakers may turn it back to you, as a donation; but that should be their choice. Some societies offer a

272

free membership which entitles them to a monthly newsletter and other benefits.

One speaker I am acquainted with asked me to be specific about the outline of the program, and not throw in a workshop after the presentation. Other suggestions he made:

- print handouts as given.
- consider transportation costs.
- confirmation near date.
- refreshments...perhaps a beverage before speaking.

I suggest the program leader give the speaker some idea of the needs of the group, perhaps suggest a few questions he might use to direct his talk. We are considering a talk on the courthouse, but we are afraid the lawyer may use a lot of jargon. I would suggest that he take us on an imaginary tour of any courthouse, outlining the various sections and what they house. Then he could be specific about his own situation, and we could put it in perspective.

Some groups may have a question box for the speaker. This allows shy members some input, encourages attentive listening, and the speaker may study the questions during the business meeting.

We have recently drawn up CERTIFICATES of APPRECIATION in two forms: one for **member**/speakers which states we are fortunate to have you as a member, and entitles them to a one-year paid membership. The other for **visitor**/speakers states we respect your background of experience and time in preparation. We hope you will visit us again. We include a check in this one.

Most genealogical society meetings I have attended in other places have some excellent speakers, but that seems to be the only reason they convene. The gatherings represent the typical formal business meeting set-up, as this seems to make everyone feel professional, serious and intellectual. Often the seating is stationary and it limits your possibilities. This is a carry-over from the old school where the teacher was authoritarian and all wisdom in that room was going to emanate from him/her.

Now learning takes place only when you realize that one way does not suit all. For all you organized people, yes we must

have structure, but it should not control you...you control it!
"Managers do things right; leaders do the right thing!" So say the
writers, Warren Bennis and Burt Nanus in their book,
"LEADERS—Strategies For Taking Charge."

We need enough structure for continuity and organization,
but enough freedom to welcome new ideas. People learn in many
different ways and styles. They are as varied in adults as they are
in children. The key to learning is communication, and the setting
I just described is usually one-way. If good questions are asked,
specific needs can be met...but some people are hesitant to speak
up. If visuals are used, the talk is more supported. If hand-outs
are given, time does not have to be spent taking notes.

Don't overlook one of your best resources...each other!
There is so much to gain by coming together to share our gifts of
expertise, experience, and resources, as well as support and
fellowship when we need it. Our gifts are returned in many ways,
and in proportion to our giving. If you work on a committee,
your contacts are sources of help. But you must communicate
your needs: exchange problems for solutions, books for
conversation, questions for clues. We have a lot of answers in
each of our members.

CLIMATE OF OPENNESS

We feel this is best accomplished by creating a climate of
openness where you are encouraged to share. Here are some
suggestions:

1. Set up a BROWSING TIME prior to the business
meeting. Members are asked in the newsletter, which is mailed
prior to the meeting, to bring related items to display and share.
This is a deliberate effort to keep each gathering unique. We never
know who will bring what, and we don't want to miss anything.
If you want to be sure SOMEONE is bringing something, call a
few and request their contribution.

2. We meet in the MEDIA CENTER of a school because
there are tables and chairs for grouping, and media equipment if
we need it. The computer room is adjacent when we've had
demonstrations. Of course, the presence of books always makes
us feel at home.

3. Since this browsing time is on-going, members can
come at the time most convenient. It is a good time for committees

274

to hold short *corner meetings.* VISITORS come into a room filled with friendly conversation and activity, where they can easily be welcomed and oriented in advance of the meeting. We encourage first-time visitors to bring a family chart to help introduce themselves. This assures them an immediate response. Though some may think this time unnecessary, let me point out that this develops communication and creates avenues for assisting each other. A casual mention of a problem may get you a lot of help. I've been told many times, that they didn't tell me because I never asked!

4. We issue NEW MEMBER PACKETS at the time they join. These are prepared by the membership chairman with sample charts, library hours, shelf list, committee needs, cards for the surname index, a reminder to send queries to the newsletter, and a sample newsletter.

A yearly award could be presented to the person bringing in the most new members. The chairman introduces any new members during the business meeting.

5. We keep two GUEST BOOKS...one for visitors with addresses and one for speakers as a record for future programs. Badges are issued and collected from members. Stick-on badges are given visitors.

6. A new BROCHURE was prepared which is a bright yellow twice-folded legal sheet. Inside the first fold is stated the when, where, why of the meetings, and the purpose of the organization. When fully opened, the four sections are as follows: PREVIOUS PROGRAMS, ACTIVITIES, OFFICERS, APPLI-CATION FOR MEMBERSHIP. We have nothing printed on the back of the application, so it can be torn off and mailed in with the dues. It could be stapled and mailed as such, but we decided to draw a map for the back instead. A good brochure advertises for you, and is something that can be referred to and passed on to others. I never leave home without one. It represents the business we're in, if they ever need us.

7. Our SURNAME INDEXES have evolved from a card file to a computerized double listing...one by surname, and one by locality, both alphabetical. After two or three years of submitting names, the two lists were bound into spiral paperbacks and sold to members. They become obsolete after three more years, as research is completed and members change, so revision is inevitable.

8. We exchange NEWSLETTERS with nearby counties, and have these items and other indexes on a browsing table. Members are encouraged to bring in their library materials on a one-time basis for others to preview.

9. Members are asked to assist the PUBLICITY chairman by distributing fliers announcing the coming meetings. The newspaper announcements are clipped for the Scrapbook. We also utilize the Cable TV Bulletin Board.

10. A SALES TABLE is maintained offering members forms, charts, inexpensive paperbacks, "how-to" books, and new publications which can be ordered at a quantity discount. Members who have found an additional item may offer to send in an order with their own. This often includes archival materials.

11. CAR POOLS are organized by members who are attending a workshop, or a distant library. Much is shared going to and from the destination that increases our background of experience. FIELD TRIPS are organized twice a year by one member who takes reservations up to 14 for a van trip.

12. A BULLETIN BOARD is brought to each meeting for posting more details on items in the newsletter or announced at the meeting. Many cartoons and news articles are also displayed, as well as sign-up sheets.

13. Articles are collected and written by the NEWSLETTER editor for publication once a month. It includes a calendar of local genealogical events, research hints, recent field trips by members, personality sketch of a member, book reviews, news items of national genealogical interest, and previews of the upcoming meeting. Members can then come prepared in the spirit of anticipation.

14. HANDOUTS are planned for every meeting. Only those attending receive them...this is to encourage attendance.

OUTREACH

We have four outreach projects that tie us to community. This proves the validity of our organization in bringing people together.

EDUCATION: One member prepares lessons in genealogy to teach elementary and middle school-age students. She also has prepared a unit with the local historical society library and museum. A letter has been sent to the social studies department of

276

the school system encouraging genealogy to be used as a springboard into history.

BIBLE COPYING: Twice a year one member coordinates this project, securing photographer and library space, and publicity for the copying of these valuable records. These records are later filed in the library.

LIBRARY: Some libraries consider genealogists an asset; however our public library director considers us an outside group. So it was impossible to liaison and set up a working relationship. We asked permission to share space at the county historical society for our small collection of books. We also wanted to have a place to hold workshops, meet with beginning researchers, and be available to visitors who have questions. For a while we set up a Saturday Seminar Series which attracted beginners who later joined our group. Both societies have profited by sharing not only space, but also expertise and fellowship.

We donate about 20 books yearly and these are shelved adjacent to the historical society's collection. The librarian, Mary, is a member of both organizations, so that keeps it running smoothly. Kathy's family has lived in the area for generations, so she helps with local history as a regular volunteer

CEMETERY: This committee has had the continuing leadership that has published seven volumes of cemetery transcriptions in this county. Since increased building of homes has threatened small family gravesites, these volumes have acted as a registry to protect them. They are consulted regularly before a permit is issued.

We are working on getting more permanent legislation all over our state—Maryland. If you have found answers to this problem in your state, please let me hear from you.

SPECIAL COMMITTEES

Two more special committees have been formed from the interest of three members:

The COMPUTER INTEREST GROUP is headed by Charles, who tries to familiarize himself with all genealogy software and shareware. He is then prepared to give assistance to anyone interested in getting into computer records and charts.

The CABLE COMMITTEE is headed by a couple, Dan and Anne, who have obtained grants, written scripts, directed, produced, and edited nine half-hour programs for our local cable channel. The programs are all on facets of the joy of genealogy, from publishing your own book to telling about your black sheep.

Concerning black sheep, you probably don't know there is even a Society for the descendants of the Illegitimate Sons and Daughters of the Kings of Britain. (DISDKB) This group of 260 members can show acceptable proof of descent from same. Their aim is to encourage high quality in genealogical research, rather than slipshod work so common in the past in hereditary societies.

Another member wants to make up MEMBER YELLOW PAGES. A blank was handed out for each to fill and return to him. On it you would fill in name, address, phone, and where you felt you had a degree of experience to pass on, what library books you would be willing to consult, or share, whether you could present a program, etc.

At the end of the year, we once sponsored a GENEA-FEST. This was really another name for Open House to show the public what we are about. Headings were made for different tables, and we displayed samples of each category from the members. We took slides and turned what we did that day into a rear-projection slide/story. This was used later at the mall to publicize our society. We also handed out brochures, and ancestor charts to encourage everyone to join us.

To get everyone acquainted, we once had a MEMBER SEARCH. As members came in, they took a sheet and tried to get all the blanks filled. Note that each person can only sign ONE TIME. As you watch the person sign, you have time to connect the name and the face...if you will. Also when the sheet is completed, you have a reference if you ever want to have a little help on the topics.

278

```
              MEMBER SEARCH
    Our members have varied research experiences that can help
    us. Find each below and get their signatures, only once.
    Include yourself.
    1. Researching in Canada..................................
    2. My ancestors settled the Midwest......................
    3. My ancestors migrated to KY or TN.....................
    4. My family's from Carolina.............................
    5. Researching Germans...................................
    6. I've done Polish research.............................
    7. West VA searcher......................................
    8. I'm strong on PA......................................
    9. Looking for Scandinavians.............................
    10.A Mayflower descendant................................
    11.Quakers are part of my heritage.......................
    12.I have Texas ties.....................................
    13.Ask me about New England..............................
    14.I research New York...................................
    15.I represent a VA family...............................
    16.I help with military research.........................
    17.I have French/Acadian ancestry........................
    18.I can translate some languages........................
    19.I have a Howard Co.ancestor...........................
    20.My ancestors came from Ireland........................
    21.I've done overseas research...........................
    22.I have a Huguenot ancestor............................
    23.I organize notes on computer..........................
    24.I have a black sheep in my family.....................
    25.I'd like to be president next year....................
```

When you want to give an award or thank all the leaders for their support, you may want to issue the GOLDEN "G" AWARD. This is a wooden letter spray-painted gold with a pin glued to the back. As you wear this pin and people ask you what the "G" is for, you'll have a reason to talk about Genealogy. Hardly anyone ever gives us an opportunity.

I see the role of a genealogical society as three-fold—as a board to **motivate**, as members to **communicate**, as a society to **educate** the community to preserve family history. With the mix of beginner and experienced, new and old members, timid and gregarious, we've provided a framework of choices. Diversity is our strength, and we learn from it.

GETTING OTHERS INTERESTED IN GENEALOGY

Doing the research involved in a **thorough** study of one's family is not for everyone, as it involves a lot of time and record-keeping. And until one begins, it appears to be **only** that. But it is my feeling that everyone becomes curious about his roots, and wishes he could find something interesting about his past.

What motivates people to study their family history? I surveyed many genealogists to find a wide variety of reasons. Perhaps you will identify with some. Some, like Dick, find old documents with new and unusual information. In his case, emigration papers listed his grandfather with an entirely different surname. Carolyn and I were reminded of the need for records when a relative passed away. Others, including Ed, Mary, and Marvin, were given research papers of older cousins or grandparents, and they felt responsible for finishing the project.

Goals vary from Robert's, who wants to find his family's original coat-of-arms, to Dick, who wants to complete a 100-year history of his great-grandparents who came to America in 1890. Mary and Bill are planning to start a computer search business. This would be especially helpful for Peter and Robert who want to locate every person in the U. S. who shares their family name.

Finding out her ancestor was tried for witchcraft just piqued Doris' curiosity for more. To balance out, she later found she also shares the ancestry of several presidents and one Mayflower immigrant. John is proud of his lighthouse keeper, as is Lee of his railroad pioneer. Carolyn was given a personalized tour of the historic Massey house, and her husband, Charles, descends from an early covered bridge builder.

Serendipity seems to guide others, like Jim and Anne, to accidently discover ancestors while browsing through old cemeteries. John and Eileen have taken trips overseas to track down those Irishmen; and Kathy often combines business with pleasure, doing research and bringing back brochures for us.

It's safe to say, all of us do some traveling...New England, Texas, Wisconsin, overseas, to the ends of the earth and over the rainbow, if the answers were there.

Notebooks seem to be the best way to organize our findings; and we usually make every effort to compile one for each of our grandparent's family lines. If there is enough interest from others in the family, we have each notebook printed or published, and include any input we can gather from the descendants.

So you see, we're not sitting in a monastery somewhere working over our manuscripts, but out and about trying to "put flesh on the bones" of our ancestors, and telling stories you wouldn't believe...until you join us!

So I don't turn every conversation into a genealogy *soapbox,* and bore my friends; I decided to offer to hold orientation classes for anyone as they become interested. By advertising in the paper once a month, it would remind people that instruction is available on a regular basis, and others are very actively pursuing this study...why not you?

I would encourage you to do this in your community, by following these simple suggestions:

• If you are a beginner, seek out the library or genealogical society and suggest that they sponsor a workshop. Or find the town historian or genealogist and ask him to start one.

• I like the term *workshop* as it implies two-way communication as opposed to lecture. Make sure you allow time for individual questions.

• Be sure to term it a workshop for **"beginners"** to attract the largest number of people who feel they will not be intimidated. Most people with any experience will have already oriented themselves and possibly joined a society. However, you may want to word it to include those who have recently moved into the area, and are beginning in a new location.

• I always encourage people to call my number in advance to register for materials and secure information. At this time, I can assess their needs, mention the donation and handouts, make suggestions of things they may want to bring, or visits to take prior to the workshop.

• Take down the name and phone number of each caller, in case of emergency, or for future reference. However, I have asked others to fill in for me when I found I could not be there.

• I hold these workshops in the library of the historical society, which is where we house books on local history and genealogy. It is smaller than the public library and not as widely used. I have volunteered there for many years, helping patrons as they dropped in. It occurred to me that holding the workshops there would acquaint others with the inventory and provide another suggestion for research. The larger public library does not have space for small groups, but does sponsor one three-day workshop a year on genealogy, and one of the librarians, Sylvia Waters, is a Genealogical Specialist.

Our county also has a community college which offers a course each semester in genealogy. We support each other by suggesting further instruction on different levels.

Here is an outline of topics and materials I cover in a typical workshop session.

1. Get acquainted with what goals each person would like to accomplish with their family history, so I can help them achieve these goals. Some bring charts and documents which piqued their interest, and they begin to respond to each other. This is a great opportunity to point out the rewards only communication can give.
2. That then gives me an excuse to tell them that in ten

years I have found 101 rewards in my experiences.

3. I explain the importance of staying organized, with use of forms, documentation, notebooks, or computer.

4. Five-Generation Chart and how to fill it in properly.

5. One-Family Chart and importance of siblings for clues.

6. Examples of letters sent for information from a new cousin or a library or archives.

7. Listing of all major libraries and archives in area, hours, addresses and phone numbers.

8. How To Get The Most From A Library...procedures to assist you in obtaining information from the facility or librarian...anywhere.

9. How and where to look for clues...a checklist.

10. Sampling of kinds of books where information is available...county histories, marriage, cemetery records, wills, newspaper abstracts, etc.; allow time for browsing.

11. Invitation to join the County Genealogical Society and return to the library for research. I also encourage them to call me if they have further pitfalls.

By this time, I feel they sense my sincerity, and have received handouts and as much as we could get in to two hours. Their donation would be appreciated and will help us to buy another book.

This book is about creating opportunities. We seem to want to tackle things in our own independent way, write our book, do our research OUR way, at our own pace. So once we get these creative juices flowing, just give us room and we'll turn out something unique. Also, a creative group does not perpetuate itself, but continually evaluates its unique needs and satisfies them with achievable goals. People tend to think the experts are from out-of-town, but remember, "Every meeting of persons is an exchange of gifts." Find out what gifts you can share.

PRESERVING YOUR COMMUNITY

13

WHATEVER HAPPENED TO THE GOOD OLD DAYS?

"Things ain't like they used to be"...(and never was!)
"All the good things are gone"...(gone or just replaced?)
"I hardly know anyone anymore"...(maybe we need introductions!)
"You can't go home again"...(then where is home?)
"Whatever happened to the good old days?" (Why, they're stored away...waiting to be discovered again!)

I've said all those things myself, and those are the best answers I can come up with. I'm pleased my husband and I grew up in a small town because we knew what it meant to have an *extended family* long before it became something you had to cultivate. The whole town was your extended family; they knew you well...and you'd better not change without their permission. (I don't think you'd ever get it anyway!)

You never had to have your credit checked, unless you had recently moved in. Then you were under suspicion until you were *sponsored* by a long-time resident. We're sure you're not going to appreciate the town, because you aren't *from here*. You're going to be like a renter, instead of an owner...you haven't known the town enough to appreciate it.

Well I know now, that a new resident brings with him lots of experience in many fields that may enrich the town with his expertise. He may help us see with new vision what we have taken for granted all these years. You sometimes have to take a trip around the world to appreciate what was in your own backyard.

If a new resident is smart, he will try to work with the *natives* first, and get acquainted with their viewpoint, before he suggests any changes. The first thing the native wants to say is, "If you didn't like it the way it was, why did you come here?" It is security to those of us who were born in the town to be able to hang on to as much as we can support, but we must be willing to attend discussions concerning same. We are challenged to defend our motives...are we being practical or just sentimental?

The only thing *constant* is change; if we don't go forward, we will go backward, but we will change. My bones tell me that every day!

We're always hoping to bring back the *good old days* when everything seemed better, but was it really...or wasn't it the things we could always count on being there? The people who became *players* in our Game Of Life when we understood the rules. The places we frequented and the school and church we attended, with that same group of people. They made the days we spent there special, and it's hard to imagine the town without them. But they did go, a lot of them, and we need to change the rules.

So I'm of the opinion that we need both *roots and wings* as do our children. We will always feel at home with our earlier friends, but we need wings to feel free enough to be inventive and open to new ideas, experiences and friends. We may be cheating ourselves and missing out on something if we don't! So enjoy the best of both worlds...you're the link...as you are between the past and the future.

If we consider the past so important to remember, we should do all we can to keep a record of its people, history, activities, industry...anything that we value and want to share with future generations. Not only our children, but the new residents, will appreciate knowing the way it used to be, and we'll have something to pass on to them all. It's good to know a town has pride, and here are some ways to show it.

Genealogists and history students may come to your town needing information on its early residents and growth. Any person whose ancestors once lived in the town may return to find clues to the past. There are many places they will look. Perhaps you will be one of them...or you may be someone who will make sure the records are there for them.

TOWN RECORDS:
Are the early land and tax records at the town hall or in the county courthouse? Perhaps a Historical Commission can be appointed to organize and keep the records in a file open to researchers, by appointment. The ultimate is to have some local records copied and put in a library.

In our home town, the commission, headed by the Rev. Austin Cooper, and eventually Mary Margrabe, did a remarkable book on the history of the area. The book includes the leadership positions in business and government as they affected the growth of the town. The book strikes a nice balance between documented fact and recollection, giving credit to those most qualified on particular topics. They spent a lot of time getting residents to come together and reminisce, and took excerpts from the tapes they made. Using the local paper, they asked for photos and stories about the town. It's good to see a group of dedicated people unify the community in a project of that magnitude. Now when we get a family chart in every household, we'll have our history recorded *up close and personal.*

Even very small communities have an unofficial historian who has always taken an interest in the area, and studied it on his/her own. He may offer his expertise when there are inquiries. Sometimes this has been a young person, who, early in his life, enjoyed the Indian folklore or the excitement of nearby battlefields, and led tours for visitors. As a local genealogist, I have left a card for referral when needed. As a visitor, this will give you a friend who is acquainted with local resources.

National and state park rangers have programs, as do the scouts from time to time. If one is stationed near you, ask what background they can provide. Seek out history professors at nearby colleges to share their expertise and speak to the community. Ask if they would be willing to act as resource persons should the need arise, and construct a list to be consulted at the library or town hall. All of these things come under the heading of Public Relations, and leave visitors with positive feelings for the area.

NEWSPAPERS:
Where are back issues of the local paper kept? Someone could clip the obituaries from available issues and drop them into envelopes marked alphabetically. After a goodly number have been accumulated, several are photocopied on sheets of paper for preservation. Newsprint crumbles after a while.

Choose a favorite topic of your own to collect a history of in your community...the railroad, sports, school. Headline resumes of each year are usually printed in the December 31st issue.

Marriages and births, anniversaries, details of disasters, articles on the early history, awards, and outstanding citizens should be preserved. Make at least one copy of everything.

PERSONAL COLLECTIONS:

These are hard to find initially, but need to be noted and eventually donated to a library or museum. Scrapbooks and albums kept by teachers, ministers or anyone who's a saver. The longer we save, the more valuable it becomes. (My husband certainly hopes so...he's tired of building rooms on to the house!)

Photo collections—We had one man, Myer Kaplon, who enjoyed taking photos of everything and everybody...long before anyone anticipated the building would burn or the bridge would be replaced. His photos are housed at the local library as irreplaceable treasures. You could start making a photo history now of *your* lodge, workplace, street, or just the accidents, fires or natural disasters that called the community together. The fire company and ambulance crews would have documentation over the years. Yes, the newspaper does some of that, but your collection would specialize, and include your personal additions. These could be donated to the library or museum later, when back issues are hard to gain access to.

Another storekeeper, turned historian, gathered graduation photos for every class from our local high school. When there weren't group photos, he composed them by putting single ones into a composite. Though it took him several years and a personal monetary investment, the town is now indebted to Marion Burns for his unique contribution. His albums are in the museum for everyone to enjoy.

Other townspeople have collections of memorabilia that will find protection and preservation in the local museum.

TOWN MUSEUM:

This grew out of a festival situation where citizens displayed collections and crafts amongst food and drink. When a building became available, and there was enough interest in having a place where the artifacts could be housed, the museum took shape. Start small, and the rest of the town can help it grow and expand.

People feel needed in a small town, and those with the time and enduring interest can make things happen. Once in place, the museum and town can establish special days and celebrations. This is a good time to visit and see if your family is represented in the collections. You may be inspired to offer your help as a volunteer to catalog, be a docent, or donate some articles of his-

290

torical interest yourself.

At festival times, perhaps a registration table could be set up to help those interested in family history. A simple notebook, organized alphabetically by pioneer family, would provide space to register the visitor's name and address with the family they represent. (You may find some new cousins that way.) Another column may ask if they would like instruction in completing a family tree, or if they have one they would share, if contacted. This register could be kept in the reference section of the library for more daily use. Genealogists refer to these registers to find contacts they may interview or correspond with.

This information could be incorporated into a regular visitor register at the museum, but have the person indicate pioneer or visitor by checking a particular column, mentioning the family they descend from. I feel this shows everyone that we do have pride in our beginnings, and are always anxious to know more about the past.

Festival times are times to enlist the aid of some of the oldest residents who would like to share their memories and stories from the past. Give them identifying buttons which say, in BIG letters, "I've Been A Resident for ___ Years!" Station them at locations they know the most about. It gives such a personal touch for a visitor to hear stories first-hand. You generally judge a whole community by the few people you meet. On a trip west, I found myself not liking the whole state of Kansas because the nasty gas station attendant was the only one I had met! We don't realize how important first impressions are.

SCHOOLS:
Contact the Alumni Association to see if the records are available on the history of the local schools. Has anyone kept a record of the teachers before there were yearbooks? Perhaps the county Board of Education has some listing or history you could consult. Though reunions are primarily concerned with high school staff, it was the elementary teachers who knew you best. You spent most, if not all, your year with the same teacher. I know several who kept large scrapbooks of photos and classwork of note.

Other mementoes of general interest would be autograph books, programs, playbills, award ceremonies...anything that involved a great many students. You may be able to have the local

291

auction house call you whenever they receive what appears to be worthless paper, so you can sort through it for material of historical interest.

If you have school class photos that you are unable to identify, ask the local paper to run them with your name and phone number. It may remind others to do the same. The citizens of Winchester, Virginia got together all of the books and family papers they could find, and in one year they had the beginnings of one of the finest collections in Virginia. I believe the motivation came from the historical society, but would have been impossible without everyone's help. Once started, it isn't hard to convince others that you are seriously interested in preservation, and you, like they, would draw patrons from everywhere. Visit the Handley Public Library there and see.

If you have taken the time to make a collection you value, please leave instructions somewhere inside the cover, in your will or safe deposit box for its future care. Often out-of-town relatives do not realize their value to the community and your friends. Several years ago, a stranger presented the local library with a scrapbook of photos and poems put together in 1942 by our sixth grade teacher, Ms. Compton. He found it in a box of papers he had cleaned from her house when it was sold. Though he lived 100 miles away, he felt it really belonged to the town. We were fortunate he took the time to return it, and thanked him with a picture article in the paper. I hope this will encourage others to earmark some things for donation.

CHURCH RECORDS:
Church registers are sometimes kept at the church, but the very early records have usually been sent to the central archives of that particular denomination. Contact the particular minister for details.

Encourage your church to create a booklet on its history, if it hasn't already been done. It creates a pride to see its early beginnings, and the families who are responsible may still have descendants as members. Don't leave out the choir directors and organists...I was one, and sometimes both, for 35 years in three different Methodist churches. Perhaps there are special bulletins for services of dedication or remembrance of an historical event. Some now have booklets containing photos of all the families presently attending. Wouldn't we love to find some of those from the 1800's?

CEMETERIES:
Have the cemetery inscriptions been copied? If not, suggest it to a scout troop or do it yourself, as Mr. Holdcraft did for ALL of Frederick County, Maryland. This makes a ready reference for those who are not sure where the stone is located. It also is a permanent record should the stone be vandalized or eroded by weather. Titled NAMES IN STONE, these three volumes are indexed alphabetically, and cross-indexed at times.

If your local cemetery has not been recorded, all it takes is a notepad and pencil to create a record for your church or town. The usual form is to print in capitals, and place a slash (/) at the end of a line. Include any poetry, symbols, and try to pinpoint the location in the cemetery. This is done by diagramming in sections that relate to the road, fence, trees, and other landmarks. Record stones as they are located...do not alphabetize the record, only the index to the record. Placement of plots may indicate relationship. Be sure to sign and date the record.

Where I am living, we can hardly keep people from selling the land and building houses on the graves. In fact, just last month we saw grave stones being sold in a flea market. The seller said they were discarded when a local cemetery was *cleaned up.* He told us there was no law in our state against this. However, we are going to report it to the cemetery he named. We need better legislation to prevent this; speak to your representative.

Help to restore your local cemetery, so it will never be termed *abandoned.* Recently the JC's decided to sponsor a project by getting the town to donate the equipment, publicizing the day in the paper; and together they mowed, cleared and restored the town graveyard. Perhaps a community could do what New Orleans does...declare a festival day when all representatives of the families buried there come together and clean and decorate the graves. I call that real community!

Maybe attention can be called to special persons buried there by placing flags, or markers for the earliest burials, mayors, ministers, etc. A one-page map could orient a visitor. No, it has never been done before...but that's why **your** cemetery will be remembered. You show that just because they're gone, they're really not forgotten!

293

Another example of what a motivated person can do is Beulah Buckner. The day I met her was her first time at the county historical society library. She went through every file she could find, searching for black family history. I admitted that we had very little; that we only file what patrons give us. I told her that we would gladly accept any she could find elsewhere. Only one book had ever been written on our local black families. We had poll books which included blacks and manumission records we had published. But we had had no researchers specializing up to this point. She declared that from that day on, everything she finds she will copy for our files. We agreed that a black researcher would be able to extract more information from black citizens.

I have seen her many times since, doing research in every library she can find. I have offered her rides to new places. To date, she has located every black cemetery, black church and "colored school" in our county, traced many of the families, and even plans to write a book. She has also made appointments with the school superintendent to offer to provide units and lectures in the classroom. As secretary of the newly formed Central Maryland Chapter of the African-American Historical and Genealogical Society, she is supporting the renovation of a vacant, old "colored school" to become their Center for the county.

FUNERAL HOME:
Does the local establishment have records that they can share with family historians? What are the years covered? Who has operated the business from its inception at this location? Where did it exist prior? Could anyone speak on a comparison of the early burial customs as compared to today...or perhaps prepare a booklet? I'm sure some of you remember that the body lay in the parlor of the home, and a ribboned swag was hung outside the door. I can remember being asked to play quietly whenever I saw one.

LIBRARY:
Does the local library have a section for county and town histories? Would it consider accepting genealogical files for reference? Could a local genealogist volunteer to assist with the collection of these files, and act as consultant when visitors have questions?

When you research your family, the size of the library and its holdings is not important...it's whether they have any information on YOUR family! I have been to the Library of Congress many times, but my lucky day was when I visited a small two-room library that had formerly been a butcher shop in Lovettsville, Virginia. They had one black notebook containing five genealogies. Three of them were families I was researching. Is there a possibility they would add microfilm of the census to their holdings? As a citizen, consider making a bequest to the library as a memorial gift. If books are suggested or donated, a special plate will be printed and placed inside the book, if you so desire.

(See Chapter 11 for more detail on libraries.)

ORAL HISTORY:

Many historical groups would like to have oral histories completed by some of its oldest residents. This would be a wonderful way to record the operation of the industries of the early town, the transportation, schools, festival times and just general recollections of the past. Particularly eventful and filled with emotion would be the times of flood, fire, or accident...anything that brought the town together in concern as a family.

Taping these stories could be an assignment made to a willing volunteer, but it could be more meaningful if done by a member of the family. It would be more relaxing for the subject, and more valuable to the family member to hear it firsthand. These tapings are usually transcribed, so they can be referred to with or without a recorder. It also serves as an index to the tape.

My father had four drawers of reel-to-reel tapes he made of town celebrations, speeches, musical programs, church rallies, as well as personal family events. These need to be recorded on cassette to be contemporary and better preserved. Eventually, they should be housed at the library or museum, where a recorder is available. He found this an interesting hobby and did it on his own. With each reel, he included a printed program or label with the date, location and name of the event.

I think any historical commission should realize that while they are preserving the past, they are making history today that should be saved. It would be well to assure that every significant community milestone is taped and photographed by a designated person. The newspaper often has conflicting schedules and space limitations. Perhaps there are persons who would enjoy doing that service.

If you have an idea in the name of preservation, you may be able to receive a grant of money to back your project. One couple wanted experience in producing videos on genealogy for the local TV channel. After writing up a request, attending hearings, and receiving the grant, they developed a series of nine programs.

This same medium could be used by the town's Commission on History, to develop an appreciation and a positive image of the town and how they want to be perceived. It is much better than running the Police Docket in bold type to sell gossip. That is like me publishing my family history, and putting the black sheep in headlines! We all have them, and they got there the same way...wrong choices!

HOMES AND PEOPLE:

You can't separate these two because to find one is to find the other. I keep trying to tell that to historical societies when they don't understand what we genealogists do. I say, "You know those buildings that you have documented on your historical registers? Well, we research the people who built and lived in them." I don't see how historians can study buildings and businesses and not get interested in the drama of the families who lived and worked in them. I guess there's only so much you can study!

I'd really enjoy dressing up in costume and welcoming visitors to some of those mansions (that I never could have afforded!). Maybe I could get the historical society to put a framed family tree somewhere in the house. I think it would help visitors visualize the family members as they show the rooms they used.

Historical and genealogical societies share the same focus...to record the history of an area; so we complement each other.

296

You really need both to get a true picture of a person's life. We read old **wills** and **inventories**, which listed everything in the house as collateral. The amount and kind tells you what was considered his worth, his tools often indicating his line of work. To find the location, you use the census and **deeds**, and if necessary, land maps and **grants**. If the house had historical significance and was on the register, you would find a complete review of its history and usually a floor plan and description.

In the census listing, take note of the names of the **neighbors**, listed before and after your owner. These people may be related, or often involved in the lives of your family.

From a community standpoint, longtime residents simply know the houses as the Smith house, the Jordan house, whoever built the house...no matter how many times it is sold afterward. But once some historical attention has been given it, tours advertised, and articles written, it becomes a source of pride to the whole community. Maybe the house was once considered **haunted**...why? Take a look at a book by David Weitzman, MY BACKYARD HISTORY BOOK, a book for the child in all of us who has not learned to see history in our own town. Like anything else, we just have to become aware.

Someone knowledgeable about **architectural styles** can see unique features to call to everyone's attention. Some news-papers may print photos of just the eaves, or the window, or the fanlight, or the unusual Victorian siding patterns, and ask the readers to identify the locations. This points out pretty quickly that you haven't been observant, or you thought a lot of houses were the same. Things sometimes become invisible when they are familiar.

Before many more days go by, I'm going to sit down with my newly retired husband and **diagram** the whole **main street**. I think computer paper would be perfect. You see, as I've said elsewhere, he lived on West Potomac Street, a mile from me on East Potomac Street. It may interest someone someday to know who had homes and businesses along that mile. It was the street with the theater, fire hall and all the stores at the time. Why don't you do that project with an older family member soon? They'll tell you what they thought of old "Mr. So and So," and where they were when the YMCA burned down, and lots of other opinions. You just keep naming those little boxes, but leave space for previous businesses at that same location. Someone will invariably say, "Well, first it was a barber shop, and then it was Harrington's Shoe Shop."

RECREATION, FESTIVALS, CHURCH SUPPERS, CELEBRATIONS:
Were sports teams a popular pastime in your town? Adult or Little League? Did they compete with other towns? Win any trophies? Have you kept a history of the players?
Did you have soapbox derbies?
Did the service organizations sponsor carnivals?
Were church suppers and socials held the same time every year?
Were there any outstanding musicians in town? Bands, choruses of adults? Were talent shows and dances a regular event?
What annual celebrations were held? We boasted the largest parade in the county on Veterans' Day. It lasted two hours...and where did it go...right down Potomac Street! We used to have a family reunion right on Lee's front porch.

Other festivals are being initiated in order to bring people together. The railroad that was our main industry has passed us by, literally. Our town grew out of a need for a stop halfway between Washington, DC and Cumberland, Maryland for steam locomotives to be serviced. Also this was where new trains were *made up* as cars were switched into new destinations. Then came the change to diesel power and trains could make longer runs. Around the late 50's it was no longer lucrative enough to run as many passenger trains, so there was less work, and the town started losing support from the railroad.

During one of the summer heritage festivals, my husband and I, former teachers in the town, offered to set up a one-room school reproduction. We used one of the emptied classrooms of the elementary school, put two semi-circles of chairs and desks around a borrowed pot-bellied stove. On the front row of primary chairs, we placed slates with string tied for around the neck. On the back row, we placed BlueBooks with *Ciphering Book* printed on them, and also reproductions of the graded McGuffey Readers.

298

These larger chairs were turned from the front to encourage concentration. A lectern up front simulated the teacher's desk on which we placed an ink well and quill pen. By the door was a pail of water with a dipper beside, and on the back coat rack were two shawls and bonnets and lunch buckets on the shelf above. Up front, a dunce stool and cap, one map, a painting of George Washington, and a Bible motto, "The fear of God is the beginning of wisdom," completed the scene. At the appointed time, I went into the hall, and rang the hand bell. As each **student** entered I asked him or her to sit in either the primary or upper class seats. From then on we had lots of fun playing school, coming up to chant the lesson, practicing the art of penmanship, and getting put on the dunce's stool. They were all our friends and half of them older than we.

Prior to the day, we had written all the retired teachers to join us and bring any albums or memorabilia they had of **school days**. After school we gathered in the back to share stories and albums; and Lee copied photos from them for us to have negatives. No one worried whether it was completely authentic; it was fun, and it got us together. I'm so glad we thought to do it because many of the teachers have since passed away. The Alumni Association may sponsor something like this on the afternoon of their annual banquet.

I tried to get a listing that day of all the teachers who had ever taught in our schools. I taped large sheets of poster board to the chalkboard, and filled in as many faculty names as I could. Everyone who attended was asked to write others in the appropriate years. I checked the county office of education and found that they did not keep information after a teacher retires. So someone needs to...maybe **YOU**!

Another preset celebration of the past is the annual Distinguished Citizens' Luncheon which honors those of our community who have led outstanding lives. At least six persons are given awards and recognition. Since many have been living elsewhere, it is a sort of *homecoming* for all of the townspeople to renew ties.

So-o-o...it may not be what it used to be, (nothing is...) but it's the only *home* we've ever known...both of us. So be ready when someone talks about YOUR good old days! Get out the photos, scrapbooks, tapes, and records and rediscover your past! Put them in a safe place, so they can educate in the future!

A CEMETERY IS A PLACE FOR THE LIVING

We cannot forget the past as long as there is a cemetery in our midst, for though we preserve the buildings in our community, here lie the persons who built them. A cemetery is a visual reminder of all that lived out their daily lives and made the town what it is. Its story is never finished as long as there are memories, and it can tell us much about the past.

My earliest memory of burial grounds was the town cemetery, which was about one mile from our house. I suppose I thought of it as a park, for I recall asking permission to pack a lunch and take my two brothers on a walk there and back. I can remember making the sandwiches for the three of us, and becoming very excited that I was going to lead this expedition for the first time. I must have been about nine years old. The walk was shady and pleasant, and we had to be careful to stay to the side when a car would pass. When we arrived, we pretended we had been walking for days and days, and had gotten pretty hungry. We chose the first flat tombstone to sit on, and ate our lunch as though it were ambrosia from the gods. The return trip was safe and uneventful, so I felt I'd proved I could take care.

To **walk the paths** of that same cemetery today is to visit the final resting place of those we once knew as neighbors, family, leaders, sports figures, and any who took part in our life in the town. As many of the graves are in family plots, you can reconstruct whole families who lived down the street. Often the adjacent space holds the family of the wife.

It's like reading the local paper as you spy the name of the little boy who was hit by a car, or the one involved in the school bus accident. The whole day of those events flashes into your memory, and it seems like yesterday. You wondered then how the family could accept it, and now you know they managed to find a way.

Oh, and here is the mayor's grave. I remember the day we were building our house and we needed four strong men to hold up the wall until it was nailed into place. About that time, the mayor came riding by in the police car on one of his rounds. This time he included checking on the progress of Smith's house. After accepting the invitation to help, we had him autograph the beam in the basement, along with the other fellows. I wonder if the new owners have seen it.

Walking on through the cemetery I notice the stones for the storekeeper where I bought penny candy, the teacher who listened while I played my piano lesson for her. One by one we visit with them as though they were still on the porches or clerking in the stores. It is a visual sociogram of neighbors who shared over the back fence, of classmates who married, or poignant moments that brought us together in community.

The town cemetery brings us together in concern and respect for each family. When any loss occurs we turn out in large numbers to help, and for a time that family is our focus. We need the tombstones and location as reminders, to bring generations together as we walk down grassy aisles. Like beads on a rosary, we pause at each stone; we remember, and pray.

I would hope everyone would go back home to the town where he grew up and take this walk with someone close with whom you could reminisce—someone a generation older and another a generation younger. The group of you can share stories in the first person, and hear the drama in the event, the feelings at the time. You cannot reproduce them secondhand, it's better to be there.

If the younger is your child, he will listen as you discuss how you felt and what you remember about your own ancestors. It can reinforce some of the background that may have been left out when you talked about them at home. Perhaps your child can record the data from the stones as you are talking, thereby having an active part. Years later you may hear him say, "I remember the day we went to the cemetery and Grandma told us..." You will be glad you created the moment for generations to share.

While you're there, **take photos** of the family sites to keep in your album. The composition will be more meaningful if you can include the church in the background. Try to use an angle that will cast shadows into the inscription, making it easier to read.

301

Once you have located these family plots, it would be a very good thing to diagram on paper. Large cemeteries may already have these, so ask at the office and mark them for your records. To draw your own, simply mark the perimeter by noting any trees, the church, or houses. Draw the main access roads that divide it into sections. I used o's and x's to note the number of stones when helpful, the x's being my family in particular. There was a time when I even had to help the grave digger over the phone, and a diagram would have been a big help. My brother and I ended up walking at night through a foot of snow, reading the stones with a lighted match, while my husband shined the car headlights to help us. Now we have a diagram! It is an important part of our records.

This may get to be a very emotional trip for your relatives; any memory is usually tied to the highs or lows of our life. But provide a listening ear and an understanding heart; it may be just what your relative needs. You may direct her attention to any other graves nearby, sensing the time to move on. I just tell my family that my goal is to record all the wonderful memories they have of their loved ones so they won't be forgotten. You need to keep the rosary together lest the chain break, and the beads be lost.

Needing this information will give you a reason to visit cemeteries any day...not only Memorial Day and Easter. In fact, I remember a friend of mine whose family made it a tradition to visit the family cemetery at Christmas. As they stopped at each grave they sang a carol and placed some greens.

If other family reunions are held near the cemetery, favorite hymns could be sung and children could place a rose.

When we genealogists say "Gone but not forgotten," we mean it! We'll go almost anywhere to find the family burial spot. Often you find yourself searching in unfamiliar territory, so we have unique experiences...tramping through cow pastures, watching where we step...opening three gates (and closing them) before coming to the spot.

It has been nearly dark on some occasions, and we have carried a lantern or flashlight to see. When the thought occurred to us that we might be mistaken for grave robbers, we shortened our visit. Poor planning, you say, but often it just took us that long to find the location of the cemetery.

What was once a small rural gravesite may be sitting in the low-rent district of a city now. Once, when we located the address, it was in a ghetto, and the high cement wall around it was covered with graffiti. When we found the gate was locked, for protection, did we leave? Of course not! While Lee kept the motor running, I climbed up on the hood for a view over the wall...only to find all the stones facing the other way! I had to come home and write a letter to the historical society to get a list of burials—a safer, but less exciting way to get information! So, you see, this is not always just an intellectual pursuit...it is a *James Bond* challenge in many ways. But we always get our man...or woman!

Realizing that our young people are our historians of the future, our county schools are promoting projects to increase student awareness of **cemeteries as historic sites**. One school, Glenwood Middle School, has been involved in taking the 7th grade classes out to a very old graveyard (Oak Grove Cemetery) that is near the school. Since the project involves the whole day, the students take a lunch and walk to the site. (Sounds a little like my first trip!) However, English teacher, Carla Beachy, involved her whole department in planning a lesson and including persons from the community to help with various fields of expertise. I think this showed the students that learning also takes place in the community, and all of us are teachers in some way.

At the school, I was given an itinerary sheet with a schedule of activities, was introduced to everyone, and was asked to accompany them on their quarter-mile walk to the cemetery.

I was pleased to be included as president of the genealogical society to tell the students why **we** are interested in the stones. This included a definition of genealogy as a study of the family that everyone *can* and *should* do, the information that we hope to find inscribed, clues you get from the quality of the stone—its size, location—and where we might look and record.

I also showed a copy of the inscriptions from that same cemetery that we have published in one of seven volumes. These then act as a registry for anyone not able to come to the location in person. The registry is a permanent record should the stones be eroded or vandalized. I was pleased to answer questions from both the students and the parent-chaperones, after which I stayed on for the other activities.

After my presentation, the students went to another location for a demonstration of tombstone rubbing. They were given materials, and working in pairs, they each completed one to take home.

After eating a box lunch, they listened to an actress dressed in an ominous-looking, black hooded cape perform Poe's poem, *The Raven.* She positioned herself under a huge old oak tree to add to the *eerie* effect.

This was followed by a historical society member who gave background on the early history of the neighborhood. The sexton of the Union Chapel church followed with facts about the church itself and how it represented nearby families.

For the last activity, teachers handed out sheets for a treasure hunt of information from the stones...the oldest, the youngest person, military marker, vocabulary "consort," "relict," any foreign language or country of origin named. They noted special symbols and art work, old script and unusual epitaphs. Two of the boys even found a SMITH stone for me!

It was an impressive lesson, and filled with practical ideas for active students. Hopefully, they will try to do some of these same things at their own family cemeteries. As for me, I handed out blank ancestor charts to four parents and gave some for the teacher to distribute to the students who wanted them. I sold a copy of the published records to the sexton of the church, who wanted to keep it available for visitors.

I met another parent who recently moved to the farm across the road, and wanted to know where to find the history on the family who built the old dwelling. I was able to tell her I would meet her at the historical library later in the week to find the records.

CLUES ON A TOMBSTONE

The cemetery holds many clues to help with your family history. Let me list the things you can look for on a tombstone:

1. Record (print) the complete name and inscription, using slashes to indicate the end of each line. If in a foreign language print it and have it translated later. Clues may be there as to country of origin or parentage.

304

2. Verses may be clues to the condition of the deceased, such as one of ours which said,"her vision clouded, has now been made clear"...indicated she was blind. Some verses are lyrics of a hymn. When lettering was eroded, my choir experience helped me decipher.

3. The size and material of the stone may be a clue to the economic position of the family.

4. Symbols on the stone may show affiliation with an organization or lodge.

5. Military units named with person give clues to further research in the service unit and the war.

6. Inscription may mention line of work or standing in the community, i.e., mayor or minister.

7. Wife's maiden name and parents may be given.

8. Shape of the stone may give a clue to the ethnic background, especially in the very early graves.

9. Folk art symbols have special meaning.

10. Some vocabulary you may encounter:
    Relict: spouse of a deceased mate.
    Consort: spouse of a living mate.

11. Age may be expressed in years, months, days; in his 67th year means he was already 67.

12. Several wives may be buried with same husband. Look for infant grave which indicates wife died in childbirth. Death dates will coincide. This was common.

13. Many deaths in the same year may give clues to an epidemic or disaster of some sort.

14. Take note of families in nearby plots; may be relatives of the wife, and a clue to her surname.

15. If cemetery is church affiliated, take note of denomination of family for future research. Locate the church, address, and phone, if available.

16. Family home may have been close by.

17. Take a photo of all sides of the stone that have information. Try to include the church in the background.

18. Make a diagram of the cemetery for quick location of stones in the future.

19. If print is hard to read because of erosion, your aim is to distinguish the hollows of the letters. This can be assisted by reflecting light at an angle (flashlight or white card), or by darkening the hollows with muddy soil and brushing off the excess. Spraying water may darken the cut areas of some stone.

Pressure sensitive paper rubbed with a dollar bill may be the answer. This paper is purchased from monument companies.

20. This equipment is recommended for recording gravestones:
Always go prepared for poor conditions
Bug spray for mosquitoes
Gloves to remove poison ivy, briars
Trowel to clear soil and grass away from buried stone
Crow bar to surface a buried stone, or raise a toppled one.
Flashlight or white card to reflect light
Scrub brush (no wire) to clean lichen, etc.
Spray bottle with water
Boots for mud
Old blanket to kneel or sit on
Clipboard with paper, pencil, and rubber band to keep pages from blowing
Rubbing paper (or shelf paper) and large or flat crayon (If desired as memento, add location of site and data)
Masking tape to hold the paper securely as you rub
A cardboard tube with rubber band to hold finished rubbing
I carry all of these in a bag called "The Graveyard Shift" to keep them altogether. One more thing...always secure permission first if a caretaker is close by. He may save you some time by assisting you or showing you the records.

Once you have recorded the inscriptions, here are some sources you can investigate next:
Newspapers—now that you know the exact day of death, consult newspapers at the library or paper office. Obituaries may give cause of death, names and addresses of surviving family, church that handled burial, pall bearers, membership in organizations. Consult many different papers of area.
Funeral home records—may have more detail.
Church from which person was buried may have birth and marriage records for same family.
Death certificate—send for copy to see where he died, name of parents, cause of death, verify dates, person who gave information.
Military records—have details of service record, family names, pension application, bounty land.
Probate of will—may have family names and distribution of property; clue to economic background.

307

So you see, there are many clues to be found in the cemetery and I always like to think that my ancestor was glad I took the time to remember he lived and looked him up. He seems to be saying,
"Remember me as you pass by,
As you are now, so once was I.
As I am now, soon you will be;
Prepare yourself to follow me."

Related subjects to this topic of cemeteries would include: history of burial practices, meaning of symbols & motifs, collections of epitaphs, and the role of archaeology in preservation. We have touched on all of these through speakers, books or concern for community.

PRESERVING CEMETERIES

How do we know that our family cemeteries will be there when we finally pinpoint the location? Only if someone has had the foresight to treat it as *sacred ground*. In the past, it has been taken for granted that no one disturbs a cemetery. Laws are on the books concerning vandalism, but someone has to be there, see the damage, and then try to rectify it. Land is becoming more and more valuable to the owner and the builder, and if someone is not paying for the privilege of occupying space, the grave is removed for some money-making project.

This is one of the reasons that genealogical societies everywhere are taking an interest, not only in copying and publishing the inscriptions, but getting involved in the protection of the same. After routinely copying all of the obvious cemeteries in our county for the past eight years, our county society noticed that the building of new homes was creeping closer and closer to small family graveyards.

We started putting notices into the paper that we would welcome calls from anyone who knew of small cemeteries that we could record. We asked if the Health Department would consider our volumes to be a registry of existing cemeteries when asked to issue building permits. They agreed, and member Clyde Pyers and they drew up a map with red dots indicating cemeteries.

Ironically, we find that some large family organizations and churches do not fully maintain their own old sections, which certainly sets a poor example for the private citizen. At present, our county government is concerned at the speed with which land is being developed, and is considering a moratorium on growth until a plan can be developed. We, as a society, are trying to record all the stones to get them on the registry. We've had some reported, but need to record an official location.

We plan to get publicity whenever we go on our recording trips, so that everyone is aware of our quest and will notify us. One person called us to put up a fence around a small set of stones in a plowed field. But we had to tell her that we don't put up fences; we try to notify heirs, as we would have the builders do.

To date, each county has to confront the problem when it becomes one. We are encouraging each county to set up a registry such as ours. Once the stones are recorded this is proof that they existed at that location, whether they are eroded, destroyed or vandalized in the future.

Recently the police called us as they had discovered a tombstone which had been thrown along the road. By reading us the inscription we were able to check our volumes and tell them where it belonged. Family members from all over the U.S. write us asking if we have members of their family buried in our county. A quick look at the indices allows us to send a prompt reply, and a photocopy should they desire it.

We also presented legislation to the state suggesting more stringent laws to prohibit builders from securing permits until an attempt is made to relocate graves. Ideally, we hope heirs could be consulted, but our main concern is that they not ignore the presence of a graveyard and simply bulldoze over it. We plan to rewrite the bill and have it submitted again this year with representation from more of the state.

One more remarkable effort was motivated by one woman, Barbara Sieg. She lives in a nice neighborhood, not too far from the old Whipps family graveyard. Many of the family had passed away or left the area, the graveyard was sorely neglected, and was occasionally used as a dumping ground. She had always dreamed it could be restored as it was in the early 1800's; it wasn't until new houses were built adjacent to the site, that she started into a project of restoration, protection and preservation. It seems that the new residents found tombstones in their backyard when they dug for a garden. Barbara realized that there must be more to the area than the builder was admitting. So with the community association behind her, and genealogist friend Charles Ahalt, they combed the courthouse records and the lot itself to try to redefine its boundaries. They found the deeds and an early account that mentioned the graveyard as a haven with plants and birds.

She had local nurseries and landscapers destroy the poison ivy and clear the large debris, but **most** of the clearing was done by community volunteers. Scouts volunteered to do service projects and help clean up the area. Plants were donated and put in by garden clubs. Tombstones were reset, repaired, and recorded. Descendants of the family were contacted. With each addition, she was motivated to do more...but the beauty of the project is the way she had everyone working together. One of our members, Jim, had suggested we start an "Adopt A Cemetery" project, and it seemed this would be a pilot.

When things were mostly in place, she had a plaque erected to name the area and to thank the largest contributors. TV crews came to do a short segment for the evening news. When winter came and it was impossible to do much work, she put out a newsletter giving background on what had been done, what was planned for the future, and included articles on the history of the Whipps family. When spring temperatures would allow, she gathered up a crew and set out to evaluate the damage, if any, that winter had done to the new plantings. Work began again, putting down pathways of pine bark throughout the one-acre area. Research was done on the iron fencing and whether it could be replaced. An historic gate and fencing were found and brought to the site from two locations. A local company is going to reproduce the original ironwork that defines family plots.

Barbara has kept her eye out for nearby sites that are about to be bulldozed, and asked permission to have plants that were in the way. So she leaves no proverbial *stone unturned* if it can be used in the Whipps cemetery.

Before Memorial Day, she put out another issue of the newsletter, this time reporting on the species of plants that had survived the winter, and the current needs of the project. Plans have been made to hire a gravestone restorer to mend the broken stones. If monies are donated, people know in advance what they are needed for. She is always careful to mention the names of those who have contributed time or materials to help.

This time she invited everyone to bring flowers and decorate the graves on Memorial Day, giving the background on the first Decoration Day in 1868. She had Girl Scouts dressed in Victorian dresses and bonnets to welcome us and answer questions. Small blossom bouquets were placed on each tree-shaded grave. It had become just what she had visualized thus far...a shady resting place for those here now and from the past.

One person can make a difference, and what a difference! Who would ever let it go back to weeds again when someone cared so much? To complete a similar project, refer to A GRAVEYARD PRESERVATION PRIMER, Lynette Strangstad, American Association for State and Local History, Nashville, TN.

A cemetery still speaks to the living in many ways...Can you imagine your community without one?

Boder, John, RUBBINGS AND TEXTURES
Gillon, Jr., E. V., EARLY NEW ENGLAND
   GRAVESTONE RUBBINGS
Andrew, Laye, CREATIVE RUBBINGS
Wust, Klaus, FOLK ART IN STONE

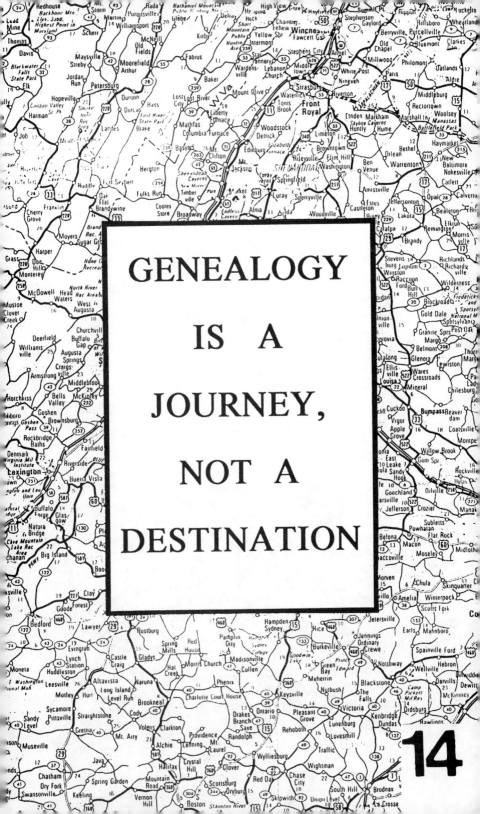

GENEALOGY

IS A

JOURNEY,

NOT A

DESTINATION

14

GENEALOGY IS A JOURNEY,
NOT A DESTINATION

Just as life is a journey that takes you down many roads you have never traveled, so it is with genealogy. The route is not already planned for you, so you will find yourself needing many people to help you along. You will learn to *ask directions and communicate your needs* if you want to reach your goal. And just like life, you'll have unexpected pleasures along the way, experiences with people and places that will enrich your life.

As a genealogist, you will no longer take trips just to see the mountains in the fall or the seashore in the summer. You will pinpoint all the family villages and plan to see the scenery in between. However, if the right cemetery or library looms up along the route, you will opt for them instead of the vistas.

They tell us that we are happiest when we have overcome some obstacle in our lives and proved we could be victorious. Well, genealogy challenges you every step of the way. Finding these ancestors with little known clues in towns that no longer exist and names that were spelled at least 21 ways is like a Lewis and Clark expedition. Each time you discover a new ancestor, you have two new parents to start looking for. Some people are content to look for a new rock, mineral, or feathered bird; but these are MY people, MY ancestors, and once I find their burial grounds and record it, it will be a permanent part of MY family record.

ANCESTRAL JOURNEYS

Actually, genealogy is the story of the journey of our ancestors; only you travel back into the past over present roads, looking for signs along the way. We retrace it as we search for clues that take us to their beginnings. Research in the old country is much easier because families didn't take journeys far from their homeland until wars and famine forced them.

Here in America we find ourselves planning literal research journeys back to areas where our ancestors lived and worked. Somehow we feel we'll see something, or find someone who can fill in some blanks, give us some clues. Once there, we can take photos, stand on hallowed ground, listen for voices from the past, and wait for their spirits to direct us.

It doesn't hurt to get the facts first-hand, go to the scene of the crime (so to speak). You can check the records for yourself, read the tombstone for things that may have been overlooked, get a sense of the area and not have to trust a letter from whomever happened to be on duty that day. If the census taker can make mistakes, so can others.

PLANNING A FIELD TRIP

When you plan to take a genealogy field trip, here are some guidelines to help you make the most of your time:

1. Assess the areas that you need information about. Write them down. Secure the phone numbers and addresses and contact all persons who can gather materials to help you. Find out when it would be convenient for you to visit. Carolyn and Charles stay at a bed and breakfast, where they become oriented to the area by the hosts.

2. Check the phone directory to see if anyone with the family name is still there; give them a call to tell them of your quest, and ask if they know of a published family history.

3. Visit the homeplace; talk to the current resident. He may offer you a tour inside. Take old photos with you to compare. Take new photos of today's evidence of old areas.

4. Go to the local library and ask for any help they can give you on your family name; are there any collections of local family history? Look at county maps for cemeteries and churches.

5. Visit cemeteries of the denomination of your ancestors; take photos and rubbings as mementoes.

6. If you find any cousins, record any stories they can tell you; share your ancestral chart.

7. Locate the school site where they attended.

8. Keep a record of your photos in a notebook, or on tape, so you may label them when developed.

9. Is there a town historian who would enjoy talking with you about the early days. Check out some of the family stories you've heard.

10. When you visit the courthouse or town office, have your needs down on paper so they will be easy to retrieve.

11. Always carry your four-generation chart with you to show any interested party. It will show them many names they may be able to relate to.

12. Ask if there is an experienced genealogist in town. They will direct you to other repositories in the area, such as seminary and college libraries, state archives, and historical societies. They may call attention to special fees, parking, hours, routes that will be helpful. Offer to do the same for them when they come to your state.

13. This *on location* research is perfect for the whole family, as it is activity-oriented. Children will relate better in the future when they hear the older folks speak of this area. They can do a tombstone rubbing, keep a trip log, get autographs of the relatives...perhaps with a word of advice about growing up. They may find flowers to press, a stone from the creek, a slate that fell off the roof, an old photo, and best of all, a road map of the area with the route marked in red. This could be material for a school project in the fall.

14. If you are there over Sunday, you may want to attend a service in your family's old church. Later you could inquire about records.

15. Don't be discouraged if you don't uncover a lot of material. You can always go back to the records in the national collections, passenger lists, and LDS libraries, and maybe eventually, a trip overseas. At least for a while, we walked with our ancestors and tried to bring our records to life.

Of course, we highly recommend an RV for these journeys so you are ready for most anything. They have their drawbacks down narrow country roads that involve covered bridges; that's an oft proven fact! But we have everything there, no matter where we find ourselves needing any of life's necessities.

The biggest advantage of the RV is the choice of activities it allows us. We never need a guest room should we find a new cousin. In fact, we can offer transportation for a tour around the area, and a snack afterward. There's space for my research papers, the camera, recorder, tombstone rubbing materials, and the camcorder as well.

When we return to the nearest campground, we spend time organizing what we found that day, and making plans for the next.

In the future, I plan to put out my shingle at any campground announcing, "Want to talk genealogy? Come to Site 12!" As we travel roads that once were trails for immigrants, we say the motor home is just a modern covered wagon with the horsepower of a 460 engine.

ANCESTRAL HOMES

If you become a genealogist, you will have many new experiences as you discover the homes of your ancestors. We had no idea of the exciting stories we were about to unfold. In one case, my grandmother's birthplace on Virginius Island at Harpers Ferry is now a walking trail in a national park. I tried to imagine the streets and homes being so close to the river, and how desperate they must have felt when the flood waters were rising.

In another instance, we found my husband's great-grandfather's brick home boarded up by the Park Service. It was so close to the stone fort on Maryland Heights that the Civil War generals had used it for headquarters. We also learned that the house was believed to be haunted because Lee's great-grandmother had died a violent death there. The obituary said she was blind and had caught her clothes on fire. The ranger opened the house for us to tour one day, but, unfortunately, Sarah didn't show up; I had a lot of things to ask her!

On a third occasion, we traced a family line back to the Rev. Jeremiah Moore, an early Baptist minister who lived in Vienna, Virginia. His estate, named Moorefield, has been placed on the Historic Register and a history of the home and family has been printed. I proudly added that to our collection, and announced to my Baptist sister-in-law, Nancy, that we had finally arrived!

Often there is a family graveyard on the property of old country homes. But when you haven't researched enough to know who and where your ancestors are, their graves may be dug up or covered over with housing or roads or simply plowed under. This is why we should try to protect all graveyards from vandalism of any kind. Somewhere there are family members who may be searching for their location. If we take care of the ones in our area, we hope someone is doing the same for our ancestors.

ETHNIC VILLAGES

Perhaps you will include a visit to a *living history museum* that recreates some portion of your ancestor's life. Here you could get a feel for the mores of those times, the occupation, the dress, customs, architecture, foods; and perhaps you'll want to buy a few items that represent your heritage. Listed below are some of the leading ethnic villages of America:

Danish—Solvang, CA, settled 1911
German—Hermann, MO, settled 1837; Maifest,
    Octoberfest, also Leavenworth, WA
French—Shandaken, NY
Greek—Tarpon Springs, FL, settled 1850; Epiphany,
    Easter
Indian—Russell Cave Nat. Mon.; Bridgeport, AL
American Industry—Agrirama, Tifton, GA
Spanish—St. Augustine, FL; coast of CA
Canal Town— Coshocton, OH (Apr-Dec)
Gold Rush Days—Columbia St. Pk, CA all year
    Wickenburg, AZ; About Feb 10-12
Pioneer Village—Harold Warp, Minden, NE
Old World Wisconsin—Eagle, WI (Norwegian,
    Finnish, German, Danish, Yankee)
Cuban—Miami, FL
Dutch—Holland, MI - 1847
Jewish—Brooklyn, NY - 1900
Irish—Boston, MA - 1840
Chinese—San Francisco, CA
Italian—New York City, Baltimore, MD
Japanese—Seattle, WA - 1890-1924
Portuguese—Newark, NJ - also FL and RI
Swedish—Lindborg, KS - 1870-1880

If you really want to role play *pioneer,* join a wagon train and take the same trails they used. Trips vary from one day to six. The most authentic is:

Oregon Trail Wagon, Rte. 2, Bayard, NE 69334

Two others include:

Old West Tours, Box 7467, Dept. BHG, Jackson, WY 83001

Flint Hills Overland Wagon Train, Box 1076, Dept. BHG, El Dorado, KS 67042

YOUR PERSONAL JOURNEY

While you're keeping records on your ancestor's past, whole years of your own life are becoming history. Try to find some time to record **your** life as well. So why not start keeping a log of your journey through life...that's what a person's genealogy is! When you take a trip, you write down all the events that took place, outstanding or otherwise. Take a *sentimental journey* through your life and record the people and places that hold a special meaning.

—To The Homeplace

Record what made your own home unique and a place where you felt special. It probably has nothing to do with the style of the house, but the people and activities that took place in it.

Check the history of the house: who built it, how long did your family live here, were any changes made in the rooms and when? Has the road or street leading past the house been altered? Were there outbuildings? List their purposes. Who were the neighbors? Were they friendly? Did they go to school with you? Did you move to other houses as a child? Where?

—To The Home Church

As you think about the church of your childhood, who do you see every Sunday? Were there important events held there? Did you have recitations and songs you sang? Did you attend funerals or weddings there? Whose? What about picnics and festivals?

320

Were you comfortable attending church? Did you look forward to it? Did you have responsibilities each Sunday? Did you sing in the choir? What are your favorite hymns? When the service was over, did you have a different routine from the other days of the week? Has your religious faith been important to your life?

—To The Schoolhouse

Your socialization began with school, so how was this experience? Did it come hard or easy to you? I was amazed to find out that my teacher/principal husband had to be threatened every step of the way on his first day. The school was only two blocks away. He must have learned to enjoy it, as he spent the next 54 years in the schools of Maryland.

Your choices of friends, favorite teachers and activities tell a lot about you. Were there special events that were embarrassing, rewarding, or memorable?

Where were the buildings located? Was there ever a fire and other changes in the routine of classes? It was a great disappointment to me that we would not have All State Chorus because there would be no bus transportation. Gasoline was rationed during W.W. II., and none was allowed for school functions.

I was quite proud to have started the first cheerleaders in our school. It was really so we three girls could go to all the basketball games. My cousin, Virginia Lee, taught me all the cheers from her school, and I passed them on. But the principal didn't think much of the short skirts with the red rayon undies we'd bought at the local *dime store*...A bit risky for the 40's!

If you go to college, a great deal of your education is learning to live together in the dorm. I had to work my way through, as my father felt that money would be wasted on a girl. I only had money enough to come home three times a year, so I have a lot of letters from my mother I've saved. Other than your studies, what memories do you have of your school years that you want others to appreciate? What has improved in the schools of today?

—To The Workplace

As you think about your work, your career, what about it is, or was, satisfying? The people you worked with were a team, and together you were to put out a product. What are some of the highlights of your years in your chosen work? What would you have changed, if you could?

Who were your co-workers?...name them. Did they represent characters in a daily script...as mine did? Though I was an elementary music teacher and enjoyed bringing music in some form to all 500 students, it was the programs over the years that I enjoyed the most...about 60 total. Working with adults in choir and community choruses brought new opportunities to cast singers as voice types for certain pieces of music. We usually wrote the programs to go with whom we had to cast.

I guess that's how a personnel director sees a well-run office. Do you feel you were cast well, or should have had a different opportunity to show what you could do? Nowadays, people are writing their own job descriptions. What would yours say?

I hear a lot of older people talk about the shabby way they feel their old job is being done today. Indeed, some of the work of the past is no longer needed at all. That doesn't mean that it was not a necessary step toward the work of today. Who will ever appreciate the fact that your work was important to the improvement of the company, if you don't describe your part in it?

There has never been a change that didn't have some good in it...but it must build on the past as its foundation. You can give validity to the past and show where the present has come from.

MAPS AND CHARTS

Every journey needs a map, a goal of some sort to give the traveler direction and a feeling of accomplishment when he arrives. I feel that is what a chart does for the genealogist. It provides goals and a sense of direction as we set them, keeping us on track and showing how far we've gone. When our research hits a dead end, it's as though the highway ran out, and we have to study to see where we made a wrong turn.

Sometimes we find unexpected clues in a will, for instance, and we go off in another direction for a while. This is true with any trip. It is the foolish traveler who does not allow himself time to enjoy the unexpected pleasures along the way. He may even change the time of his arrival to spend more time when the attraction warrants it.

The chart is the means to an end, not the end in itself! Just like a road map, many of the charts I have passed on have been put into a drawer. If they are ever brought out, they are referred to, as is a reference book or dictionary. "Did Aunt Bess die before or after Thanksgiving?" "We need Uncle Harry's birthdate for his obituary." "What's the name of Bob's little girl; they're coming for a visit?" That is respect in itself.

Genealogy's fascination is that you seldom find the routes already charted, and you are traveling through virgin territory. It means taking risks; will you find the wilderness too much for you...or will you make friends with an Indian guide? Now I'm getting into movie script material, but you get the picture!

THESE ARE THE DAYS OF OUR LIVES

From your window, from your observation, from your experiences, this is how you saw it and lived it. Though you may have been brought up with 12 children, your viewpoint is your own; your development and innate qualities are your own. But because your ancestors contributed in many ways, you want to give credit to those who came before you. Like you, they were a combination of nature and nurture, and have their stories to tell.

"Southern Living" magazine, December 1986, featured four pages of the "rituals of remembering." These stories of personal history are called gifts of a lifetime. But don't be content to read of other's lives and deeds; they are no more important than you are to your own family. Of all the 500 names on my charts, there would be 500 very different stories to tell. Only YOU can tell yours!

Ruth Kanin, in her book, WRITE THE STORY OF YOUR LIFE, convinces us that writing a narrative will be an act of sharing, a conversation with your family communicating your thoughts and teaching from experience. It will be a tribute to those who helped you, a legacy for generations to come. Writing is therapeutic because it helps you organize your thoughts and make a statement. For me, it has been a vehicle for both my husband and me to assess the past, create new goals, and share in the excitement.

Taking all these journeys, meeting all these people from the present and the past, sharing all these rewards are very important to us. But I guess you have to experience it to know what it's like. I guess you have to be a genealogist!

Kanin, Ruth, WRITE THE STORY OF YOUR LIFE. Baltimore, MD: Genealogical Publishing Co., 1986

Thomas, Frank P., HOW TO WRITE THE STORY OF YOUR LIFE. Cincinnati, OH: Writer's Digest Book

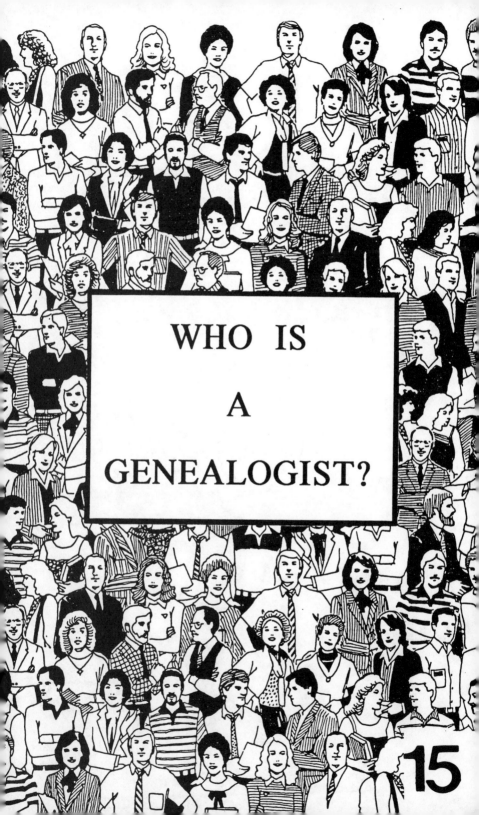

WHO IS A GENEALOGIST?

15

WHO IS A GENEALOGIST?

A **GENEALOGIST** is a person who has enough pride in his/her family to want them to be remembered for generations to come. He knows that they are important in his own genetic background, and wants to know more about them. This fills him with anticipation.

He is willing to spend many hours, even years, to find all the information he can to reconstruct their lives. In doing so, he finds that each is truly a unique individual influenced by his genetics, birth order, ethnic makeup, economics, natural disaster, and local and national history. But the events that shaped his life most of all were the choices he made.

A **GENEALOGIST** learns more about himself as he follows the lives of his ancestors. He begins to identify with a lot of the struggles that accompany the ancestor's lifestyle, and becomes more tolerant of everyone.

While researching the past and interviewing relatives, he realizes that he can be a catalyst to unify the present-day family. He organizes reunions and stimulates discussion between members, producing collections of audio and video tapes, charts, and photographs that bring them closer together. They become acquainted as friends, and not just names on a family tree!

A **GENEALOGIST** is an inquisitive person—a persistent person who is on a quest for identity and the place his ancestors had in the history of this country. He is an intellectual person who chooses to invest his personal time in the study of records and history in order to document his family's story. Therefore, he is always learning, growing, and bringing factual credence to some of the old *folk tales* in the family.

GENEALOGISTS are creative individuals who have chosen to take on this pursuit, working at their own rate, and choosing the form it will take. They often meet with others to exchange ideas concerning new references and pitfalls; they share expertise and stories of unusual ancestors they have just discovered. Clues are found in such unusual places, and at serendipitous times that no two tales are ever the same.

Genealogy can be a springboard into other careers for those who have leadership skills. Some GENEALOGISTS lead tours to the countries of origin, taking people to large research libraries there. Some, like Mary and Bill, become so adept at using the computer they set up an index service for other seekers. Others become speakers, teach classes, assist with desktop publishing, copy antique photographs, or become certified genealogists who do the searching for a fee.

GENEALOGISTS like a challenge and believe that it gives life purpose, filled with the anticipation of new discovery. Many retirees lose their vitality for life because they no longer have a measurement of their worth. We are in control of the amount of pressure we want to bring to our task. (I may never get all those Smiths sorted out. They are probably the reason we have social security numbers; too bad they didn't think of them in 1812. My troubles would be over.)

A GENEALOGIST takes an unwritten oath to be truthful in thought, word, and deed. This means if we write it, it should be because we KNOW and can PROVE it by our references. You never know who may use your charts, and be led astray by the wrong names or dates. So we can be creative in other ways, but not on those charts.

GENEALOGISTS have two qualities that each brings to his tasks...**motivation** and **enthusiasm**! It is amazing the work you can turn out, and enjoy every minute of it! I am continually amused by all the talk today of people who have to *find themselves*. They switch jobs, colleges, majors, husbands, wives, psychiatrists, self-help groups, all in a quest to discover **who they are.** The best way to satisfy their search is to work on their genealogy, and they may get a clue. I have no problem with **nature/nurture**. I think you should **nurture your nature**...if you can recognize it in time. There's a lot of it you can change, but there's a heck of a lot of it you're stuck with! Blame it on Grandma Ella and get on with your life! I think we only *find ourselves* when we relate to life's experiences, and find we have the capacity to **grow** with them!

So, who is a **GENEALOGIST?** It could be YOU! You have everything to gain by celebrating the life of your family. It is something only **you** can do, and it grows more valuable over the years. Anything of value takes time, but the joy of discovery will be well worth it...so go for it!

Enjoy your journey, and send me a post card when you have time!

L. Duane Smith

Quotes and Notes

Carpe diem–record your memories TODAY!

Remember YOU are # 1 on the chart!

History without Genealogy is only Geography!

Accentuate the positives in your family; try to forget the negatives!